THE WITNESSES
TO THE
HISTORICITY OF JESUS

THE WITNESSES

TO THE

HISTORICITY OF JESUS

BY

ARTHUR DREWS, Ph.D.

PROFESSOR OF PHILOSOPHY IN THE TECHN. HOCHSCHULE, KARLSRUHE

(author of "The Christ-Myth," etc.)

TRANSLATED BY JOSEPH McCABE

"Woe unto you, lawyers! for ye have taken away the key of knowledge: ye entered not in yourselves, and them that were entering in ye hindered."—LUKE XI, 52.

Fredonia Books
Amsterdam, The Netherlands

The Witnesses to the Historicity of Jesus

by
Arthur Drews

ISBN: 1-4101-0339-0

Copyright © 2003 by Fredonia Books

Fredonia Books
Amsterdam, The Netherlands
http://www.fredoniabooks.com

All rights reserved, including the right to reproduce this book, or portions thereof, in any form.

In order to make original editions of historical works available to scholars at an economical price, this facsimile of the original edition is reproduced from the best available copy and has been digitally enhanced to improve legibility, but the text remains unaltered to retain historical authenticity.

CONTENTS

	PAGE
PREFACE	ix

THE JEWISH WITNESSES

1. PHILO AND JUSTUS OF TIBERIAS	2
2. JOSEPHUS	3
3. THE TALMUD	10

THE ROMAN WITNESSES

1. PLINY AND SUETONIUS	18
2. TACITUS	20
(a) Evidential Value of the Passage	22
(b) Question of the Genuineness of *Annals*, xv. 44	24
I. Arguments for the Genuineness	25
II. Arguments against the Genuineness	37
(a) General Observations	37
(b) The Criticisms of Hochart	41
(c) Possibility of Various Interpretations of *Annals*, xv, 44	49
3. "LUCUS A NON LUCENDO"	56

THE WITNESS OF PAUL

1. PROOFS OF THE HISTORICITY OF JESUS IN PAUL	65
(a) Simple Proofs	69
(b) The Appearances of the Risen Christ	77
(c) The Account of the Last Supper	80
(d) The "Brothers" of the Lord	84
(e) The "Words of the Lord"	91
2. PAUL NO WITNESS TO THE HISTORICITY OF JESUS	98
3. THE QUESTION OF GENUINENESS	102
(a) Emotional Arguments for Genuineness	103

		PAGE
(b) Arguments for Genuineness from the Times	-	106
(c) The Spuriousness of the Pauline Epistles	-	116

THE WITNESS OF THE GOSPELS

1. THE SOURCES OF THE GOSPELS — 123
2. THE WITNESS OF TRADITION — 130
3. THE METHODS OF HISTORICAL CRITICISM — 134
   - (a) The Methodical Principles of Theological History — 134
   - (b) The Methods of J. Weiss — 136
4. THE "UNIQUENESS" AND "UNINVENTIBILITY" OF THE GOSPEL PORTRAIT OF JESUS — 142
5. SCHMIEDEL'S "MAIN PILLARS" — 144
6. THE METHODS OF "THE CHRIST-MYTH" — 156
   - (a) The Literary Character of the Gospels — 156
   - (b) The Mythical Character of the Gospels — 161
7. THE MYTHIC-SYMBOLIC INTERPRETATION OF THE GOSPELS — 169
   - (a) The Sufferings and Elevation of the Messiah — 169
   - (b) The Character and Miracles of the Messiah — 174
   - (c) John the Baptist and the Baptism of Jesus — 183
   - (d) The Name of the Messiah — 194
   - (e) The Topography of the Gospels — 200
     - I. Nazareth — 200
     - II. Jerusalem — 205
     - III. Galilee — 209
   - (f) The Chronology of the Gospels — 212
   - (g) The Pre-Christian Jesus — 216
   - (h) The Transformation of the Mythical into an Historical Jesus — 228
   - (i) Jesus and the Pharisees and Scribes — 235
   - (k) Further Modifications of Prophetical and Historical Passages — 245
8. HISTORIANS AND THE GOSPELS — 247

CONTENTS

		PAGE
9. THE WORDS OF THE LORD		249
(a) The Tradition of the Words of the Lord		249
(b) The Controversies with the Pharisees		253
(c) Sayings of Jesus on the Weak and Lowly		258
(d) Jesus's Belief in God the Father		262
(e) Love of Neighbours and of Enemies		266
(f) The Sermon on the Mount		271
(g) Further Parallel Passages		277
10. THE PARABLES OF JESUS		280
11. GENERAL RESULT		288
12. THE "STRONG PERSONALITY"		290
13. THE HISTORICAL JESUS AND THE IDEAL CHRIST		296
14. IDEA AND PERSONALITY: SETTLEMENT OF THE RELIGIOUS CRISIS		301
APPENDIX		309
INDEX		317

PREFACE

THE present work is an abbreviated and amended version, for English readers, of the volume which the author recently published as the second part of *The Christ-Myth* (English translation, 1910, Fisher Unwin). The author described this part as "an answer to his opponents, with special reference to theological methods," and dealt in the early part of it with the theological critics who had assailed the results and the methods adopted by him. It will be seen that the fault of method is entirely on the side of the opponents, and that theologians can maintain the historical reality of Jesus on methodical arguments only when their methods are pre-arranged to lead to that result. It is not the author's intention wholly to omit the points of this controversy, as in this respect there is no difference between the theologians of Germany and those of other countries. The chief aim of the work, however, is to collect, examine, and refute the arguments which are advanced on the theological side for the historicity of Jesus. In spite of their arrogant behaviour, the German theologians have not been able to produce one single decisive reason for the historicity of Jesus. It remains to be seen whether the English authorities can adduce better proof of the validity of the Christian belief than their German colleagues have done. Besides doing this necessary critical work, it is hoped that the book may also provide a better explanation of the rise of the Christian religion than historical theology, as it is called, has yet afforded. In this respect the author is indebted to the very stimulating and informing works of Mr. J. M. Robertson (*Christianity and Mythology, Pagan Christs,* and *A Short History of Christianity)*, and to the American writer Professor W. B. Smith, whose works, *Der vorchristliche Jesus* and *Ecce Deus*, ought to be in the hands of every student of the Christian religion.

The question of the historicity of Jesus is a purely historical question, and, as such, it must be settled with the resources of historical research. This procedure is, however, in view of the close connection of the subject with emotional and religious elements, not inconsistent with the fact that the final decision belongs to an entirely different province, that of philosophy, which also controls subjective feeling. In this sense, the question whether Jesus was an historical personage coincides with the question of the significance of personality in the general order of the world, and of the roots and motives of the inner religious life generally.

The controversy in regard to the Christ-myth is at the same time a struggle for the freedom and independence of the modern mind, and of science and philosophy. Let there be no mistake about it: as long as the belief in an historical Jesus survives we shall not succeed in throwing off the yoke of an alleged historical fact which is supposed to have taken place two thousand years ago, yet has profoundly affected the science and philosophy of Europe. What a situation it is when the deepest thoughts of the modern mind must be measured by the teaching of Jesus, and referred to a world of ideas that has nothing to recommend it but the antiquity of its traditions and the artificially engendered appreciation of everything connected with it!

At the same time the Christ-myth controversy is a struggle over religion. Religion is a life that emanates from the depths of one's innermost self, an outgrowth of the mind and of freedom. All religious progress consists in making faith more intimate, in transferring the centre of gravity from the objective to the subjective world, by a confident surrender to the God within us. The belief in an historical instrument of salvation is *a purely external appreciation of objective facts*. To seek to base the religious life on it is not to regard the essence of religion, but to make it for ever dependent on a stage of mental development that has long been passed in the inner life. Those who cling to an historical Jesus on religious grounds merely show that they have never understood the real nature of religion, or what "faith" really means in the religious sense of the word. They see only the interest of their Church, which assuredly profits by a confusion of true religious faith, of a trustful surrender to the God within us with the intellectual acceptance of certain facts of either a dogmatic or an historical character; they only deceive themselves and others when they imagine that they are promoting the interest of *religion*.

Our science has not hitherto suffered the indignity of being placed after theology in the hierarchy of culture, and so being compelled to justify its deepest thoughts and achievements from the theological point of view, or concern itself about theology at all. Our philosophy, however, allows faith to be set above knowledge, in spite of the fact that faith is born of the thirst for knowledge and consists in a view of the world; in this way theology comes to exercise control over the whole province of philosophical knowledge. A philosophy that thus comes to terms with theology, a "perfectly safe philosophy" which seeks to live in peace with theology, is unworthy of the name. For it is not the work of philosophy merely to prepare academic theses, and deal with things that have no interest for any person outside the lecture-hall and the study: its greatest cultural task is to defend the rights of reason, to extend its sway over every province of knowledge, and to rationalise faith. In the words of Hegel, its task is "to disturb as much as possible the ant-like zeal of the theologians who use critical methods for the strengthening of their Gothic temple, to make their work as difficult as possible, to drive them out of every refuge, until none remains and they must show themselves openly in the light of day." It is from no accident, but in the very nature of things, that a philosopher thus came to denounce the truce which has so long and so artificially been maintained with theology, and sought to show the untenability of its central belief in an historical Jesus.

Meantime we may reflect with comfort on the words of Dupuis: "There are large numbers of men so perversely minded that they will believe everything except what is recommended by sound intelligence and reason, and shrink from philosophy as the hydrophobic shrinks from water. These people will not read us, and do not concern us; we have not written for them. Their mind is the prey of the priests, just as their body will be the prey of the worms. We have written only for the friends of humanity and reason. The rest belong to another world; even their God tells them that his kingdom is not of this world—that is to say, not of the world in which people use their judgment—and that the simple are blessed because theirs is the kingdom of heaven. Let us, therefore, leave to them their opinions, and not envy the priests such a possession. Let us pursue our way, without lingering to count the number of the credulous. When we have unveiled the sanctuary in which the priest shuts himself, we can hardly expect that he will press his followers to read us. We will be content with a happy revolution, and we will see that, for the honour of reason, it is so complete as to prevent the clergy from doing any further harm to mankind."

ARTHUR DREWS.

THE WITNESSES TO THE HISTORICITY OF JESUS

THE NON-CHRISTIAN WITNESSES

IN view of the vagueness, defectiveness, and vulnerability of the evangelical accounts of Jesus, as far as his historical reality is concerned, the witnesses in non-Christian literature have always occupied a prominent place in the question of his historicity. As early as the first few centuries of the present era pious Christians searched the Jewish and pagan writers for references to Jesus, convinced that such references ought to be found in them; they regarded with great concern the undeniable defects of tradition, and, in the interest of their faith, endeavoured to supply the want by more or less astute "pious frauds," such as the Acts of Pilate, the letter of Jesus to King Abgar Ukkama of Edessa,[1] the letter of Pilate to Tiberius, and similar forgeries. Greater still was the reliance on the few passages in profane literature which seemed to afford some confirmation of the historical truth of the things described in the gospels. As these so-called non-Christian witnesses are again brought forward to rebut the denial of the historicity of Jesus, in the discussion which has followed the appearance of *The Christ Myth*, and are even pressed upon us as decisive testimony, we must make a comprehensive inquiry into the value of those references in profane writers which seem to support the belief in an historical Jesus.

---

[1] Eusebius, *Ecclesiastical History*, I, 13.

THE JEWISH WITNESSES

1.—PHILO AND JUSTUS OF TIBERIAS.

LET us begin with the witnesses in Jewish literature. Here we at once encounter the singular circumstance that Philo (30 B.C. to 50 A.D.) makes no reference to Christ. Philo, the Alexandrian philosopher and contemporary of Jesus, was by no means a secluded scholar who took no interest in the fortunes of his people. As envoy of the Alexandrian Jews to Caligula, he pleaded the interests of his co-religionists at Rome, and, in all probability, himself visited the land of his fathers. He even in one place makes an incidental reference to Pilate, who had caused an agitation among the Jews at Jerusalem by some offence against their religious ideas.[1] We are further indebted to him for some important information on the Palestinian sect of the Essenes, who in many respects closely resembled the Jessenes and Nazarenes, as the Christians were at first called. His own views, in fact, have so unmistakable an affinity with those of the contemporary Jewish-Gnostic sects,[2] and some of these, such as the Cainites, are so fully described by him[3] that it is in the highest degree improbable that Philo was unacquainted with the Nazarenes, on the supposition that they really were an important body in his time, and caused as serious an agitation among the Jews as is commonly believed.

It may be suggested that Philo had no occasion to speak about them.

How can we explain, then, that the Jewish historian

[1] Schürer, *Geschichte des Jüd. Volkes*, 4th ed. III, p. 678, etc.
[2] Gfrörer, *Philo und die Jüd.-Alex. Theologie*, 1835.
[3] M. Friedländer, *Der vorchristliche Jüd. Gnostizismus*, 1898, p. 19, etc.

Justus of Tiberias, another contemporary and a closer fellow-countryman of the alleged historical Jesus—he lived at Tiberias, not far from Capernaum, where Jesus is supposed to have been especially active—is also silent about them? Justus wrote a chronicle of the Jewish kings down to the time of Agrippa II. The original work has been lost. We know it only from a reference in Photius, a patriarch of Constantinople of the ninth century. Photius assures us, however, that he read through the Chronicle of Justus in search of references to Jesus, and found none; he attributes it to "the disease"—that is to say, the unbelief—of the Jews that such a man as Justus does not mention the appearance of Christ, the fulfilment of the prophecies by him, and the miracles he wrought. As, however, we learn from Photius that the chronicle was merely a brief treatment of a subject that had no direct connection with the life of Jesus, we must not lay too much stress on the absence of any reference. Still the fact remains that Photius himself believed there ought to be some mention of Jesus, and was surprised to find none.

2.—JOSEPHUS.

We have next to see how we stand in relation to the Jewish historian Flavius Josephus (37–100 A.D.), the contemporary and political opponent of Justus of Tiberias. He is the first profane writer who can seriously be quoted for the historicity of Jesus. Josephus wrote three large works—the history of the Jews, the history of the last Jewish war, and a defence of the Jewish religion. In these, according to the theological view, he cannot have had any occasion to deal with the appearance of Jesus, an episode of no significance in the history of the Jews, or with Christianity. At the time when he wrote the body was almost extinct as a Jewish sect, and in any case of no consequence whatever. Moreover, the theologians say, it would have been very difficult for him to deal with it from the point of view of either side.

But Josephus has mentioned much less important persons who, like Jesus, set up a messianic movement, and suffered death for it.

Josephus has left us a luminous portrait of Pilate. He depicts him in all his brutality and unscrupulousness.[1] Can we suppose that he refrained from telling how, in the case of Jesus, his compatriots forced the proud Roman to yield to them? Or did he know nothing of any such occurrence? Is it possible that he never heard of the exciting events which, as the gospels relate, occurred in the metropolis of Judæa—the triumphant entrance of Jesus into Jerusalem, while the people acclaim him as the expected Messiah, the growing anger of the ruling parties, the taking of Jesus by night, the disturbance before the Governor's house, the abandonment of one of their own people by the Sanhedrim to the hated Roman authorities, the disappearance of the body from the grave, etc.? It would not be very easy to show that Jesus and his affairs would seem "insignificant" to Josephus in writing the history of the Jews, and that the sect brought into existence by him would seem unworthy of mention. At that time the Christian movement is supposed to have reached a prominent place in public life and attracted general attention. Can it be called an insignificant thing when a new religious sect enters into such rivalry with the old religion, from which it has sprung, as is ascribed to early Christianity in the *Acts of the Apostles*,[2] and this a very short time after the death of its founder? We have only to recall the three thousand souls who are supposed to have been baptised in one day at Jerusalem, in the very heart of the Jewish cult! It is, of course, an enormous Christian exaggeration; but, in any case, Christianity must have made great progress before the

---

[1] *Jewish Antiquities*, xviii, 3, 1 and 2; 4, 1, etc.   [2] ii, 41.

destruction of Jerusalem, if we are to put any faith whatever in the account of its early years given in the New Testament.

It has been suggested that Josephus concealed the whole messianic movement among his people from the Romans, and wished to represent the Jews to them as extremely harmless, peaceful, and philosophical citizens; and that this explains his remarkable conduct. In other parts of his works, however, Josephus does not make the least difficulty about the messianic agitations of the people of Palestine. In the *Antiquities*,[1] for instance, he gives the episode of the false Messiah who induced the Samaritans to go up with him to the holy mountain Gerizim, where he would show them the sacred vessels which Moses was supposed to have buried there, and thus he could inflame them to rise against their Roman masters. He tells of Judas the Gaulonite, who stirred up the people against the census of Quirinius.[2] He also relates how Theudas pretended to be a prophet and said that he could by his sole word cause the waters of the Jordan to divide, and so allow those who followed him to cross over in safety.[3] Does anyone seriously believe, in fact, that Josephus could have concealed from the Romans, who had long ruled over Palestine and were most accurately informed as to the disposition of their subjects, the messianic expectations and agitations of his compatriots, and represented them as harmless, in works which were especially concerned with their strained relations to their oppressors? It would be much the same as if a Pole, writing the history of his country, were, in order to avert unkindly feeling from his compatriots, to say nothing of their dream of a restoration of the ancient kingdom of Poland, and represent the Poles as "extremely harmless, peaceful, and philosophical citizens"!

[1] xviii, 4, 1.
[2] *Antiquities*, xviii, 1, 1; 1, 6; xx, 5, 2; *Jewish War*, ii, 8, 1.
[3] *Antiquities*, xx, 5, 1.

As a matter of fact, it is hardly less ridiculous to make any such tender feeling for the sensitiveness of Rome the ground for the remarkable silence of Josephus, as Weinel and many other theologians do, than for von Soden, another theologian, to declare that Josephus would have been "embarrassed" to pass judgment on the Christians and the head of their sect from either side.[1] What sides does he mean? From the Roman side? But it might be a matter of complete indifference to them what judgment a Josephus would pass on what was—so von Soden would have us believe—in the eyes of the Jewish historian, the insignificant sect of the Christians? Does he mean from the Jewish side? They would entirely agree with him if he condemned it. Is it suggested that he had a favourable opinion of the Christians? This is, in point of fact, the view of J. Weiss, and it harmonises very well with the predilection of Josephus for the Essenes. It seems to him an indication of "a friendly, or at least impartial, disposition" that Josephus does not mention the Christians and their founder. He therefore rejects the view, put forward by Jülicher, that Josephus said nothing about the Christians because their sect might discredit the Jewish faith. According to Jülicher, it is "not difficult to guess" why Josephus omitted the Christian sect from his narrative: "not from shame and not from hatred, but because he could not very well *at the same time* represent the Jews, in whom he was primarily interested, as supporters of the Roman monarchy and of human civilisation, and describe the Christians (of the first century), who were regarded as enemies of the whole world, as an outcome of his pacific Jews. To be silent about them was a cleverer tactic than vigorously to shake them from his coat-tails" (!). It is remarkable what astounding things these theologians will say. Would not Josephus have done better, if he were minded

---

[1] *Hat Jesus gelebt?*, 13.

as Jülicher says, to have separated himself as widely as possible from the Christians? "In the same way as he condemns the zealots," says Weiss, "who were responsible for all the misfortunes of his country, he would have had a fitting occasion to brand the fools or fanatics who had drawn such false conclusions from the sayings of the prophets; to him especially the Christians must have been the fittest lightning-conductor." According to Weiss, therefore, the silence of Josephus is "no sign of hatred of the Christians, but rather the reverse. An enemy of the Christians would certainly have drawn attention to them in order to relieve Judaism of the charge of having anything to do with the sect." "His silence is all the more puzzling" (p. 90). May not the simple explanation be that in the time of Josephus the Christians did not differ sufficiently from official Judaism to require special mention? Must we not conclude from this silence of Josephus that he knew nothing about Jesus, though, if Jesus had really existed and things had occurred as tradition affirms, he ought certainly to have heard of and mentioned him, just as he mentions a John the Baptist and refers to other pretenders to the messiahship and disturbers of the people? Weinel maintains that Josephus would only count as a witness against the historicity of Jesus if he spoke of Christianity and was silent only about Jesus (p. 107). But what if he had no occasion to speak of it because our whole modern view of the rise of Christendom, and the part it played during the first century, is radically false?

Josephus, however, is not silent about Jesus. In his *Jewish Antiquities* (xviii, 3, 3) we read: "About this time lived Jesus, a wise man, if indeed he should be called man. He wrought miracles and was a teacher of those who gladly accept the truth, and had a large following among the Jews and pagans. He was the Christ. Although Pilate, at the complaint of the leaders of our people, condemned him to die on the cross, his earlier followers were faithful to him. For he appeared to them alive again on the third day, as god-sent prophets had foretold this and a thousand other wonderful things of him. The people [sect?] of the Christians, which is called after him, survives until the present day."

Here, it would appear, we have what we seek. Unfortunately, the genuineness of the passage is by no means admitted. There are two opinions on it. According to one view, the whole passage is an interpolation; according to the other, it has merely been altered by a Christian hand.

Let us examine the words of Josephus which remain after the expurgation of the supposed possible interpolations. They are as follows: "About this time lived Jesus, a wise man. He had a large following among the Jews and pagans. Although Pilate, at the complaint of the leaders of our people, condemned him to die on the cross, his earlier followers were faithful to him. The sect of the Christians, which is called after him, survives until the present day." Immediately before this Josephus tells of a rising of the Jews, due to a bitter feeling at the conduct of Pilate, and its bloody suppression by the ruling power. The words that immediately follow the passage are: "Also about this time another misfortune befel the Jews"; and we are told of the expulsion of the Jews from Rome by Tiberius on account of the conduct of some of their compatriots.

What is the connection between the reference to Jesus and these two narratives? That there must be some connection, if Josephus himself has written the passage about Jesus, goes without saying, in view of the character of the writer. Josephus is always careful to have a logical connection between his statements. The repression of the Jews by Pilate must, naturally, have been regarded by Josephus as "a misfortune." We likewise understand the concern of the Jewish historian at the expulsion of his compatriots from Rome. These two episodes are directly connected by their very nature.

But what have the condemnation and crucifixion of Jesus to do with them? If Josephus really considered the fate of Jesus as a misfortune of his people, why was he content to devote to it a couple of meagre and lifeless sentences? Why was he silent about the followers of Jesus? We have already seen that the reasons usually advanced for this silence are worthless. From a rational point of view, Josephus had no occasion whatever to put the passage about Jesus in the connection in which we find it. That, on the other hand, the later Christians had every interest in inserting the passage, and inserting it precisely at this point, where there is question of events in the time of Pilate and of the misfortunes of the Jews, is clear enough; it must have been to the Christians a matter of profound astonishment and concern that in such a connection there was not a word about Jesus, whose name was for them intimately connected with that of Pilate. And was not the condemnation of Jesus at the demand of the Jewish leaders really the greatest misfortune that the Jews had ever incurred?[1] In the edition of Origen published by the Benedictines it is said[2] that there was no mention of Jesus at all in Josephus before the time of Eusebius (about 300 A.D., *Ecclesiast. Hist.*, I, 11). Moreover, in the sixteenth century Vossius had a manuscript of the text of Josephus in which there was not a word about Jesus. It seems, therefore, that the passage must have been an interpolation, whether it was subsequently modified or not. We are led to the same conclusion by the fact that neither Justin, nor Tertullian, nor Origen, nor Cyprian ever quotes Josephus as a witness in their controversies with Jews and pagans. Yet Justin, at least, could have had no better argument than the testimony of a compatriot in his dialogue with the Jew Trypho. Indeed, Origen says expressly that Josephus did not recognise Jesus as the Messiah.[3]

---

[1] *Cf.* Origen, *Contra Celsum*, I, 47. [2] I, 362. [3] *Contra Celsum*, I, 47.

The same difficulties arise in regard to the other passage in Josephus,[1] where the Jewish historian tells how the younger Ananus (Hannas), at the time when the governor Festus died and his successor Albinus was as yet on the way, summoned a Council, brought before it James, the "brother of Jesus, who was called Christ," and had him and some others stoned for transgression of the law (62 A.D.). It is extremely doubtful whether James is understood by Josephus to be the corporal brother of Jesus, as brotherhood might very well mean only that he belonged to the Jesus-sect. In that sense Josephus would merely be saying that James was a "brother of Jesus," or leader of those who venerated the Messiah (Christ) under the name of Jesus. It is more probable, however, that this passage also is a later interpolation, as Credner[2] and Schürer are disposed to admit. Weiss also (88) regards this passage in the text as a Christian interpolation; and Jülicher too says, in his essay on "Religion and the Beginning of Christianity," in Hinneberg's *Kultur der Gegenwart* (2nd ed. 1909), that Josephus leaves Jesus "unmentioned" (*loc. cit.*, 43).

We understand, therefore, why Origen knows nothing of the passage. In his polemical work against Celsus he does not mention it when he comes to speak of James,[3] though he refers to another in which Josephus represents the destruction of Jerusalem as a punishment of the Jews for having put James to death; which certainly does not accord with the facts.

3.—THE TALMUD.

When we have thus excluded Josephus from the number of witnesses to the historicity of Jesus, there remains only the question whether there may not be some evidence in the other Jewish literature of the time: in the body of Rabbinical writings collected under the name

---

[1] *Antiquities*, xx, 9, 1.   [2] *Einl. ins N. T.*, 1836, p. 581.   [3] I, 47.

of the Talmud, which cover a period from about 200 B.C. to 600 A.D. The answer is that no information about Jesus is to be found in the Talmud. One would suppose that, in works intended solely for a Jewish public, the Rabbis of the time would not fail to take the opportunity of attacking Jesus, if he spoke and acted as the gospels describe. Instead of this, they almost entirely ignore him, and, when they do mention him, their references have not the least historical importance. Von Soden declares that they had no opportunity of dealing seriously with him, as the oldest collection, entitled "Sayings of the Fathers," contains only moral sentences. Nevertheless, all these moral aphorisms, definitions of religious law, and ritual prescriptions are closely connected with the meaning of the work. They partly relate to the same subjects as the sayings of Jesus. They bring together the opposing views of the various famous Rabbis. Why is the Talmud silent about Jesus in this connection? Why is there not the slightest definite reference to the man who expounded the law more subtly than any other Jewish teacher, and made the most serious attack upon the orthodox conception?

It is poor consolation for the supporters of the historicity of Jesus when an expert on the Talmud, Chwolson, says that there was no contemporary Rabbinical literature. In the extant Rabbinical literature of the second century there is, on his own showing, much material and many sayings that "belong to the Rabbis of the second and first centuries of the Christian era."[1] In fact, there are supposed to be among them three valuable references of the first and beginning of the second century—the experience, namely, of the Rabbi Eliezer ben Hyrcanus, the brother-in-law of Gamaliel II., with the Judæo-Christian James of Kefar-Schechania, of whom it is said that he was a "pupil" (disciple) of Jesus, and had healed

---

[1] *Ueber die Frage ob Jesus gelebt hat*, p. 11.

the sick in the name of Jesus. Then there is the explanation by Jesus of a difficulty in the law, which the said James put to him, and which Jesus settled by a certain verse, after the fashion of the Rabbis. Lastly, there is the doubt of the Rabbi as to the orthodoxy of Jesus and the disdain he himself incurred by becoming a Christian. But who doubts for a moment that at the close of the first century and in the first half of the second sayings and explanations of the law were current in the name of Jesus, that the name of Jesus was used in exorcisms, and that sympathy with the Jesus-sect might in certain circumstances have very unpleasant consequences for a Rabbi?[1]

There is no room for doubt that after the destruction of Jerusalem, and especially during the first quarter of the second century, the hostility of the Jews and Christians increased, as not only Chwolson himself (*Das letzte Passahmahl Christi*) and Joel,[2] but also Lublinski, has recently shown.[3] Indeed, by the year 130 the hatred of the Jews for the Christians became so fierce that a Rabbi, whose niece had been bitten by a serpent, preferred to let her die rather than see her healed "in the name of Jesus." But when Chwolson says that we see from these passages that the Rabbis of the second half of the first century, or the beginning of the second, were "well acquainted with the *person* of Christ" (13), he clearly deceives himself and his readers, if the impression is given that they had any personal knowledge of him.

On the other hand, the Rabbis are said to have possessed, as early as the year 71 A.D., a gospel which,

---

[1] Moreover, it is by no means established that the Jesus whom James of Kefar followed was the Jesus of the gospels. Neubauer, in his text of the Talmud, read, instead of Jesus ha-Nozri (the Nazarene), Jesus Pandira, who was supposed to be a contemporary of the Rabbi Akiba (p. 135). *Cf.* K. Lippe, *Das Evangelium Matthaei vor dem Forum der Bibel und des Talmud*, 1889, p. 26.
[2] *Blicke in die Religionsgeschichte*, II, 1883, especially p. 73, etc.
[3] *Die Entstehung des Christenthums aus der antiken Kultur*, 1910.

according to Chwolson, "was probably the original gospel of Matthew." About that time a judge appointed by the Romans, "undoubtedly a Judæo-Christian of Pauline tendencies," though he is not expressly described as such, quotes *Matthew* v, 17, in the Aramaic language, where it is said that Christ did not wish to abolish, but to supplement, the Mosaic law. In his work *Jesus, die Häretiker und die Christen nach den ältesten jüdischen Angaben* (1910, p. 19, etc.), Strach has given us a literal translation of this passage.[1] It runs:—

> Imma Salom was the wife of the Rabbi Eliezer, the sister of Rabban Gamaliel. Among his acquaintances was a "philosopher" who had the reputation of being incorruptible. *They wished to make him ridiculous. Therefore* she [Imma] brought to him a golden candlestick, and said: "I desire a part of the family property." He answered them: "Divide it." Then he [R. Gamaliel] said: "It is written for us[2] that, where there is a son, the daughter inherits nothing." He answered: "Since ye were driven from your land the law of Moses is abolished, and there is Avon-gillajon [Evangelium = the Gospel], in which it is written, 'Son and daughter shall inherit together.'" On the following day he [R. Gamaliel] on his own part brought him a Libyan ass. Then he replied: "I have searched further in the Avon-gillajon, and it is written therein: 'I, Avon-gillajon, have not come to do away with the Thora, but to add to the Thora of Moses have I come.' And it is further written therein: 'Where there is a son, the daughter shall not inherit.'" Then she said: "Thy light shineth like a candle." And R. Gamaliel said: "The ass has come, and has attached the candle"

—*i.e.*, someone had spoiled the effect of a small bribe by giving a larger one.

It is possible that we really have here a reference to the text of *Matthew*, and this is the more likely when we consider the play upon the candlestick, in reference to *Matthew* v, 14–16. That there is no question of our *Matthew* is certain, as there is no such passage in any of

---

[1] *Babyl. Talmud Sabbath*, p. 116, etc. [2] *Numbers* xxvii, 8.

our gospels that the son and daughter shall inherit together; Jesus, on the contrary, often expressly dissuades from mingling in these quarrels about inheritance.[1] But what right has Chwolson to put the witness of this "Primitive Matthew," which seems to be referred to in the anecdote, about the year 71 A.D.? Chwolson relies on the fact that R. Gamaliel (died about 124) was the son of the R. Simeon ben Gamaliel who is known to us from *Acts* v, 34, where he cleverly speaks for the Christians, and *Acts* xxii, 3, as a teacher of the Apostle Paul, and who was executed about 70 A.D. with other Rabbis who had taken part in the rising against the Romans. He gratuitously assumes that the passage in the Talmud refers to the quarrel about the property of the dead father, which would be divided about the year 71. This is plausible enough if there is question in the passage of a *genuine* quarrel about inheritance. But that is precisely what the text of the passage excludes. It is expressly stated that they wished to bring ridicule upon the "philosopher" who had an unmerited repute for incorruptibility. There is question, therefore, of a purely *fictitious* quarrel about inheritance, and there is no reason to suppose that this would necessarily be about the year 71. Indeed, the text itself shows that it was not, as the Jews were not yet expelled in 71; so that Chwolson finds himself compelled to change the expression "driven from your country" into "lost your country." Hence Chwolson's statement that there is evidence of a Gospel of Matthew in 71 A.D. breaks down. Moreover, even if the existence of such a gospel at that time were proved, it would have no bearing on the historicity of Jesus. The saying in *Matthew* v, 17 is not at all quoted in the Talmud passage as a saying of Jesus, as one would gather from Chwolson. "We see," says Chwolson emphatically and in large type, "from this important reference that not only was there

---

[1] *Luke* xii, 14.

a Gospel of Matthew in existence about the year 71 A.D., but it was already well known to the Christians of the time." As you please; but one would like to know what this proves in regard to the historicity of Jesus.[1]

In addition to the few first-century references quoted by Chwolson, and regarded by him as "of great historical value," the Talmud contains a comparatively large number of references to Jesus, mostly of the third and fourth centuries. They have, of course, as Chwolson admits, "no historical value whatever" (p. 11). They are rather caricatures of Jesus, when they do plainly refer to him; though this, on account of the cryptic phrasing of the Rabbis, does not seem to be the case quite as frequently as is generally supposed. Derenbourg has shown that the much-quoted Stada or ben Sat'da is not originally identical with Jesus, and Strach also admits that the scanty material in regard to Jesus which earlier students found in the Talmud shrinks still further on more careful inquiry.[2] Jülicher, however, has pointed out that, as the caricatures of the Jesus-story are familiar to R. Akiba, we may conclude that the Christian tradition itself is much older. Now, Akiba met his end, in old age, on the occasion of the bloody rising of the Jews under Bar Kochba, in the year 135. It is not disputed that the *evangelical tradition* existed in the first third of the second century, when the hostility of the Jews and Christians was at its height. What "proof" is there, then, of the historicity of Jesus in the fact that Akiba, a fierce enemy of the Christians, spoke bitterly of Jesus at that time? Certainly he regards him as an historical personage, just as the Talmud generally never doubts that Jesus had really existed. But Joel has, in this connection, shown that the Talmudists of the second century were careless about everything except the study of the

---

[1] Compare Steudel, *Im Kampf um die Christusmythe*, 1910, p. 83, etc.
[2] There is a complete collection of the relevant passages in H. Laible, *Jesus Christus im Talmud*, 1891, 2nd ed. 1900.

scriptures and the law, and pointed out that it is "one of the most curious and astonishing consequences" of this indifference that they were so poorly informed in regard to events in the time of Jesus.[1] The Talmud derives all that it knows of the origin of Christianity from the little that has reached it of the gospel tradition and from the impression it has of the life of Jesus from the events of the second century; and it changes its statements, as time goes on, in harmony with the changes in the Christian tradition. Thus Akiba, for instance, followed the narrative of the Synoptics in regard to the death of Jesus, and put the execution on the Feast-day. On the other hand, the somewhat later *Mischna* iv, 1, and the *Gemara* give the later version of the Gospel of John, that the death was on the Day of Preparation for the Passover. Hence the Talmud has *no independent tradition about Jesus;* all that it says of him is merely an echo of Christian and pagan legends, which it reproduces according to the impressions of the second and later centuries, not according to historical tradition.[2] That is, moreover, the view of Jülicher in *Kultur der Gegenwart*, where he says that the Talmud has "borrowed" its knowledge of Jesus from the gospels. The Talmud is, in fact, so imperfectly acquainted with the time and the circumstances of Jesus that it confuses him with the Rabbi Josua ben Perachja, or a pupil of his of the same name (about 100 B.C.), and even makes him a contemporary of Akiba in the first third of the second century. Can we, in such circumstances, pretend that there is any evidence for the historicity of Jesus in the fact that the Talmud does not question it?

It is not true, however, as has recently been stated, that no Jew ever questioned the historical reality of Jesus, so that we may see in this some evidence for his existence. The Jew Trypho, whom Justin introduces in

---

[1] *Loc. cit.*, p. 54.   [2] Joel, *loc. cit.*, p. 54, etc.

his *Dialogue with Trypho*, expresses himself very sceptically about it. "Ye follow an empty rumour," he says, "and make a Christ for yourselves." "If he was born and lived somewhere, he is entirely unknown."[1] This work appeared in the second half of the second century; it is therefore the first indication of a denial of the human existence of Jesus, and shows that such opinions were current at the time.

---

[1] viii, 3. Compare also K. Lippe, *Das Evangelium des Matthäus*.

THE ROMAN WITNESSES

1.—PLINY AND SUETONIUS.

WE now come to the Roman witnesses to the historicity of Jesus.

Of the younger Pliny it is hardly necessary to speak further in this connection. He was dragged into the discussion of the "Christ-myth" at a late stage, merely to enlarge the list of witnesses to the historicity of Jesus. No one seriously believes that any such evidence is found in Pliny.[1] In his correspondence with the Emperor Trajan, which is believed to have taken place about the year 113, and which is occupied with the question how Pliny, as Proconsul of the province of Bithynia in Asia Minor, was to behave in regard to the Christians, he informs the Emperor that the adherents of the sect sing hymns to Christ at daybreak " as if he were a god (*quasi deo*)." What this proves as regards the historical reality of the *man* Christ we should be pleased to have rationally explained.[2] What has been said on the subject up to

---

[1] It is characteristic of the tactics of our opponents that certain Catholic writers have begun to appeal to Porphyry, the Neoplatonic philosopher, who lived 232-304 A.D. He wrote many works against Christianity, which we know only indirectly from the refutations of Methodius and Eusebius. No one can say precisely what they contained, as the Emperor Theodosius II. prudently ordered them to be burned in public in the year 435. What does that matter to the theologian as long as he can bring one more name into the field?

[2] Moreover, the genuineness of this correspondence of Pliny and Trajan is by no means certain. Justin does not mention it on an occasion when we should expect him to do so, and even Tertullian's supposed reference to it (*Apol.*, cap. ii) is very doubtful. The tendency of the letters to put the Christians in as favourable a light as possible is too obvious not to excite some suspicion. For these and other reasons the correspondence was declared by experts to be spurious even at the time of its first publication, at the beginning of the sixteenth century ; and recent authorities, such as Semler, Aubé (*Histoire des Persécutions de l'Église*, 1875, p. 215, etc.), Havet (*Le Christianisme et ses Origines*, 1884, iv, 8), and Hochart (*Études*

the present is merely frivolous, adapted only to an utterly thoughtless circle of readers or hearers. Yet even a man like Jülicher does not hesitate to quote Pliny among the profane witnesses. He also mentions Marcus Aurelius, who expresses his anger against the Christians in his *Meditations* (about the year 175!), and assures us that what is meant there by Christianity is the community of those who believed in the Jesus of our and their gospels as their God and Saviour (p. 17). We are grateful for this "information," but we should have expected that a scholar like Jülicher would have something more serious to tell us on the subject.

There seems to be more significance in the words of the Roman historian Suetonius (77–140 A.D.), who tells us in his *Life of Claudius* (c. 25) that that emperor "expelled from Rome the Jews because, at the instigation of Chrestus, they were perpetually making trouble" (Claudius Judæos impulsore Chresto assidue tumultuantes Roma expulit). If we only knew precisely who is meant by this Chrestus! The name in the text is not "Christus," but "Chrestus" (and in some manuscripts Cherestus), which is by no means the usual designation of Jesus, while it is a common name, especially among Roman freedmen. Hence the whole passage in Suetonius may have nothing whatever to do with the question of Christianity. It may just as well refer to any disturbances whatever caused among the Jews by a man named Chrestus, and it does not say much for the "scientific" spirit of theologians when they interpret it in their own sense without further ado.

An attempt has been made to connect the passage in Suetonius with the messianic expectation of the Jews, and to interpret it in the sense of referring either to

au Sujet de la Persécution des Chrétiens sous Néron, 1885, pp. 79–143; compare also Bruno Bauer, *Christus und die Cäsaren*, 1877, p. 268, etc., and the anonymously published work of Edwin Johnson, *Antiqua Mater*, 1887), which have disputed its authenticity, either as a whole or in material points.

quarrels in the Jewish community at Rome owing to the belief of those who held that Jesus was the Messiah they all expected, or to a general agitation of Roman Judaism on account of its messianic ideas and hostility to the pagan world. The first alternative, however, is not very helpful in view of the fact that, when Paul came to Rome about ten years afterwards to preach the gospel, the Jews there seem to have known nothing whatever about Jesus; and, according to the account in *Acts*, his arrival led to no disturbance among them.[1] The second alternative, on the other hand, contains no evidence for the historicity of Jesus, as, even if we substitute Christus for Chrestus, "Christus" is merely the Greek-Latin translation of "Messiah," and the phrase "at the instigation of Chrestus" would refer to the Messiah generally, and not at all necessarily to the particular Messiah Jesus as an historical personality.[2]

In any case, however we interpret the passage of Suetonius, it has no bearing whatever on the question of the historicity of Jesus. Jülicher and Weinel admit this when they omit Suetonius in their enumeration of profane witnesses. J. Weiss also admits: "The passage in Suetonius relating to Jewish disturbances at Rome in the time of Claudius 'impulsore Chresto' betrays so inaccurate a knowledge of the facts that it cannot seriously be regarded as a witness" (p. 88).

2.—TACITUS.

The passage in Suetonius leaves it uncertain who Chrestus is, and cannot, therefore, be advanced as a

---

[1] *Acts* xxviii, 17, etc.
[2] In his *Geschichte der Römischen Kaiserzeit*, Bd. I, Abt. I (1883), p. 447, Hermann Schiller also connects the expulsion of the Jews under Claudius with their domestic disturbances, and says: "It is time to desist from the practice of identifying the *impulsor Chrestus* in Suetonius with Christ. Words ending in 'tor' stand for a constant property, or an act that impresses a definite and permanent stamp on the subject in question; in neither case can we refer this to Christ, who had never been in Rome, and was no longer living; the activity of the *impulsor* can relate only to the *assidue tumultuantes* referred to."

THE ROMAN WITNESSES

proof of the historicity of Jesus. It is very different with the evidence of Tacitus. In the *Annals* (xv, 44) Christ is expressly mentioned as an historical personage. The historian has related what measures were taken by Nero to lessen the suffering brought about by the great fire at Rome in the year 64, and to remove the traces of it. He then continues: "But neither the aid of man, nor the liberality of the prince, nor the propitiations of the gods, succeeded in destroying the belief that the fire had been purposely lit. In order to put an end to this rumour, therefore, Nero laid the blame on and visited with severe punishment those men, hateful for their crimes, whom the people called Christians [Ergo abolendo rumori Nero subdidit reos et quæsitissimis pœnis affecit quos per flagitia invisos vulgus Christianos appellabat]. He from whom the name was derived, Christus, was put to death by the procurator Pontius Pilatus in the reign of Tiberius [autor nominis ejus Christus, Tiberio imperitante, per procuratorem Pontium Pilatum supplicio affectus erat]. But the pernicious superstition, checked for a moment, broke out again, not only in Judæa, the native land of the monstrosity, but also in Rome, to which all conceivable horrors and abominations flow from every side, and find supporters. First, therefore, those were arrested who openly confessed; then, on their information, a great number, who were not so much convicted of the fire as of hatred of the human race. Ridicule was poured on them as they died; so that, clothed in the skins of beasts, they were torn to pieces by dogs, or crucified, or committed to the flames, and when the sun had gone down they were burned to light up the night [Igitur primum correpti, qui fatebantur, deinde indicio eorum multitudo ingens, haud proinde in crimine incendii quam odio humani generis convicti sunt. Et pereuntibus addita ludibria, ut ferarum tergis contecti laniatu canum interirent, aut crucibus affixi, aut flammandi, atque ubi defecisset dies, in usum nocturni luminis urerentur]. Nero had lent his garden for this spectacle, and gave games in the Circus, mixing with the people in the dress of a charioteer or standing in the chariot. Hence there was a strong sympathy for them, though they might have been guilty enough to deserve the severest punishment, on the ground that they were sacrificed, not to the general good, but to the cruelty of one man."

(a) Evidential Value of the Passage.—When Tacitus is assumed to have written, about the year 117, that the founder of the sect, Christus, was put to death by the procurator Pontius Pilate in the reign of Tiberius, Christianity was already an organised religion with a settled tradition. Even the gospels, or at least three of them, are supposed to have then been in existence. Hence Tacitus might have derived his information about Jesus, if not directly from the gospels, at all events indirectly from them by means of oral tradition. That was the view of Dupuis, who writes: "Tacitus says what the legend said. Had he been speaking of the Brahmans, he would have said, in the same way, that they derived their name from a certain Brahma, who had lived in India, as there was a legend about him; yet Brahma would not on that account have lived as a man, as Brahma is merely the name of one of the three manifestations of the personified god-head. When Tacitus spoke thus in his account of Nero and the sect of the Christians, he merely gave the supposed etymology of the name, without caring in the least whether Christ had really existed or it was merely the name of the hero of some sacred legend. Such an inquiry was quite foreign to his work."[1] Even J. Weiss observes: "Assuredly there were the general lines of even a purely fictitious Christian tradition already laid down about the year 100; Tacitus may therefore draw upon this tradition" (p. 88). It has been said, on the authority of Mommsen, that Tacitus may have derived his

---

[1] *Ursprung der Gottesverehrung*, p. 223; *cf.* also p. 227.

information from the Acts of the Senate and the archives of the State, and it has been suggested that his authority was Cluvius Rufus, who was consul under Caligula. Weiss says, however: "That he or any other had seen a report from Pontius Pilate in the records of the Senate is a hypothesis I should not care to adopt, as it would be complicating a simple matter with an improbability." "Archival studies," we read in the *Handbuch der klassischen Altertumswissenschaft*, "are not very familiar to ancient historiography; and Tacitus has paid very little attention to the *acta diurna* and the records of the Senate."[1] In fact, Hermann Schiller says, in his *Geschichte des Römischen Kaiserreichs unter der Regierung des Nero* (1872): "We are accustomed to hearing Tacitus praised as a model historian, and in many respects it may be true; but it does not apply to his criticism of his authorities and his own research, for these were *astonishingly poor* in Tacitus. *He never studied the archives*."[2] It is, moreover, extremely improbable that a special report would be sent to Rome, and incorporated in the records of the Senate, in regard to the death of a Jewish provincial, Jesus. "The execution of a Nazareth carpenter was one of the most insignificant events conceivable among the movements of Roman history in those decades; it completely disappeared beneath the innumerable executions inflicted by the Roman provincial authorities. It would be one of the most remarkable instances of chance in the world if it were mentioned in any official report."[3] It is the sort of thing we may expect from a Tertullian, who, in his *Apology for Christianity* (c. 21), tells one who doubts the truth of the gospel story that he will find a special report of Pilate to Tiberius in the Roman archives. In the mouth of a modern historian such a statement is frankly ridiculous.

[1] viii, 2 Abt., Heft 2, under "Tacitus."
[2] Work quoted, p. 7.   [3] Weiss, work quoted, p. 92.

There is nothing, then, in the records of the Senate, and of Cluvius Rufus we know next to nothing. As Bruno Bauer ironically observes: "That the founder of Christianity was put to death under Tiberius by the procurator Pontius Pilate must have been discovered by the historian—who was not otherwise a very assiduous searcher of the archives—in the same archive which, according to Tertullian, also gave the fact that the sun was darkened at midday when Jesus died."[1] In any case the reference in Tacitus is no proof of the historicity of Jesus, because it is far too late; it is almost certain that the Roman historian simply derived it from the Christian legend. Tacitus could in 117 know of Christ only what reached him from Christian or intermediate circles. In such matters he merely reproduced rumours in whatever light his subject seemed to him to demand.[2]

Here we might close our investigation into the profane witnesses. We have reached the same result as J. Weiss: "*There is no really cogent witness in profane literature*" (p. 92). Weinel comes to the same conclusion when he says that not much importance can be attached by either side to non-Christian witnesses: "As there can be no doubt that at the time when the *Annals* of Tacitus, the letters of Pliny, and even the historical works of Josephus, appeared, Christianity was widely spread in the Roman Empire and traced its origin to Jesus, the man of Nazareth, who was crucified under Pontius Pilate" (p. 104). Jülicher also, in the above-mentioned essay in *Kultur der Gegenwart*, denies altogether the evidential value of the Roman profane witnesses.

(b) The Question of the Genuineness of "Annals," xv, 44.
—It is, however, not superfluous, perhaps, to consider more closely what is regarded as the most important profane witness for the historicity of Jesus—that of Tacitus. Such witnesses still seem to make a great impression on

---

[1] *Christus und die Cäsaren*, p. 155. [2] Schiller, work quoted.

the general public. Even theologians who are themselves
convinced of the worthlessness of such witnesses as
regards the problem we are considering do not fail, as a
rule, to repeat them to "the people" as if they gave
some confirmation of their belief in an historical Jesus.
That would be prevented once for all if it could be proved
that the whole passage is not from the pen of Tacitus at
all. However, this statement, which I advanced in the
Christ Myth in accordance with the view of the French
writer Hochart, has been so vehemently attacked, even
by those who, like Weiss and Weinel, admit the worthlessness of the passage as far as the historicity of Jesus
is concerned, that it seems necessary to inquire somewhat
closely into the genuineness of *Annals*, xv, 44.

I. ARGUMENTS FOR THE GENUINENESS.

There can, of course, be no question of any impossibility
of interpolating the passage in the *Annals* on the ground
of "the inimitable style of Tacitus," as defenders of the
genuineness repeat after Gibbon.[1] There is no "inimitable" style for the clever forger, and the more unusual,
distinctive, and peculiar a style is, like that of Tacitus,
the easier it is to imitate it. It would be strange if a
monastic copyist of Tacitus, occupied with his work for
months, if not for years, could not so far catch his style
as to be able to write these twenty or twenty-five lines in
the manner of Tacitus. Teuffel, in his *Geschichte der
Röm. Literature* (5th ed. 1890, ii, 1137), commends
Sulpicius Severus for his "skill" in imitating Tacitus,
among others, in his composition. Such an imitation is
not, in his opinion, beyond the range of possibility.
Moreover, as far as the historicity of Jesus is concerned,
we are, perhaps, interested only in one single sentence of
the passage, and that has nothing distinctively Tacitan
about it.

---

[1] *Decline and Fall*, ch. xvi.

Equally invalid is the claim that the way in which Tacitus speaks of the Christians excludes all idea of a Christian interpolation. Von Soden thinks that Christians "would certainly have put early Christianity in a more favourable light, as they always did when they falsified the story of the rise of Christianity in the historical works they read." He overlooks the fact that the injurious epithets on the new religion and its adherents would probably, in the opinion of the forger, tend to strengthen its chances of passing as genuine. They are just what one might suppose to be in harmony with the disposition of Tacitus. The expressions, moreover, are at once enfeebled by the reference to the sympathy that the Romans are supposed to have felt for the victims of Nero's cruelty. It is a common occurrence in the accounts of the Christian martyrs for the pagan opponents of Christianity to find their hostility changed into sympathy, and recognise the innocence of the persecuted Christians. We need quote only the description of Pilate in *Matthew* and *Luke*—his "I find no blame in him" and "I am innocent of the blood of this just man"—and the supposed words of Agrippa when Paul is charged before him: "This man doeth nothing worthy of death or of bonds."[1] So Pliny the younger condemns the Christians in his letter to Trajan, although he acknowledges their innocence. This, it is true, is not the case with Tacitus; he seems rather to regard the Christians as guilty, whether or no they were the authors of the fire. But he allows the spectators to be touched with pity for the executed Christians, and thus awakens a sympathetic feeling for them in the readers of his narrative.

It is said, however, that Tacitus, "on account of the difficulty of his style and his whole attitude, was not generally read by Christians," so that his text is, "in the

[1] *Acts* xxvi. 31.

general opinion of experts, the freest from corruption of all the ancient writings." So at least von Soden assures us (p. 11). In this, however, he is merely repeating the opinion of Gibbon. As a matter of fact, none of the works of Tacitus have come down to us without interpolations. This supposed "purity of the text of Tacitus as shown by the oldest manuscripts" exists only in the imagination of Gibbon and those who follow him. It is, further, not true that the Christians did not read Tacitus. We have a number of instances in the first centuries of Christian writers who are acquainted with Tacitus, such as Tertullian, Jerome, Orosius, Sidonius Apollinaris, Sulpicius Severus, and Cassiodorus. It is only in the course of the Middle Ages that this acquaintance with the Roman historian is gradually lost; and this not on account of, but in spite of, the passage in Tacitus on the Christians. This testimony of the Roman historian to the supposed first persecution of the Christians would be very valuable to them for many reasons.

Are there, however, no witnesses to the genuineness of the passages of Tacitus in early Christian literature? There is the letter of Clement of Rome belonging to the end of the first century. According to Eusebius,[1] it was sent by Clement, the secretary of the Apostle Peter, and the third or fourth bishop of Rome, to the community at Corinth, in the name of the Roman community; as is also stated by Hegesippus (c. 150) and Dionysius of Corinth.[2] The point is so uncertain, nevertheless, that such distinguished authorities as Semler, Baur, Schwegler, Zeller, Volkmar,[3] Hausrath,[4] Loman,[5] Van Manen, Von den Bergh van Eysing,[6] and Steck,[7] have disputed the

---
[1] *Eccl. Hist.* III, 16.   [2] *Op. cit.* iv, 22, 1-3; iv, 23.
[3] See his essay on "Clement of Rome and the Subsequent Period," *Tübinger Theol. Jahrbücher*, 1856, 287-369.
[4] *Neutestamentl. Zeitgesch.*, III, 99, Anm. 5.
[5] "Quæstiones Paulinæ," in *Theol. Tijdschrift*, 1883, p. 14, etc.
[6] *Onderzoek naar de achtheid van Clemens' ersten brief aan de Corinthers*, 1908.
[7] *Der Galaterbrief nach seiner Echtheit untersucht*, 1888, p. 294, etc.

genuineness of the letter; and it was reserved for the modern believers in Jesus to discover grounds for regarding it as genuine. Volkmar puts the letter in the year 125; Loman, Van Manen, and Steck do not admit its composition earlier than the year 140. The letter cannot, therefore, be regarded as a reliable document on that account.

But what do we learn about the Neronian persecution from the letter of Clement? " Out of jealousy and envy," he writes to the Corinthians, " the greatest and straightest pillars were persecuted and fought even to death "; as in the case of Peter, " who, through the envy of the wicked, incurred, not one or two, but many dangers, and so passed to his place in glory after rendering his testimony," and Paul, " who showed the faithful the way to persevere to the end; seven times was he imprisoned, he was banished, stoned, he went as a herald to the east and the west, and he reaped great glory by his faith. The whole world has attained to a knowledge of justice; he went even to the farthest parts of the west, and gave his testimony before them that held power. Then was he taken out of the world and went to the holy place, the greatest model of patience."[1]

It is clear that we have here no reference to the persecution of the Christians under Nero. It is not even stated that the apostles named met with a violent death on account of their faith, as the word " martyresas " (" after rendering his testimony ") need not by any means be understood to mean a testimony of blood, because the word " martyr " originally means only a witness to the truth of the Christian faith in the general sense, and is equivalent to " confessor," and was only later applied to those who sealed their faith by a violent death.[2] If the expression in the above text is usually taken to refer to

---

[1] *Neutestatamentl. Apokryphen*, edited by Hennecke, 1904, ch. v.
[2] See Hochart, *Études au Sujet de la Persécution des Chrétiens sous Néron*, 1885.

the execution of the apostles under Nero, it is not because
Clemens says anything about this execution, but merely
because, according to Christian tradition, Peter and Paul
are supposed to have been put to death at the time of the
Neronian persecution. This tradition, however, is not
only relatively late, but extremely doubtful in itself.
That Peter was never in Rome, and so did not meet his
end there under Nero, must be regarded as certain after
the research of Lipsius.[1] As regards Paul, the tradition
is, according to Frey,[2] certainly not earlier than the end
of the fifth century; before that time it was certainly
said that he and Peter died under Nero, but not that Paul
was a victim of the Neronian persecution.[3] How, then,
could the Roman Clemens about the end of the first
century connect the death of the two apostles with the
Neronian persecution? That he does so is supposed to
be shown by the succeeding words, in which he says:
"These men were accompanied on the heavenly pil-
grimage by a great number of the elect, who have given
us the noblest example of endurance in ill-treatment and
torment, which they suffered from the envious. On
account of envy women were persecuted, Danaids and
Dirces, and had to endure frightful and shameful ill-
treatment; yet they maintained their faith firmly, and
won a glorious reward, though they were feeble of body."
"These words," says Arnold, in his work *Die Neronische
Christenverfolgung* (1888), which supports the genuineness of *Annals*, xv, 44, "are seen at a glance to be a
Christian complement of the description of Tacitus; he
also speaks of 'most exquisite tortures,' of the shame and
derision with which the victims were treated when they
were put to death, and of the satisfaction it gave to the
crowds' lust for spectacles."[4] But would Tacitus, with

---

[1] See his *Chronologie der Röm. Bischöfe*, p. 162, and *Die Quellen der Röm. Petrussage*, 1872.
[2] *Die letzten Lebensjahre des Paulus*: Bibl. Zeit- u. Streitfragen, 1910.
[3] *Loc. cit.* p. 8; see also *Neutestamentl. Apokryphen*, p. 365.
[4] Work quoted, p. 37.

his well-known taste for spectacular stories of that kind, have refrained from giving us the ghastly picture of the Dirces torn on the horns of oxen? And what is the meaning of these Danaids, in whose form Christian women are said to have been shamed and put to death? Can anyone seriously believe that the patient water-drawing daughters of Danaos would provide a fitting spectacle for the satisfaction of the crowd's lust for display and blood? Or does the writer of the letter merely intend by the words "Danaids and Dirces," which have no connection with what precedes and follows in the text, to set the Christian women-martyrs in contrast to the frivolous performers of the ancient myth? Further, what does he mean when he says that these numerous men and women were ill-treated "out of jealousy and envy," and puts the lot of the Christians in this respect on the same footing as that of Cain and Abel, Jacob and Esau, Joseph and his brothers, Moses and the Egyptians, Aaron and Miriam, Dathan and Abiram, and David and Saul? Renan suggests the hatred of the Jews for the Christians; but Joel has successfully defended his co-religionists against such a charge, and Tacitus does not give it the least support. Arnold suggests "denunciations by Christians with party passions."[1] According to Lactantius, it was Nero's jealousy at the success of their propaganda that induced the emperor to persecute the Christians. But is it not possible that the writer of the letter had seen the Acts of Peter and other apocryphal writings, according to which Simon the magician, who had entered upon a struggle with Peter out of jealousy, may have been the cause of the persecution of the Christians? And may not the whole ambiguous passage, with its rhetorical generalities, not really refer to the Neronian persecution, but rather throw back upon the time of Nero the martyrdoms that Christian men and

---

[1] Work quoted, p. 69.

women had suffered in later persecutions? In any case, it does not follow from the letter of Clemens that the "number of the elect" who "had endured shame and torture on account of jealousy," and been "added to the company" of the apostles Peter and Paul, died at the same time as they. This assumption arises simply from an association of ideas between the death of the apostles and the supposed Neronian persecution—an association that in all probability did not exist in the time of Clemens. How could the supposed Clemens, about the year 95, make Peter and Paul die under Nero, when the former had never been in Rome, and the latter did not die until after 64? And how can the very scholars who dispute the presence of Peter in Rome and do not admit the death of Paul in the Neronian persecution regard the letter of Clemens as genuine, and as establishing the Neronian persecution?

This, then, is the situation: either the letter of Clemens was really written about the year 95, and in that case the supposed reference to the Neronian persecution must, if it really is such, be regarded as a later interpolation; or this reference is an original part of the letter, and in that case the letter cannot have been written until the tradition as to the death of the apostles in the Neronian persecution had taken shape—that is to say, not before the middle of the second century. In either case, the so-called letter of Clemens is no evidence of the fact of a considerable persecution of the Christians under Nero.[1]

---

[1] As the reference of the part quoted to the Neronian persecution is the only detail for fixing the date of the letter, if we refuse to admit the passage the date of the letter is altogether uncertain, and it may belong to the fourth century just as well as the first—the "great century of literary forgeries" (*Antiqua Mater*, p. 304). The reference in I, 1, where there is question of perils and hardships that have suddenly come upon the Roman community, to the Domitian persecution in the year 93 is anything but certain. It is by no means proved that the so-called Domitian persecution was a persecution of the Christians. The text of Dio Cassius (67, 14) which is relied upon points at the most to a persecution of those who, like Flavius Clemens, the emperor's cousin, leaned to "atheism" or the Jewish faith. "If we rely on Roman sources, we find no persecution of the Christians under Domitian; if we rely on Christian

The belief that the Neronian persecution of the Christians belongs to the realm of fable is further confirmed by the fact that the other witnesses that are quoted for it are just as vague and indecisive. What propagandist material would not the details of this first persecution of their faith have furnished to the early Christians! Yet what trace of it do we find in them? Let us take the evidence of Melito of Sardis. In his writing to the Emperor Marcus Aurelius, in which he endeavours to explain to the Emperor how beneficial Christianity had been to Roman power, we read: "The only emperors who, seduced by evil-minded men, sought to bring our religion into evil repute, were Nero and Domitian, and from their time the mendacious calumny of the Christians has continued, according to the habit of people to believe imputations without proof." In these words, which, moreover, are only known to us from Eusebius,[1] there is no question of a general persecution of the Christians under Nero; it is merely stated that Nero tried to bring the Christians into bad repute. Dionysius of Corinth (about 170) also, and the presbyter Caius, who lived in the time of the Roman bishop Zephyrinus (about 200), affirm only, according to the same Eusebius,[2] that Peter and Paul died the death of martyrs "about the same time" at Rome,[3] which does

---

sources, the persecution goes far beyond Rome, as, according to Hegesippus, the grandsons of Judas, being relatives of Christ, were brought from Palestine to Rome and condemned, and, according to Eusebius and, possibly, Irenæus, the apostle John was then banished to Patmos. In this case it cannot be said that Rome alone was affected by the persecution, and so there is no analogy with the description given in the letter " (Steck, work quoted, p. 297). It seems, then, that it was the imagination of the apologists and fathers of the Church, who wanted to make the sufferings of Christianity begin as early as possible, that deduced from the letter this persecution of the Christians as such. (Br. Bauer, work quoted, p. 288; also see Joel, work quoted, II, 45.)

[1] *Ecclesiastical History*, VI, 33.   [2] *Ibid*. II, 28.

[3] In this connection it may be observed that all these references in Eusebius must be regarded with the greatest suspicion. This man, whom Jakob Burckhardt has called "the first thoroughly dishonest historian of antiquity," acts so deliberately in the interest of the power of the Church and the creation and strengthening of tradition that far too much notice is taken of his historical statements. "After the many falsifications, suppressions, and fictions which have been proved in his

not necessarily mean on the same day or the same occasion, or that the "trophies of their victory" are to be seen on the Vatican and the road to Ostia. Of the Neronian persecution they tell us nothing. In Tertullian's *Apologeticum*[1] we read that Nero, cruel to all, was the first to draw the imperial sword against the Christian sect which then flourished at Rome. He thinks it an honour to himself and his co-religionists to have been condemned by such a prince, since everyone who knows him will see that nothing was condemned by Nero that was not especially good. But there is nothing in his words to show that he was thinking of anything besides the death of the apostles Peter and Paul. Indeed, he says expressly that the apostles, scattered over the world at the master's command, after many sufferings at length shed their blood at Rome through the cruelty of Nero, and he urges the pagans to read the proofs of this in their own "Commentaries"; which is much the same as when Tertullian refers to the Roman archives those who doubt the gospel narrative of the execution of Jesus.[2] We read much the same in the same writer's *Scorp.*, ch. xv: "Nero was the first to stain the early faith with blood. Then was Peter (according to the word of Christ) girded by another, as he was fixed to the cross. Then did Paul obtain the Roman right of citizenship in a higher sense, as he was born again there by his noble martyrdom."[3]

There remains only the witness of Eusebius and of *Revelation*. Eusebius, however, merely reproduces[4] the statement of Tertullian that Nero was the first of the emperors to become an open enemy of the divine religion. He writes: "Thus Nero raged even against the apostles,

---

work, he has no right to be put forward as a decisive authority; and to these faults we must add a consciously perverse manner of expression, deliberate bombast, and many equivocations, so that the reader stumbles upon trapdoors and pitfalls in the most important passages." (J. Burckhardt, *Leben Konstantins*, 2nd ed. 1860, pp. 307, 335, 347.)

[1] Ch. v. [2] Ch. xxi.
[3] See also *De Præscriptione*, cap. 36, and *Adversus Marcion*, iv, 5.
[4] *Ecclesiastical History*, ii, 28.

and so declared himself the first of the arch-enemies of God. It is recorded that under him Paul was beheaded at Rome and Peter was crucified under him." In proof of this he points to the fact that the names of Peter and Paul have remained until his time on an inscription in the burying-place at Rome. As to *Revelation*, the commonly assumed connection between it and the Neronian persecution is so little proved that Arnold speaks of it as "a most unhappy suggestion" to associate the "great crowd" of Christians executed under Nero, according to Tacitus, with the vision of John, in which the seer beholds a vast multitude, whom no man can count, of all nations, peoples, and tongues, bearing palms and clothed in white garments before the throne of the Most High.[1] The Christian parts of the so-called Sybilline Oracles, which are supposed to have been written in part shortly after this event, have, as Arnold says, no relation to the Neronian persecution, even where there would be the greatest occasion. They speak often enough of the return of Nero and his cruelties, but he is never represented, as he is afterwards in Eusebius, as the enemy of God and Christ and the persecutor of the early community. It seems very doubtful if the poets knew anything whatever of such an occurrence.[2] Hence the idea that *Revelation* is the Christian "counter-manifesto to the Neronian persecution" is of no value. Ecclesiastical tradition assigns *Revelation* to the year 96 A.D. When recent theological scholarship assigns it to the year 65, it is assuming that the work refers to the burning of Rome in 64. In that case it is clearly a vicious circle to infer the historicity of the Neronian persecution from the fact that *Revelation* was written shortly after 64. How little was definitely known of such a persecution in the first Christian centuries may be gathered from the fact that Eusebius puts it in the year 67. Justin, in spite of his

---

[1] *Revelation* vii, 9.   [2] Work quoted, pp. 75–86.

praise of the courage and steadfastness of the Christians in their martyrdoms, does not say a word about it. Even the later Acts of Peter are silent about it, while other writings go so far as to make Nero a friend of the Christians, and say that he condemned Pontius Pilate to death for the execution of Christ. Origen (185–254) says in his work against Celsus[1] that, instead of the "multitudo ingens" of Tacitus, the number of those who suffered death for the faith was inconsiderable!

But does not Suetonius speak in his *Life of Nero* (ch. xvi) of a chastisement of the Christians by the emperor as a class of men full of a new and criminal superstition (genus hominum superstitionis novæ ac maleficæ)? It is to be noted that he in no way connects this event with the burning of Rome, but with other misdeeds that were punished by Nero. Arnold has pointed out[2] that this biographer does not follow a chronological order in his work or observe the internal connection of events, but classes the deeds of the emperor as good or bad, and so puts the burning among the latter and the punishment of the Christians among the former. However that may be, no reason is given why Nero should punish the Christians on account of their religion. It is expressly allowed by historians[3] that the Roman emperors of that time were extremely tolerant of foreign religions. Suetonius himself says that Nero showed the utmost indifference, even contempt, in regard to religious sects.[4] Even afterwards the Christians were not persecuted for their faith, but for political reasons, for their contempt of the Roman State and emperor, and as disturbers of the unity and peace of the empire.[5] What reason, then, can Nero have had to proceed against the Christians, hardly distinguishable from the Jews, as a new and criminal sect?

---

[1] iii, 8.   [2] Work quoted, p. 38.
[3] See H. Schiller, *Geschichte der Röm. Kaiserzeit*, i, 441.
[4] Cap. 46.   [5] Arnold, work quoted, p. 74.

Schiller also thinks that the Roman authorities can have had no reason to inflict special punishment on the new faith. "How could the non-initiated know what were the concerns of a comparatively small religious sect, which was connected with Judaism and must have seemed to the impartial observer wholly identical with it? Apart from Jerusalem, hardly any community at this time had so pronounced a Judæo-Christian character as that of Rome."[1] If, moreover, it were supposed that by the "Christians" of Suetonius we must understand the Jews excited by messianic expectations—"Messianists" who, with their belief in the approaching end of the world and its destruction by fire, made light of the burning of Rome and so incurred the hatred of the people—the connection between them and the historical Jesus would be called into question, and the evidential value of the passage of Suetonius for the existence of Jesus would be destroyed. In fact, this supposition is negatived by the complete silence of Josephus as to any such misfortune of his co-religionists, though he does not otherwise spare the misdeeds of the emperor. Paulus Orosius also, the friend and admirer of Augustine, relies expressly on Suetonius for the expulsion of the Jews from Rome under Claudius, and even mentions the Neronian persecution, which, according to him, spread over every province of the empire,[2] but for this does not quote the witness of either Tacitus or Suetonius. When we further reflect that neither Trajan nor Pliny mentions the Neronian persecution of the Christians in his correspondence, although there was every occasion to do so, since they were discussing the judgment and treatment of the Bithynian Christians, we can hardly do otherwise than regard the passage in Suetonius's *Life of Nero* as a later interpolation.

---

[1] Work quoted, p. 585. [2] *Adversus Paganos Historiæ*, vii, 4.

II. ARGUMENTS AGAINST THE GENUINENESS.

(a) General Observations.—As regards the passage in Tacitus, the simple credulity with which it had hitherto been accepted led to a sceptical attitude, not only abroad, where the Frenchman Hochart,[1] the Dutchman Pierson,[2] the English author of *Antiqua Mater*, Edwin Johnson, the American William Benjamin Smith in *Ecce Deus* (1911), and others assailed its genuineness, but also in German science. Besides Bruno Bauer,[3] H. Schiller has drawn attention to certain difficulties in the Tacitean tradition that had been overlooked; and even Arnold acknowledges, though he endeavours to show the unsoundness of the critical view of the passage, that "this reference, which had hitherto been regarded as quite simple and easy to understand, has been very little understood."[4] According to Hochart the passage contains as many insoluble difficulties as it does words.[5] This is especially true of the sentence: "Igitur primum correpti, qui fatebantur, deinde indicio eorum multitudo ingens, haud proinde in crimine incendii quam odio humani generis convicti sunt." Schiller calls this sentence "one of the most difficult in this sententious writer," and adds: "One could almost believe that he deliberately left a riddle to posterity which he had failed to solve himself."[6]

We have first the "multitudo ingens" of the Christians. Even Arnold sees a "rhetorical exaggeration" in these words; it is opposed to all that we know of the spread of the new faith in Rome at the time.[7] The question is, who exaggerated—Tacitus, who would scarcely take any interest in the number of the Christians, or a later Christian interpolator, who would naturally have such an

---

[1] *Études au sujet de la persécution des chrétiens sous Néron*, 1885; *De l'Authenticité des Annales et des Histoires de Tacite*, 1890; *Nouvelles Considérations au sujet des Annales et des Histoires de Tacite*, 1897.
[2] *Bergrede*, p. 87. [3] *Christus und die Cäsaren*, p. 150.
[4] Work quoted, vi. [5] *Études au sujet*, etc., p. 220.
[6] Work quoted, p. 435.
[7] Work quoted, p. 40. See also Schiller, work quoted, p. 436, note.

interest, in order to demonstrate the rapid spread and marvellous attractiveness of the religion of Jesus?

Then there is the word "fatebantur." Theological writers like Renan, Weizsäcker, etc., refer the expression to the belief of those who were captured, and so make them out to have been persecuted on account of their Christianity. Von Soden also translates it: "All who openly confessed Christianity were at once arrested," etc. (p. 11). Schiller, however, rightly holds that it is not probable, in view of the close life of the Christians at the time, that some of them, apart from all the others, "had openly professed a doctrine that was not yet a peculiar creed, and would be intelligible to nobody."[1] Others, therefore, such as Arnold, think that the word "fatebantur" refers rather to the crime of setting fire to Rome. In that case, there would, as many historians, such as Neumann, admit, be no question of a persecution of Christians as such, but merely of a police procedure.[2]

In the next place, however, the Christians are not so much "convicted" of the fire as of "hatred of the human race." Holtzmann (in Sybel's *Historischer Zeitschrift*) has translated this phrase as "completely devoid of any humane and political culture," "so that they might be relieved of considerations of humanity in dealing with them." Schiller sees in it a reference to the custom of the Christians to withdraw from all intercourse with the world, celebrate forbidden festivals in secret meetings, and never sacrifice to the genius of the emperor.[3] Arnold conceives the expression as "an opposition on principle to the omnipotence of the Roman State."[4] But, as Hochart rightly asks, could Tacitus, who never took seriously the faith of the Jews, and presented the Jewish and, according to Tertullian, even the Christian God to his readers as a deity with an ass's head,

---

[1] Work quoted, p. 435.
[2] See also H. Schiller, *Geschichte der röm. Kaiserzeit*, I, 446–50.
[3] Work quoted, p. 436. [4] Work quoted, p. 23.

regard the existence of a Jewish sect, which differed in
no respect from the Jews in the eyes of the Romans, as
so menacing to the welfare of the empire that he must
call down on it the full anger of the gods of Olympus?
"It is inconceivable that the followers of Jesus formed a
community in the city at that time of sufficient importance
to attract public attention and the ill-feeling of the people.
It is more probable that the Christians were extremely
discreet in their behaviour, as the circumstances, especially
of early propaganda, required. Clearly we have here a
state of things that belongs to a later date than that of
Tacitus, when the increase and propagandist zeal of the
Christians irritated the other religions against them, and
their resistance to the laws of the State caused the
authorities to proceed against them."[1] The interpolator,
Hochart, thinks, transferred to the days of Nero that
general hatred of the Christians of which Tertullian
speaks. Indeed, the French scholar thinks it not impossible that the phrase " odium humani generis " was simply
taken from Tertullian and put in the mouth of Tacitus.
Tertullian tells us that in his time the Christians were
accused of being " enemies of the human race " (pæne
omnes cives Christianos habendo sed *hostes* maluistis
vocare *generis humani* potius quam erroris humani).[2]

[1] Hochart, work quoted, p. 214.
[2] *Apol.* 37. How just this charge against the Christians was in the
time of Tertullian may be gathered from Hausrath's excellent essay on
"The Church Fathers of the Second Century" in his *Kleine Schriften religionsgeschichtlichen Inhalts* (1883), especially p. 71. It is enough to recall
the words of a pious Father of the Church in his work *On Spectacles* (cap. 30),
where he addresses a pagan fellow-citizen, in a sweet foretaste of vengeance:
"Spectacles are your chief delight; wait, then, for the greatest of all
spectacles, the final and eternal judgment of the world. How I shall
admire, how I shall laugh and be delighted, when I hear so many proud
Cæsars, whom men had turned into gods, whining in the deepest abyss of
darkness; so many magistrates, who persecuted the name of the Lord,
melting in a more furious fire than any they had lit for the Christians;
so many wise philosophers, who taught their pupils that God cared about
nothing, burning in the glowing flames; so many esteemed poets standing
and shivering before the judgment-seat, not of Rhadamanthus or Minos,
but of Christ! Then will the tragedians roar louder than on the stage,
and the player coo more seductively when he is softened by the flames,
and the chariot-driver be seen careering—red as fire on the flaming wheel.

And even the "Thyestean meals" and "Œdipodic minglings," of which Arnold is reminded by the circumstance that Tacitus ascribes those horrors and scandals to the Christians, hardly suit the age of Nero, and have all the appearance of a projection of later charges against the Christians into the sixties of the first century—supposing, that is to say, that the writer was thinking of them at all in the expression quoted. It cannot be repeated too often that charges of this kind, if, as is usually gathered from similar expressions of Justin and Tertullian, they were really put forward by the Jews,[1] have no ground or reason whatever in the historical relations between the two during the first century, especially before the destruction of Jerusalem. The schism between Jews and Christians had not yet taken place, and the hatred of the two for each other was as yet by no means such as to justify such appalling accusations.[2] If, on the other hand, they are supposed to be brought by the pagans against the Christians, there is a complete absence of motive.[3]

But I will not look at these; rather will I turn my insatiable gaze upon those who made sport of the person of the Lord.......From seeing and rejoicing over these no prætor, no consul, no quæstor, and no priest can prevent us. These things, by our faith in the spirit and our imagination, we already have ever present to us." "It must be admitted," Hausrath observes on this, "that this kind of 'Christian charity' has an unmistakable resemblance to the 'odium humani generis' with which the pagans reproached the new sect" (work quoted, p. 92). If Roman justice proceeded with severity against people of this temper, we can hardly blame it, any more than we should blame a modern State for its severe punishment of anarchists. In any case, the number of the martyrs has, as Hausrath shows, been fearfully exaggerated on the ecclesiastical side. It appears that during the first three Christian centuries there were no more than 1,500 people put to death on account of their faith (?), whereas Duke Alba slaughtered more than 100,000 Protestants in the Netherlands, and the St. Bartholomew massacre was responsible for 2,000 deaths in Paris and more than 20,000 in the whole of France, to say nothing of the savagery of the Inquisition and the crusades against heretics, such as the Albigenses. Moreover, many of these Christians often sought death out of religious fanaticism, irritated the authorities to proceed against them when they had no need to do so, and provoked, by their own behaviour, the cruelties of the persecutors which were afterwards so loudly deplored by Christian critics. See J. M. Robertson's *Short History of Christianity* (1902), p. 130.

[1] See, to the contrary, Joel, work quoted, p. 15.
[2] See also Graetz, *Gesch. der Juden*, IV, 104.
[3] See *Antiqua Mater*, p. 23. Bruno Bauer also says: "The picture

(b) *The Criticisms of Hochart.*[1]—No one has more decisively attacked the belief in the persecution of the Christians than Hochart, and it is therefore advisable to give a summary here of the critic's arguments.

In the first place, he regards it as wholly improbable that the charge against Nero, of setting fire to the city himself, was made at all. The whole conduct of the emperor during and after the fire, as it is described by Tacitus, could not possibly have led to such a feeling among the people. Even Suetonius, who is so bent on throwing the blame of the fire on Nero, knows nothing of such a rumour, and, according to the account of Tacitus, the emperor suffered no loss of popularity with the people. Then the aristocrats, who were in conspiracy against him, did not venture to take any step against him, and the people were very far from disposed to take the part of the conspirators when they were tried. Hence the persecution of the Christians has no adequate motive, and cannot in any case have been due to the cause alleged in Tacitus. In this Schiller agrees with Hochart. In agreement also with Adolph Stahr,

given in Tacitus can only be understood in connection with the influences of the age in which he wrote his *Annals*—the age of Trajan, the second decade of the second century. At that time there were Christian elements in Rome, and he might have heard of Christ and his fate under Pontius Pilate, and supposed that the unhealthy state of things that was suppressed by the death of Christ may have broken out again and reached Rome, the place to which everything unclean went. The same influences of the time and of Tacitus are seen in Suetonius's biography of Nero (cap. 16 and 17), which mentions the punishment of the Christians, as people having a new and shameful superstition, among the police measures of the emperor" (p. 155). Lublinski has recently put very clearly the contradiction involved in the passage of Tacitus (*Das werdende Dogma vom Leben Jesu*, 1911, p. 59): "The Christians suffered a punishment that was clearly regarded as a penalty of their crimes; the murderous incendiaries were burned. Nevertheless, they are said to have been condemned, not on account of the fire, but for hating the human race. Strange to say, they could not be convicted of complicity in the fire, though they had made a 'confession.' In other words, people acknowledged themselves guilty of arson, yet could not be convicted of it; but they were nonetheless executed for arson in order to punish severely their hatred of the human race. Could anything be more confused and contradictory?"

[1] *Etudes au sujet de la persécution des chrétiens sous Néron*, 1885; *De l'Authenticité des Annales et des Histoires de Tacite*, 1890; *Nouvelles Considérations au sujet des Annales et des Histoires de Tacite*, 1897.

he regards the rumour that Nero was the author of the fire as utterly incredible. If any rumour of the kind arose, it would, he believes, have been confined to the members of the aristocratic party, with whom Tacitus was in sympathy, and would not be found among the people, who considered him innocent.[1] There was, therefore, according to Schiller, with whom even Arnold agrees on this point,[2] no reason why Nero should accuse the Christians of causing the fire.[3] In any case there can be no question of a Neronian "persecution of the Christians," even if Tacitus has discovered a statement handed down that, on the occasion of the fire, a number of Jewish sectaries, possibly including some Christians, were put to death on the charge of causing it.[4]

The expression "Christians," which Tacitus applies to the followers of Jesus, was by no means common in the time of Nero. Not a single Greek or Roman writer of the first century mentions the name: neither Juvenal nor Persius, Lucian or Martial, the older Pliny or Seneca. Even Dio Cassius never uses it, and his abbreviator, the monk Xiphilinus, sees no reason to break his silence, but speaks of the Christians who were persecuted under Domitian as followers of the Jewish religion.[5] The Christians, who called themselves Jessæans, or Nazoræans, the Elect, the Saints, the Faithful, etc., were universally regarded as Jews. They observed the Mosaic law, and the people could not distinguish them from the other

---

[1] Work quoted, p. 425. In the same way might be explained the testimony of the Prætorian leader, Flavius Subrius, who, in order to cut Nero as deeply as possible, called him, according to Tacitus (*Annals*, xv, 67), the murderer of his mother and wife, a charioteer, a comedian, and an incendiary. Bruno Bauer rightly observes on this: "Is it not possible that Tacitus, or, rather, his interpolator, merely put these words into the mouth of the brave officer? Dio Cassius, who, like Tacitus and Suetonius, represents the prince as the deliberate author of the fire, has preserved the answer of Flavius Subrius in what is probably an older and more reliable form (lxii, 24): 'I will not serve a charioteer and zither-player'" (work quoted, p. 153).
[2] Work quoted, p. 41. [3] *Gesch. der röm. Kaiserzeit*, p. 359.
[4] Arnold, work quoted, p. 34; Schiller, work quoted, p. 449.
[5] See Joel, work quoted, p. 98.

Jews. That Tacitus applied the name, common in his
time, to the Jewish sectaries under Nero, as Voltaire and
Gibbon believe, is very improbable. The Greek word
Christus (" the anointed ") for Messiah, and the derivative
word Christian, first came into use under Trajan, in the
time of Tacitus. Even then, however, the word Christus
could not mean Jesus of Nazareth. All the Jews without exception looked forward to a Christus or Messiah,
and believed that his coming was near at hand. It is,
therefore, not clear how the fact of being a "Christian"
could, in the time of Nero or of Tacitus, distinguish the
followers of Jesus from other believers in a Christus or
Messiah.[1] This could only be at a time when the
memory was lost of the many other persons who had
claimed the dignity of Messiah, and the belief in the
Messiah had become a belief in Jesus, not as *one*, but *the*
Messiah, and Christ and Jesus had become equivalent
terms.[2] Not one of the evangelists applies the name
Christians to the followers of Jesus. It is never used in
the New Testament as a description of themselves by the
believers in Jesus, and the relevant passage in *Acts*

[1] On the other hand, Arnold has attempted to ascribe to Tacitus a close
acquaintance with the Christians from the fact that Sulpicius Severus
used him as his authority in his description of the destruction of Jerusalem,
and that his statement that Titus deliberately furthered the destruction of
the temple in order to destroy at once the Christian and the Jewish religion
was taken from the last conclusion of the fifth book of Tacitus's *Histories*
(work quoted, p. 46). No less an authority than Jakob Bernays (*Über die
Chronik des Sulpicius Severus*, 1861, p. 57) has seen in this reference of
Sulpicius a literal agreement with the statement of Tacitus in the *Annals*
(xv, 44), that Judæa was the birthplace of the Christian religion, and
concluded from this that Sulpicius had Tacitus before his eyes. Bruno
Bauer has, however, observed that the ecclesiastical teachers of the fourth
century were so firmly convinced of the hostility of all the emperors after
Claudius to the Christians that the pupil of the Saint of Tours could easily
penetrate the secret design of Titus without any inspiration from the
Histories of Tacitus (*Christus und die Cæsaren*, p. 216). Hence the
inference that Sulpicius possibly took the statement from Tacitus is anything but convincing, and thus the idea that Tacitus had any close
acquaintance with the Christians falls to the ground.

[2] This general acceptation of the name Christian can, according to
Harnack, only be traced to the end of the reign of Hadrian and that of
Pius (*Die Mission und Ausbreitung des Christenthums in den ersten drei
Jahrhunderten*, 1902, p. 296).

(xi, 26), according to which the name was first used at Antioch, has the appearance of a later interpolation, belonging to a time when the term had become a name of honour in the eyes of some and a name of reproach in the eyes of others.[1] With this is also connected the peculiar way in which Tacitus speaks of the execution of Christ under the procurator Pontius Pilate. He does not know the name Jesus—which, we may note incidentally, would be impossible if he had had before his eyes the *acta* of the trial or the protocols of the Senate—takes Christ to be a personal name, and speaks of Pilate as a person known to the reader, not as an historian would who seeks to inform his readers, but as a Christian to Christians, to whom the circumstances of the death of Christ were familiar.

The Jews at Rome had gone there voluntarily in order to make their fortune in the metropolis of the empire, and on the whole they prospered. They may have been held of little account, or even despised, but no more so than the other oriental foreigners who endeavoured to make money at Rome by fortune-telling, domestic service, or trade. In any case there is so little question of a general "hatred" of the people for them that the Jewish historians, especially Josephus, do not make much complaint of the treatment accorded to their countrymen at Rome.[2] It is incredible that the Jessæans or Nazoræans amongst them, who must in any case have been few in number at the time of the fire, were the object of an especial hatred, and so would be likely to bear the blame of the fire in the eyes of the people.

Death by fire was not a form of punishment inflicted at Rome in the time of Nero. It is opposed to the moderate principles on which the accused were then dealt with by the State. The use of the Christians as "living torches," as Tacitus describes, and all the other

---

[1] See also 1 *Peter* iv, 16, and *Acts* xxvi, 28.
[2] See also Joel, work quoted, p. 106.

atrocities that were committed against them, have little
title to credence, and suggest an imagination exalted by
reading stories of the later Christian martyrs. The often
quoted statements of Juvenal and Seneca have no bearing
on this; they are not connected with the Christians, and
need not in the least be regarded as references to the
members of the new sect sacrificed by Nero.

The victims cannot possibly have been given to the
flames in the gardens of Nero, as Tacitus says. According to his own account, these gardens were the refuge of
those whose homes had been burned, and were full of
tents and wooden sheds. It is hardly probable that Nero
would incur the risk of a second fire by his "living
torches," and still less probable that he mingled with the
crowd and feasted his eyes on the ghastly spectacle.
Tacitus tells us in his life of Agricola that Nero had
crimes committed, but kept his own eyes off them. The
gardens of Nero (on the present Vatican) seem to have
been chosen as the theatre of the deed merely to
strengthen the legend that the holy of holies of Christianity, the Church of St. Peter, was built on the spot on
which the first Christian martyrs had shed their blood.[1]

Finally, there is the complete silence of profane writers
and the vagueness of the Christian writers on the matter;
the latter only gradually come to make a definite statement of a general persecution of the Christians under
Nero, whereas at first they make Nero put to death only
Peter and Paul. The first unequivocal mention of the
Neronian persecution in connection with the burning of
Rome is found in the forged correspondence of Seneca
and the apostle Paul, which belongs to the fourth
century. A fuller account is then given in the Chronicle
of Sulpicius Severus (died 403 A.D.), but it is mixed with
the most transparent Christian legends, such as the story
of the death of Simon Magus, the bishopric and sojourn

---

[1] Cf. Hochart. *Nouvelles Considérations*, 160 ff.

of Peter at Rome, etc. The expressions of Sulpicius agree, in part, almost word for word with those of Tacitus. It is, however, very doubtful, in view of the silence of the other Christian authors who used Tacitus, if the manuscript of Tacitus which Sulpicius used contained the passage in question. We are therefore strongly disposed to suspect that the passage (*Annals*, xv, 44) was transferred from Sulpicius to the text of Tacitus by the hand of a monastic copyist or forger, for the greater glory of God and in order to strengthen the truth of the Christian tradition by a pagan witness.[1]

But how could the legend arise that Nero was the first to persecute the Christians? It arose, says Hochart, under a threefold influence. The first is the apocalyptic idea, which saw in Nero the Antichrist, the embodiment of all evil, the terrible adversary of the Messiah and his followers. As such he was bound, by a kind of natural enmity, to have been the first to persecute the Christians; as Sulpicius puts it, "because vice is always the enemy of the good."[2] The second is the political interest of the Christians in representing themselves as Nero's victims, in order to win the favour and protection of his successors on that account. The third is the special interest of the Roman Church in the death of the two chief apostles, Peter and Paul, at Rome. Then the author of the letters of Seneca to Paul enlarged the legend in its primitive form, brought it into agreement with the ideas of this time, and gave it a political turn. The vague charges of incendiarism assumed a more definite form, and were associated with the character of Antichrist, which the

[1] In his *De l'Authenticité des Histoires et des Annales de Tacite* Hochart points out that, whereas the *Life of St. Martin* and the *Dialogues* of Sulpicius were found in many libraries, there was only one manuscript of his *Chronicle*, probably of the eleventh century, which is now in the Vatican. Hence the work was almost unknown throughout the Middle Ages, and no one was aware of the reference in it to a Roman persecution of the Christians. It is noteworthy that Poggio Bracciolini seems by some lucky chance to have discovered and read this manuscript (work quoted, p. 225). Cf. *Nouvelles Considérations*, pp. 142-72.

[2] Compare Eusebius, *Eccl. Hist.*, ii, 28.

Church was accustomed to ascribe to Nero on account of his supposed diabolical cruelty. He was accused of inflicting horrible martyrdoms on the Christians, and thus the legend in its latest form reached the *Chronicle* of Sulpicius. Finally a clever forger (Poggio?) smuggled the dramatic account of this persecution into the *Annals* of Tacitus, and thus secured the acceptance as historical fact of a purely imaginary story.

We need not recognise all Hochart's arguments as equally sound, yet we must admit that in their entirety and agreement they are worthy of consideration, and are well calculated to disturb the ingenuous belief in the authenticity of the passage of Tacitus. It seems as if official "science" is here again, as in so many other cases, under the dominion of a long-continued suggestion, in taking the narrative of Tacitus to be genuine without further examination. We must not forget what a close connection there is between this narrative and the whole of Christian history, and what interest religious education and the Church have in preventing any doubt from being cast on it. Otherwise how can we explain that no one took any notice during the whole of the Middle Ages of a passage of such great importance for the history and prestige of the Church? No one, in fact, seems to have had the least suspicion of its existence until it was found in the sole copy at that time of Tacitus, the Codex Mediceus II, printed by Johann and his brother Wendelin von Speyer about 1470 at Venice, of which all the other manuscripts are copies.[1] Our historians as a rule are content to reproduce the narrative of Tacitus in somewhat modified terms, without making any close scrutiny of *Annals*, xv, 44; thus does Domaszewski, for instance, in his *History of the Roman Empire* (1909), to say nothing of the numerous popular manuals of history. But our whole science of history is still, as regards the origin of Christianity, under the mischievous influence of

---

[1] Hochart, *De l'Authenticité*, etc., p. 50.

theology, and is content to reproduce its statements without inquiry. In regard to the question of the origin of the Christian religion and the historicity of Jesus it has almost entirely abdicated its function, and is actually pleased that it need not deal with this delicate theme, as Seeck candidly admits when he says in his *Geschichte des Untergangs der antiken Welt* (iii, 1900): " We have no intention of depicting the human personality of Jesus and telling the story of his life, since these problems are, in the present state of tradition, perhaps insoluble, but at all events not yet solved. Every question relating to the origin of Christianity is so difficult that *we are glad* to avoid it altogether."[1] It is true that Seeck regards the hesitation in regard to the genuineness of the writings admitted in theology as " in most cases without foundation." He accepts tradition in regard to the Tacitus narrative, and believes in the Neronian persecution of the Christians. What is the use of this, however, when he has made no close inquiry into these things, and therefore gives his verdict solely in accordance with a general belief which is possibly a mere prejudice? Assuredly we do not envy the " historical sense" and the good taste of men who would persuade themselves and others that it would be just as easy to deny the historicity of Socrates, Alexander, Luther, Goethe, Bismarck, etc., as that of Jesus, although this is shown in a very different way than the historical existence of the " god-man" of the gospels.[2]

---

[1] Work quoted, p. 173.
[2] Compare Steudel, *Wir Gelehrten vom Fach*, etc. (p. 6), and Lublinski, work quoted, p. 47. In the controversy about the Christ-myth an attempt has been made even lately to revive the much-ridiculed argument that there never was such a person as Napoleon, by which Perez fancied he could refute Dupuis, and the argument of Von der Hagen against Strauss, " that there was never any such person as Luther," in the year 1837, in order to show how one may deny the existence of any great man on " Drews' method." That such arguments rely upon the thoughtlessness of the majority of people to have any effect throws equal light upon the general intelligence, and on the frame of mind of men who can make use of such arguments.

(c) *The Possibility of Various Interpretations of "Annals," xv, 44.*—So much as to the possible spuriousness of *Annals,* xv, 44. We have now to examine the evidential value of the passage, supposing it to be genuine, and apart from all that we have said of its historical value.

In opposition to Hermann Schiller, Neumann, and other historians, Harnack regards it as "certain" that the persecution mentioned by Tacitus was really a persecution of the Christians. He believes, nevertheless, that the passage is "not altogether intelligible" in the sense that it first ascribes the invention of the name "Christiani" to the "people," and then goes on to say that "the author of the name" was Christ. "If that is so, the people acted quite reasonably in giving the name of Christians to the followers of Christ. Why, then, does Tacitus call the title 'Christians' a 'name imposed by the people'?" The circumstance is really very curious. "In order to put an end to the trouble, Nero laid the blame on those whom, hateful for their crimes, the people called Christians." However, Andresen has made a fresh study of the Tacitus manuscript, and shown that the word was at first "Chrestianos," and was later altered to "Christianos"; whereas it is written "Christus," not "Chrestus." "Now it is quite clear," says Harnack, "Tacitus says that the people call the sect Chrestiani; he, however—relying on more accurate knowledge, as Plinius has already written 'Christiani'—quietly corrects the name, and rightly speaks of the author of the name as Christ."[1]

The expression "Chrestiani" is usually regarded as a popular version of "Christiani" (compare Vergil and Virgil), just as, on this account, Suetonius is supposed to have written Chrestus instead of Christus. But, as we observed before, Chrestus was not only a familiar personal

---

[1] *Mission und Ausbreitung,* p. 296.

name; it was also a name of the Egyptian Serapis or Osiris, which had a large following at Rome, especially among the common people. Hence "Chrestiani" may be either the followers of a man named Chrestus, or of Serapis. The word "Chrestus" means "the good." Thus the Chrestiani were likely to attract the name of "the good," and it is presumed that the people gave this name to those whom they detested on account of their evil deeds. Possibly this name was given to them precisely because they were hated for their crimes. The Latin sentence, "quos per flagitia invisos vulgus Christianos appellabat," admits this interpretation, and it is often found. How came the people to give the name of "the good" to men who were in their eyes notoriously bad? Clearly, the expression must, when we examine their way of thinking, be regarded as ironical; the Roman people called the followers of Serapis-Chrestus "good" because they were precisely the contrary. We might therefore regard the name "Chrestiani" as equivalent to "the clean brethren," just as it is customary to call the scum of Paris the "Apaches."[1]

We know from history what an evil repute the Egyptian people, which consisted mainly of Alexandrian elements, had at Rome. While other foreign cults that had been introduced into Rome enjoyed the utmost toleration, the cult of Serapis and Isis was exposed repeatedly to persecution. This was due, as we learn from Cumont, not merely to political considerations, the hostility of Rome to Alexandria, but also to moral and police reasons. The lax morality associated with the worship of the Egyptian gods and the fanaticism of their worshippers repelled the Romans, and excited the suspicion that their cultus might be directed against the State. "Their secret associations, which were chiefly recruited from the poorer people, might easily, under the cover of religion, become clubs

[1] Compare Louis Ganeval, *Jésus devant l'histoire n'a jamais vécu*, 1875.

of agitators and the resort of spies. These grounds for suspicion and hatred [!] contributed more, no doubt, to the rise of the persecution than purely theological considerations. We see how it subsides and flames out again according to the changes in the condition of general politics."[1]

In the year 48 B.C. the chapels devoted to Isis were destroyed by order of the Senate, and their images of the gods broken. In 28 A.D. the Alexandrian divinities were excluded from the limits of the Pomœrium—a proscription which Agrippa extended seven years afterwards to a sphere a thousand paces from the city. In fact, in the year 49 the feeling against the Egyptians ran so high, on account of a scandal in which Egyptian priests were involved, that the most drastic proceedings were taken against the followers of Serapis. On this occasion the maltreatment fell upon the Jews also, because some of their compatriots had behaved in a similar manner; this was not due to any general hatred of the Jews, but to the fact that the Roman Jews, who mostly came from Egypt and Alexandria, were confused with the Alexandrians, and even with that Alexandrian rabble the "Chrestiani." We read in Tacitus[2] that at that time the proscription of the Egyptian and Jewish religious practices was discussed, and the Senate decided to send four thousand men infected with their superstitions, of the class of freedmen, to the island of Sardinia, to fight the bandits, in the hope that the unhealthy climate of the island would make an end of them. Josephus also says this in his *Antiquities*.[3] A few years later, under Claudius, "the Senate decreed the expulsion of the mathematicians from Italy, though the decree was not put in force."[4] The mathematicians—that is to say, astrologers—are the Egyptians and Egyptian Jews, the followers of Chrestus, as we read in Fl. Vopiscus

---

[1] *Die orientalischen Religionen im römischen Heidentum*, by Gehrich (1910), p. 98.
[2] *Annals*, ii, 85.   [3] xviii, 3, 5.   [4] *Annals*, xii, 52.

in the letter of the Emperor Hadrian to his brother-in-law Servius: "Those who worship Serapis are the Chrestians, and those who call themselves priests of Chrestus are devoted to Serapis. There is not a high-priest of the Jews, a Samaritan, or a priest of Chrestus who is not a mathematician, soothsayer, or quack. Even the patriarch, when he goes to Egypt, is compelled by some to worship Serapis, by others to worship Chrestus. They are a turbulent, inflated, lawless body of men. They have only one God, who is worshipped by the Chrestians, the Jews, and all the peoples of Egypt."

It is true that this letter is often regarded as spurious, a fourth-century forgery, on account of its absurd and confused expressions on Christianity and the Christians. In any case, it shows the close connection between the Alexandrian Jews and the Egyptians, since both are described as mathematicians and Chrestians. And is it not possible that the reference to Chrestus and the Chrestians has been too hastily applied to Christus and the Christians? And may not the absurdity be due simply to the fact that the writer of the letter could see no clear distinction between the two religions and their deities? The passage in Tacitus may, in that case, be due to a similar misunderstanding. The "Chrestiani," who were detested by the people for their crimes, and to whom the historian ascribes all the abominations that have invaded the metropolis, *are not Christians at all*, but followers of Chrestus, the scum of Egypt, the "apaches" of Rome, a "multitudo ingens," a real "object of hatred to the human race," people on whom Nero could very easily cast the suspicion of having set fire to Rome, and whose admission that they had done so is not in the least unintelligible. Hence the "people" rightly called them "Chrestians," which was, as we saw, an ambiguous name, and a not uncommon epithet in Rome at the time. Tacitus, about the year 117, confuses them with the Christians of his time, just as the Emperor Hadrian does in his letter to Servius fourteen years afterwards. Having done so, he felt compelled to add the explanatory words, "autor nominis ejus Christus," etc., and describe them as coming from Judæa, confusing the Alexandrian Jews, who were identified with them, with the Jews of Palestine. In this way the expression "appellabat" (instead of "appellat"), which seems to Harnack "remarkable," becomes intelligible. *Possibly* there is question of some popular phrase used in Nero's time which Tacitus himself did not understand; possibly, however, the sentence in which Christus is said to have been the author of the name of Christians and the whole reference to Judæa do not come from the pen of Tacitus at all, but are due to a later Christian, who identified the Chrestians of Tacitus with the Christians; and thus the whole Neronian persecution and the supposed confirmation of the historicity of Christ by the Roman historian are based upon a monstrous misunderstanding. If that is so, a new light is thrown also on the "Chresto impulsore" of Sulpicius. Chrestus was not only the name of the god, but, as frequently happened in ancient religions, also of his chief priest. May it not be that the tumults of the "Jews" under Claudius really refer to rebellious and criminal elements of the Egyptian rabble in the metropolis, under the influence of their chief priest, ending in the expulsion of the Jews from Rome? This, of course, is not the only plausible explanation of the passage. We need only say that it is a possible interpretation of what happened. In that case, the passage of Tacitus might remain substantially unquestioned, without proving what it is generally supposed to prove—namely, the fact of a Neronian persecution and the existence of an historical Jesus. In this way, at all events, we find the simplest solution of all the difficulties connected with the passage in Tacitus.

Those who do not find this interpretation of *Annals*, xv, 44, plausible have still to solve the problem whether the Chrestians or Christians of the Roman historian were

really Christians in our meaning of the word or were
distinct from them. Edwin Johnson regards the Chrestians as followers of the "good god" (Chrestus), as the
Gnostics called their god in opposition to Jahveh, whom
they looked upon as the perversely conceived creator of
the Jews. He thus traces the name to a sect, the founder
of which he considers to have been Simon the Magician,
flourishing in Rome in the time of Claudius, whose
members, as representatives of a spiritualised Judaism,
were very obnoxious to the traditional Jew.[1] He supposes
that Tacitus transferred to the time of Nero the hatred of
the Christians which animated the Jews of his own time,
and thus the Chrestians (Gnostics) were confused with
the real Christians. Possibly, however, the name is only
another expression for Messianists, and the Chrestians of
Tacitus are Jews exalted by eschatological ideas, living in
expectation of a speedy end of the world by fire, and so
contracting the suspicion of having set fire to the city.
They may have formed a "multitudo ingens" and
incurred "the hatred of the human race" by being led
in their fanaticism to express their satisfaction at the
burning of the metropolis; possibly they even took part
in it. However that may be, there is not the least proof
in any case of a Neronian persecution of the Christians.
Even in this case, Tacitus's reference to Christ as the
founder of the sect rests on a misunderstanding—namely,
a confusion of the most confident of the Jewish Messianists
with the followers of the Christus who, as Tacitus had
heard, had been crucified under Pontius Pilatus.[2]

In regard to the significance of Pilate in Tacitus, a
remarkable hypothesis has recently been put forward by
Andrzej Niemojewski in his work, *Gott Jesus im Lichte
fremder und eigener Forschungen samt Darstellung der
evangelischen Astralstoffe, Astralszenen, und Astralsysteme*

---

[1] *Antiqua Mater*, pp. 279–292.
[2] See Joel, work quoted, p. 144; also Whittaker, *The Origins of Christianity* (2nd ed., 1909), p. 21.

(1910). According to this, the Pilate of the Christian legend was not originally an historical person; the whole story of Christ is to be taken in an astral sense, and Pilate represents the constellation of Orion, the javelin-man (*pilatus*, in Latin), with the arrow or lance-constellation (Sagitta), which is supposed to be very long in the Greek myth, and appears in the Christian legend under the name of Longinus, and is in the Gospel of John the soldier who pierces the side of Jesus with a spear (*longche*, in Greek). In the astral myth, the Christ hanging on the cross, or world-tree (*i.e.*, the Milky Way), is killed by the lance of "Pilatus." Hence, according to Niemojewski, the Christian populace told the legend of a javelin-man, a certain Pilatus, who was supposed to have been responsible for the death of the Saviour. This wholly sufficed for Tacitus to recognise in him the procurator in the reign of Tiberius, who must have been known to the Roman historian from the books of Josephus "On the Jewish War," which were destined for the imperial house.[1] In point of fact, the procurator Pontius Pilate plays a part in the gospels so singularly opposed to the account of the historical Pilate, as Josephus describes him, that we can very well suspect a later introduction of an historical personage into the quasi-historical narrative.

When we take account of these many possible interpretations of *Annals*, xv, 44, all of which are as probable as, if not more probable than, the customary Christian explanation, the narrative of Tacitus cannot be quoted as a witness to the historicity of Jesus. We may say, indeed, that history has hitherto treated the passage, in view of its importance, with an absolutely irresponsible superficialness and levity. "The non-Christian witnesses," says von Soden, "can only be quoted in favour of, not against, the historicity of Jesus" (p. 14). The truth is

---

[1] Work quoted, p. 129.

that they prove nothing either for or against; they prove nothing at all.[1] J. Weiss is perfectly correct when he says, as we saw previously: "There is no such thing as a really convincing witness in profane literature." It is true that he is able to console himself for this. "What," he asks, "could Josephus or Tacitus do for us? They could at the most merely show that at the end of the first century not only the Christians, but their tradition and Christ-mythos, were known at Rome. When it originated, however, and how far it was based on truth, could not be discovered from Tacitus or Josephus" (p. 91). The orthodox pastor Kurt Delbrück adds: "What does it matter whether or no Tacitus wrote it? He could only have received the information, a hundred years after the time, from people who had told it to others. It matters nothing to us, therefore, whether the passage is genuine or not. The historical personality of Jesus Christ is proved only by the fact [?] that the earliest Christian community recognised its Saviour in him whom it had once seen alive. *We have no further historical documents.*"

3.—"LUCUS A NON LUCENDO."

It seems superfluous now to enlarge on the objection that, if no pagan writer unequivocally proves the existence

---

[1] Characteristic of the conduct of our opponents is the way in which Otto Schmiedel treats the Roman witnesses. "Tacitus," says this representative of historical theology, "mentions in his *Annals* about the year 116 the execution of Jesus [?] under Pontius Pilate, and the spread of his [?] superstitious sect in Judæa and even Rome. A passage in Suetonius written about the year 120 ('Nero,' ch. xvi) is to the same effect [!?]; and the younger Pliny, Governor of Bithynia, in 112 or 113, describes in a letter (*Ep.* x, 96) to the Emperor Trajan the wide spread of the Christians in his province and the hymns they sing to their Christ as a god [!]. The violent opponent of Christianity, the philosopher Celsus, is already [*sic*] acquainted with the whole literature of the New Testament before the year 180, and this literature is unintelligible without the person of Christ, with which it is entirely concerned." (*Die Hauptprobleme der Leben-Jesu-Forschung*, 2 Aufl., 1906, p. 13). Notice the highly-coloured phrases (the execution of *Jesus*, the *person* of Christ !) and the word "already," by means of which he tries to convey the impression that the witnesses quoted were remarkably early, and therefore deserve unlimited confidence.

THE ROMAN WITNESSES

of an historical Jesus, at all events none of them ever contested it. The objection is futile, because its assumption is false. The Gnostics of the second century really questioned the historical existence of Jesus by their docetic conception; in other words, they believed only in a metaphysical and ideal, not an historical and real, Christ.[1] The whole polemic of the Christians against the Gnostics was based essentially on the fact that the Gnostics denied the historicity of Jesus, or at least put it in a subordinate position.

Moreover, how much has survived of the attacks on Christianity by its opponents? Has not the Church been careful from the first to suppress or destroy everything that might endanger its interests? Did it not burn the anti-Christian writings of Porphyry? Was not the valuable library of Alexandria sacrificed to the zeal of fanatical monks in the year 391, and were not the greatest intellectual treasures of antiquity contained in it? Who can say what evidences against Christianity did not perish in it? Even the work of Celsus, the one attack on Christianity of which we have much knowledge, is known to us only from Origen's reply to it. This work, moreover, belongs to the second half of the second century, and is, therefore, incapable of proving anything.[2] Would it be remarkable at all that no pagan should take the trouble to contest the historicity of Jesus, assuming this to be the case? At the time when the pagan reaction against Christianity began—namely, in the second century—the Jesus-story was already firmly rooted in tradition. Like the Jews, the pagan writers confined themselves in their polemic to the Christian tradition, as they were bound to do. To make research in the archives about a subject

---

[1] See Wolfgang Schultz, *Dokumente der Gnosis*, 1910.
[2] Yet Origen himself makes Celsus say: "You feed us with fables, and cannot give them a shade of plausibility, although some of you, like drunken men, who lay hands on themselves, have modified the texts of the gospels three or four or more times, in order to escape the criticisms we direct against you" (*Contra Celsum*, II, 26 and 27).

was not the practice of ancient historical writers. "There was in ancient times," says the ecclesiastical historian Hausrath, "hardly any interest in historical truth as such, but only in ideal truth. There are very few cases in which an ancient historian put himself the question what had really happened and what was merely said to have happened."[1] Even if anyone had desired to inquire into the truth of the gospel "story" and go deeply into the subject, he would have been quite unable to do so after the destruction of Jerusalem and the dispersion of the Jews.

Finally, was no doubt expressed by pagans as to the existence of Jesus because it was firmly established, or because at the time when we look for some doubter no one really affirmed it? We await an answer to this question. Our opponents ask: If Jesus was not an historical personage, how is it that no one ever doubted his existence? We reply with the further question: Granting that he was an historical personage, how is it that not only does the Talmud never mention him, but, apart from the gospels, not a single work belonging to the early Christian period gives us any intimate detail about the life of this personage? Examine Paul's Epistles! As we shall show in the next chapter, they do not tell a single special fact about the life of Jesus. Read the other Epistles of the New Testament—Peter, John, James, Jude, and the Epistle to the Hebrews—and the letter of Clement to the Corinthians, the letter of Barnabas, the *Pastor* of Hermas, the *Acts of the Apostles*, etc. Nowhere in any single one of these early Christian documents do we find even the slenderest reference to the mere man Jesus, or to the historical personality of Jesus as such, from which we might infer that the author had a close acquaintance with it. His life, as it is described in the gospels, in all its human

---

[1] *Kleine Schriften*, p. 124.

detail, seems to have been entirely unknown to these authors. His speeches and sayings are hardly ever quoted, and where this is done, as in the Epistle of James or *Acts*, they are not quoted as sayings of Jesus. We have no feeling whatever that these documents know anything of an historical Jesus; the little that could be quoted to the contrary, such as the passage in the supposed speech of Peter (*Acts*, x, 38), is so obviously due to a later tampering with the text and so absurd that we cannot pay it any serious attention. The earlier Christian literature is acquainted with a Jesus-god, a godman, a heavenly high-priest and saviour Jesus, a metaphysical spirit, descending from heaven to earth, assuming human form, dying, and rising again; but *it knows nothing whatever* about a merely human Jesus, the amiable author of fine moral sentiments, the "unique" personality of liberal Protestantism. There is therefore nothing in the objection that no one at that time questioned the existence of such a person. Those who attach importance to such doubts simply assume the correctness of the liberal-theological view of the origin of Christianity. If this view is false, if the transformation of Jesus into an historical person only occurred at a relatively late stage (the first half of the second century), the absence of any doubt about the historical existence of Jesus before that time is quite intelligible. In any case it is logically absurd ("lucus a non lucendo") to deduce from the circumstance that no one, apparently, expressed any doubt as to the existence of Jesus the fact that he actually existed.

After this complete rejection of the evidence of profane literature in regard to an historical Jesus, we need hardly linger over the arguments that may be drawn from other supposed relics of his time and environment. There is still at Trèves the holy coat for which the Roman soldiers cast lots at the foot of the cross. There is still in the Lateran at Rome the stairway which Jesus ascended on entering the palace of Pilate. Then there are the innumerable fragments of the cross pointing to the drama of Golgotha, the innumerable holy nails, the vinegar-sponge, the veil of Veronica, the shroud in which the Saviour was wrapped, the swaddling-clothes of the infant Jesus, and, last but not least, the holy prepuce. There are indeed plenty of "historical documents"—for those who *wish* to believe. They must be sought, however, not in literature, but in churches and chapels and other "holy places," where they prove their authenticity by the "blessing" which flows from them into the Church's coffers. But we will be content with our survey of profane witnesses. The improper use that has hitherto been made by theologians of these witnesses entails a careful examination. For our part we can only regard any attempt to prove the existence of an historical Jesus by these supposed profane witnesses as a sign of intellectual unscrupulousness or lamentable superficiality.

THE WITNESS OF PAUL

THE less evidence we find for the historicity of Jesus in profane writers, the greater becomes the interest of those who maintain it in a witness by whom the historical Jesus is unequivocally affirmed. Such an unequivocal witness we have, according to the prevailing view, in the so-called Epistles of the apostle Paul. Hence Paul is the *pièce de résistance* for the theologian in regard to his belief in Jesus. He is the "surest foundation," the "unshakable cornerstone," the "irrefragable witness" for the fact that a Jesus did really live, and was crucified and buried, and rose again from the dead. So convinced indeed is historical theology of the absolute worth of this witness that it fancies it can silence all scepticism about the historicity of Jesus by merely pointing to Paul. It seems to think that no one can seriously dispose of the testimony of Paul without declaring that the Apostle's letters are spurious. We read, for instance, in von Soden's work on the Pauline Epistles: "They afford so strong a proof of the historicity of Jesus that no one but Drews has ever ventured to deny this historicity without contesting the genuineness of the Pauline Epistles" (p. 29). The orthodox theologian Beth also observes: "In this case Drews must really be charged with negligence before the tribunal of his own theory, since he admitted the genuineness of some of the Epistles and found no reason to doubt the historical existence of Paul. In order to attain his end within the limits of his own theory and destroy all the evidences for Jesus, he ought also to have contested the existence of Paul."[1]

[1] Beth, *Hat Jesus gelebt?*, p. 35.

Certainly, it would be simplest to say at once that the Epistles of Paul are spurious, and thus destroy the value of their testimony to the existence of an historical Jesus. This the theologians would assuredly like us to do, because, as things are in Germany, the genuineness of at least the four chief Epistles (Romans, Galatians, and the two to the Corinthians) is so firmly held by them that any doubt about it is at once rejected by them as "not to be taken seriously." It would thus be an excellent means of discrediting the whole tendency of the Christ-myth in the eyes of the general public, and of all who swear on the word of professors of theology. Who reads to-day Bruno Bauer's *Kritik der Paulinischen Briefe* (1852), in which the first attempt was made to show the spuriousness of all the Epistles ascribed to Paul? That inconvenient scholar has so long been slighted by theologians, who have frightened readers from him by depreciatory remarks on his work, that it was thought quite safe to continue to ignore him. When, moreover, the Swiss scholar Steck concludes, in a thorough and learned investigation, that the Epistle to the Galatians is spurious (1888), that is merely "an extraordinary perversity of criticism," an "instance of pushing radical criticism too far," an attempt that one need not linger to refute. On the other hand, the criticism of English writers (Edwin Johnson, Robertson, and Whittaker) seemed to be quite devoid of danger, as few theologians have a command of the English language. It is true that in Holland a theological school has endeavoured for thirty years to show the spuriousness of the Epistles of Paul; but why should that trouble people in Germany? Dutch is a language that one has no occasion to learn at the universities. One may, therefore, take it for granted that the works of the Dutch will not be very seriously studied in Germany. Have not the Dutch, in fact, at a "Congress of free Christianity and religious progress," thanked German historical theologians for the distinguished services which

they have rendered to the whole civilised world? We
frequently hear that kind of thing. The Dutch savants
may, therefore, be regarded indulgently when they strike
a path of their own in their own country and contest
statements which are taken for granted in Germany.

It is amusing to read German theologians writing on
their Dutch colleagues. According to Beth, "the Amsterdam writer Loman has very finely shown how one may
manufacture out of air a proof that Paul was merely
invented in the second century as a preacher of universalistic Christianity" (p. 35). According to Jülicher, it is
a sign of "uncritical temper" to doubt whether Paul
wrote the Epistles to which his name is attached—a
temper which, "as soon as it perceives a difficulty, which
may occur in such documents just as well as in a
Babylonian brick, cries 'Spurious!' and recognises no
shades of difference"; and he advises it, with equal bad
taste and foolishness, to consign itself to "work in subterraneous Acheron" (p. 25). Yet these theologians are
either totally ignorant of, or have only a very superficial
acquaintance with, the work of the Dutch. This is clear
when von Soden writes: "No one has yet attempted to
give us an intelligible account of the origin of these
Epistles in the second century" (p. 29); and J. Weiss
says: "The Pauline Epistles are, as is known [!?], denied
to the apostle Paul by the Dutch school and by Kalthoff;
but there is no plausible hypothesis as to their origin in
any other way, no chronology of the various strata of the
Epistles, and no answer to many other questions suggested
by the denial" (p. 97). Are Weiss and von Soden ignorant
of the work of van Manen, whose *Römerbrief* has been
excellently translated into German by Schläger (Leipsic,
1906), while Whittaker has given a careful synopsis of
his other books in his *Origins of Christianity* (2nd ed.,
1909)? And if they are acquainted with him, how came
they to pen such sentences, seeing that van Manen has
done in a very thorough manner precisely what they say

ought to be done by those who deny Paul's authorship? The truth is that historical theology in Germany *needs* a genuine Paul as an indispensable witness to its historical Jesus, and it *must*, therefore, ignore the Dutch and those *must*-be uncritical and confused thinkers who venture to dispute the credibility of their witness.

Historical theology finds the historical Jesus in the Pauline Epistles, because it is determined to—in fact, *must*—find him there, or else the whole of its artificial historical construction of the origin of Christianity remains in the air without any support. It accepts without scrutiny not only the truth of the evangelical accounts of Jesus, but whatever *Acts* says about Paul; and since it regards Paul as the author of the Epistles, it naturally finds it easy to see a confirmation of these things in the Pauline Epistles. It refers the mentions of Jesus in the Epistles to an historical Jesus because, *anterior to any inquiry, from the gospels* it is convinced of his reality; and it therefore never dreams of referring the passages in the Epistles which deal with Jesus to any other than their own—that is, the supposed historical Jesus of the gospels. It regards as "unmethodical" any man who would put a different interpretation on those passages, because the method employed by themselves, and regarded by them as the sole correct method, leads to the result that they desire. They are, therefore, in a vicious circle in their inquiry into the genuineness of the Pauline Epistles and their testimony to the historical Jesus.

As a matter of fact, their assertion that the existence of an historical Jesus is the very foundation of the Epistles of Paul is not the *result*, but the *assumption*, of their method. As such it originated, quite independently of their method. In all investigation the method is directed according to the assumption that is made and the end to be attained. But if an inquirer is allowed to postulate the existence of an historical Jesus and confirm this assumption by his methods, it can hardly be considered a sign of partisanship and prejudice to oppose the assumption on the ground of facts, and submit that such methods can hardly lead to a satisfactory result. Historical theology has hitherto endeavoured to interpret tradition in the sense of its historical Jesus, and has lost its way in a labyrinth of difficulties, contradictions, and insoluble problems. We raise the question whether the documents may not be better and more simply interpreted in the opposite sense, and whether there is any need at all to interpret the tradition historically. On which side the truth is found cannot be determined by the starting-point of the inquiry, but only by showing which interpretation best squares with the facts and which can be most easily established. In any case our method cannot be pronounced wrong because, starting from a different assumption, we reach conclusions other than those of the theologian; nor may one charge us with "confusion" or appeal against us in the name of "sound" investigation and science when our inquiry into the New Testament documents leads us to deny the historicity of Jesus, as long as it is not proved that our assumption is absurd.

1.—THE PROOFS OF THE HISTORICITY OF JESUS IN PAUL.

The starting-point and postulate of the Pauline doctrine of salvation is the attitude of man towards the law. The law was originally given to men by God for their good. It is to teach them what is sinful. It is to quicken their consciousness of evil and show them the way to become better. It should be to them, as Paul puts it, a teacher and breeder of righteousness. In reality it has proved a curse to them, and, instead of saving them, it has forced them deeper into the slavery of evil and sin. God therefore took pity on men, and sent to them Christ, his "son," to take from them the yoke of the law. Originally a supernatural being, buried in God and co-operating in the creation of the world, Christ, at the will of his father, exchanged the glory of heaven for the poverty and straits of earth, in order to come upon the earth in the form of a slave, a man among men, for the redemption of mortals. He gave himself freely, for the salvation of men, to death on the cross. What no sacrifice had as yet been able to accomplish (a proof of the powerlessness of the law), complete delivery from sin and from death, which had come into the world with sin—was attained by the sacrificial death of him in whom was concentrated the whole being of humanity. In his death he died the death of all. By his resurrection he triumphed over death. By the rejection and casting aside of his human nature in death the God-man resumed his essential divinity. In discarding the veil of flesh and returning to his father in transfigured form, as a pure spirit and being reunited to him, he set men an example how they were to attain their true nature by the sacrifice of their carnal personality. More than this, indeed, he thereby obtained for them redemption from the bonds of the flesh, lifted them above the limitations of earth, and secured for them eternal life in and with the father. Man has only to put himself in personal relation to him, to unite intimately with him, to accept and assimilate the belief in his redeeming death (to crucify himself with Christ), and show this by a love of his fellow-men, and he will have a share in Christ's exaltation, and so attain redemption. The law therefore ceases to prescribe his conduct. By his union with Christ he is dead to the law and released from its dominion. The demons, under whose curse he had hitherto lain, have now no power over him. The life of which he has but a limited share here on earth will be enjoyed under better conditions in heaven. Christ is therefore the "mediator" between God and man, destroying the barrier between them. He is the "saviour" who heals the maladies of earthly life, corporal or spiritual, the "deliverer" from the darkness of earthly existence and death, the "God-man," the true foundation and end of all religious action.

Any man who reflects impartially on this theory will find it difficult to believe that there is question here of an external historical process, an historical individual. The idea comes closest, perhaps, to that of the Gnostics, and especially close to that of the Alexandrian religious philosopher Philo, an older contemporary of Paul, and his principle of the Logos, which we afterwards find blended with the Christian belief in the gospel of John. Christ seems to be in Paul another name for the idea of humanity, a comprehensive expression of the ideal unity of all men, set forth as a personal being. Just in the same way Philo conceives the fullness of the divine ideas personified in the shape of the Logos, the "mediator," "son of God," and "light of the world," and blends the Logos with the ideal man, the idea of man. And just as Christ is made flesh and assumes human form, so Philo's Logos descends from his heavenly sphere and enters the world of sense, to give strength to the good, and save men from sin, and lead them to their true home, the kingdom of heaven, and their heavenly father.

This idea of the redemption of men by the "son" of the most-high God is very ancient, and was widespread in early times. In the Babylonian religion the redeemer Marduk is sent upon the earth by his father Ea to save men from their spiritual maladies and moral perversity. The Greeks worshipped similar "sons" of God and benefactors of men in Heracles, Dionysos, and Jason or Jasios (the Greek name for Jesus), who likewise had a heavenly commission to redeem men, and were taken back into the circle of the blessed after a premature and impressive death. The idea flourished chiefly, however, in the religions of nearer Asia and North Africa, among the Phrygians, the Syrians, and the Egyptians, who worshipped in their Attis, Adonis, and Osiris (respectively) a god who suffered, died, and rose again for humanity, and expressed their belief in mysterious cults which are known as "mysteries." Among the Mandæic or Gnostic sects, which cultivated a peculiar form of piety, apart from the official religion, about the beginning of the present era, and to which, in a general sense, the Jewish sect of the Essenes seems to have belonged, the belief in a divine saviour and mediator was the very centre of their religious theory. Moreover, the Jewish apocalyptic of the time, which expected a speedy end of the world, leaned towards this view, and combined the form of the mediating God with its idea of the Messiah, the expected saviour of Israel from its political and social oppression. In the prophet Daniel the redeemer is described by the Gnostic name of "the son of man." Further, this idea of a suffering and dying saviour was unmistakably connected with the course of nature. It arose from the sight of the fate of the sun or the moon, as they rose and sank in their paths, as they waned, disappeared, and rose again, in conjunction with the experience of the death and resurrection of nature every year. It was expressed by a belief in a divine son and saviour, who sacrifices himself for his fellows, incurs death, descends into the underworld, struggles against the demons of hell, and after a time rises again from the tomb and brings a new life to the world. Even the Israelitic prophets are not uninfluenced by this idea. In the fifty-third chapter of Isaiah we encounter the form of the so-called "suffering servant of God," who is mocked, despised, and sacrificed in expiation of the sins of his people, but rises again in glory, and is borne to the splendours of heaven. It is true that in this the prophet immediately contemplated the fortune of his people, which he conceived as the general expiatory victim for the rest of mankind. But, as Gunkel rightly observes, the figure of a suffering and dying saviour is discerned in the background in this passage. Gressmann has even traced the fifty-third chapter of Isaiah to a "ritual song" derived from the

THE WITNESS OF PAUL

mysteries, which was sung by the initiated on the day of the death of God, and has clearly pointed out the mystery-character of the whole passage.[1]

(a) *Simple Proofs.*—The "Christ-myth" regards the fifty-third chapter of Isaiah as the real *germ-cell* of Christianity. On it is based the Christian belief that the Messiah, whom the Jews expected, *has already appeared* in human form and servile lowliness, and sacrificed himself for the sins of his people, in order that thus the condition might be fulfilled without which the desired "kingdom of God" could not be established: the complete fidelity to the law and sinlessness of the Israelites.[2] In the fact of his previous earthly appearance they saw a guarantee of the speedy coming of the Messiah in all his heavenly majesty, and the combination of the figure of the "servant of God" with that of the "just man" in *Wisdom*[3] confirmed the belief that the judgment of the world was near, at which the just would be raised to heaven and the godless thrust into eternal damnation. Paul enlarged and deepened this idea by introducing it into a more general frame of ideas and deducing its metaphysical consequences. He gave greater clearness to the pagan idea of a suffering, dying, and risen saviour-god, which must have been familiar to the apostle from his Cilician home, and gave it life by infusing into it the spirit of the old mystery-religions.[4] It follows from this that the supposed historical fact of a crucified Jesus is not absolutely necessary to explain the origin of the Paulinian doctrine of redemption, and the question arises whether the letters which have come down to us under the name of Paul contain any reference whatever to an historical Jesus. The negative reply, which the

---

[1] *Der Ursprung der israelitisch-jüdischen Eschatologie*, 1905, p. 322.
[2] *Isaiah* lviii; lx, 21.
[3] ii, 12; iii, 10; iv, 7; and xiii, 5.
[4] This mystery-character of Paulinism has lately been put beyond question by Reitzenstein in his essay, *Die hellenistischen Mysterien-Religionen*, 1910.

"Christ-myth" gives to this question, has caused great agitation among the theologians.

What, they cry with one voice, Paul knew nothing of an historical Jesus! His Jesus Christ was merely an "imaginary being," the mere "idea" of a God-man sacrificing himself! There is no historical personage, no real event, behind the fact of the death on the cross and resurrection of Jesus Christ which is the central part of the Pauline system! Is not Christ described by Paul as a real man? "Does not," von Soden asks, "his theory of redemption through Christ imply his full humanity? God sent his son in the form of sinful flesh on account of sin, and condemned sin in the flesh."[1] The apostle speaks of the "blood" of Christ, by which men are justified.[2] "In vivid language he represents to the Corinthians the entrance of Jesus into human existence in order to stimulate them to contribute generously to the funds of the early Christians (2 *Cor.* viii, 9) : 'For ye know the grace of our Lord Jesus Christ, that, though he was rich, yet for your sakes he became poor, that ye through his poverty might be rich'; and even more vividly he represents him to the Philippians as the model of humility (ii, 5) : 'Let this mind be in you, which was also in Christ Jesus, who, being in the form of God, thought it not robbery to be equal with God; but made himself of no reputation, and took upon him the form of a servant, and was made in the likeness of man.' How can Drews say in face of such passages (to which Weiss adds the allusions to the righteousness [*Rom.* v, 18, 19], the love [*Gal.* ii, 20], and the obedience [*Phil.* ii, 8] of Jesus) : 'The whole earthly life of Jesus is entirely immaterial to Paul'?" (p. 32).

I must, unfortunately, adhere to my view in spite of the instruction given to me by theologians. What do the quoted passages prove? "That Paul is thinking

---

[1] *Romans* viii. 3. [2] *Romans* iii. 25.

of the humanity of his Christ, not in the sense of an ideal humanity, but of a real human existence" (Soden, p. 31). Certainly. But where and when did I question this? It is precisely the essential point of my theory that, in the early Christian and Pauline view, the real coming of the Messiah is preceded by his appearance in human shape. According to Isaiah, it is not due to the powerlessness of God, but to the sins of the people, that the fulfilment of the promise of a Messiah is delayed (*Is.* lviii; lxx, 1). In the fifty-third chapter the prophet had spoken of the "servant of God" who takes on himself the sins of men, and thus "justifies" them. If this figure of the servant of God and just man is associated with that of the Messiah, and the idea is inspired that the servant of God is to be understood, not in the sense of the people of Israel generally, but as a single individual who offers himself for men, in the same way as in heathenism originally one individual has to sacrifice himself annually for all, it would naturally follow that the individual who thus sacrificed himself would not merely have human features, but would have to be a real man, otherwise he could not expiate the sins of men. None but a man could, according to the general feeling of antiquity, take on himself the guilt of other men. Only as man was "the just" in Solomon's *Wisdom* conceived, and he calls himself "servant of God" (ii, 13) and represents God as his "father" (xvi, 18). Indeed, even the suffering servant of God in Isaiah was so unmistakably described as man that the most resolute elevation of his figure to the supernatural and metaphysical world, such as we find in Paul, could not obliterate his human features. The question is, whether these features are those of a *real*, that is to say *historical*, man : whether the heavenly being which must appear as a man according to Paul came upon the earth *at a definite moment in history*.

Are the above-mentioned characters of the Christ-figure such that they necessarily imply an historical personality?

A man must be absolutely wrapped in theological prejudice not to recognise that they are wholly borrowed from the figure of the servant of God in Isaiah: his love, his righteousness, his humility,[1] his obedience, his poverty, and even his position under the law (*Gal.* iv, 4), which follows at once, in the case of a Jew, from his obedience, and was for Paul the necessary condition for releasing from the law the rest of men who were subject to it (v). This, as a matter of fact, was pointed out to the "historical" theologians by their colleague Wrede. "Only in one contingency," he says, "would the human personality of Jesus be a model: if the doctrine of Christ represented an idealising and apotheosis of Jesus in such wise that the historical reality were visible through it. *This is certainly not the case* [!]. Are the humility, obedience, and love which abound in the son of God, when he exchanges heaven for the miseries of earth, a reflection of the compassionate and humble man Jesus? Has Paul transferred the various traits of the character of Jesus to the heavenly form? *This has been affirmed, but it is not true.* Christ is said to be obedient because he did not oppose the divine will to send him to save the world, although it cost him his divine existence and brought him to the cross; humble, because he stooped to the lowliness of earth: and love must have been his motive, since his incarnation and death were the greatest service to mankind. Such service is naturally inspired by the desire to serve—by love. *All these ethical qualifications are, therefore, not derived from an expression of the moral character of Jesus, but originate in the apostle's own theory of redemption.*"[2]

---

[1] This is also shown by the first Epistle of Clement, in which the servant of God of Isaiah is represented as the "prototype" of Christ, and it is said: "If the Lord [!] was so *humble*, what ought we, who have been brought by him under the yoke of his grace, to be?" (xvi, 17). It is very remarkable that Clement, instead of appealing to the behaviour of Jesus to show his humility, relies on the prophet Isaiah.

[2] *Paulus, Religionsgesch. Volksbücher* (1904), p. 85. *Cf.* Martin Brückner:

But Paul represents Christ as "of the seed of David" and born "of a woman" (*Rom.* i, 3). Is not that a plain reference to an historical individual? Unfortunately, descent from David is merely one of the traditional features of the Messiah, and consequently of his human appearance; and, if the Pauline Christ was to be a man at all, from whom could he have been born if not from "a woman"? If Paul seems to lay stress on this trivial and necessary circumstance, he may have been induced to do so by Gnostic tendencies, which aimed at dissociating the figure of the saviour from all earthly limitations, and turning it into a purely metaphysical conception; and he therefore did not merely make use of a familiar Jewish expression—"born of a woman"—which occurs more than once in the Bible.[1] We may add that at least liberal theologians are, to a great extent, convinced that the "historical" Jesus *did not descend from David*, and that the genealogies in the gospels, which purport to prove such descent, are later fabrications made with a view to establishing the Messianic character of the Christian saviour. Thus Paul would have departed from the truth if he had sought to represent Christ to the communities as a descendant of David!

I need not linger to show that the many passages which mention the death and crucifixion of Jesus do not, as Weinel affirms, prove the historicity of Christ. When von Soden emphatically calls attention to the vividness with which Paul saw the details of the life of Jesus, pointing to the first Epistle to the Corinthians (xv, 4), in which he expressly [!] says that Jesus was buried after death (p. 32), we must say that the procedure of our opponents becomes rather humorous. Weinel charges me with saying that theologians based the historicity of Jesus on the account of the appearances of the risen

---

Der Apostel Paulus als Zewge wider den Christusbild der Evangelien in *Protest. Monatshefte*, 1906, 355 *ff*.

[1] *Job* xiv. 1; *Matthew* xi. 11.

Christ (1 *Cor.* xv, 5), and concealing the fact that it was the preceding verses, which speak of the death and burial of Jesus, that were in question (p. 108). I must admit that I had had too high an opinion of the theological method of reasoning. The theologians really base the historicity of Jesus on his death and burial—in spite of *Isaiah* liii, 9, where there is question of the grave of the servant of God. In fact, they even base it on the (equally historical!) fact of the resurrection, which, according to Beth, is one of those "features" [*sic*] of Jesus "which presuppose his humanity" (p. 36). What idea must theologians have of the mental level of their readers when they expect to make an impression on anyone with such quotations as these from Paul!

All that is shown by these arguments adduced by the theologians is, as I said before, that they *assumed* the existence of the historical Jesus and the truth of the gospel narrative *before they began their research;* on this account they at once, in the most uncritical way, refer every passage in which Paul touches upon the humanity of Christ to an historical individual, and interpret in the sense of the gospel narratives everything that is said about this man. Weiss says that the "impartial reader" must recognise "the historical fact of the incarnation and the crucifixion" as the foundation of Paul's creed. The word "historical" is, however, an addition for which as yet no justification has been found in the text; to say nothing of the circumstance that hitherto no one, except a theologian, has regarded the incarnation of a god as an "historical fact." In fact, Paul himself, according to Weiss, was not in a position to conceive "purely a real and entire incarnation of the heavenly Christ," and he rightly points to *Phil.* ii, 7, where the apostle does not say: "He became man and was a man in his whole behaviour," but "he was made in the likeness of a man, and was found in fashion as a man"—an expression that has really a distinctly docetic colour, and suggests the

Gnostic conception of the Saviour.[1] Moreover, Paul's creed portrays not only the man Jesus, but also the man Adam. These two "men" complete each other, according to Paul: just as all men sinned in Adam, the first man, so they will be saved by the second man, Christ. Anyone who regards Paul as taking the man Christ to have been an historical fact must consistently also take Adam to have been an historical reality, as Dupuis rightly observed.[2] When the orthodox hesitate to admit the historicity of Adam, because it is too much out of harmony with modern views, they deprive themselves of the second support on which they base their belief in the historical Christ and his work of redemption. For Paul one is just as much a reality as the other. This should be enough to open the minds of our theologians to the character of this "reality" and its relation to history.

The "evidence" which we have so far examined from Paul for the existence of an historical Jesus may be best described as "simple." We may trust that it is not very seriously advanced by its supporters, and is rather intended for the edification of the general public. Probably they will also not attach much weight to the fact that Paul reminds the Galatians (iii, 1) how "before their eyes Christ hath been evidently set forth, crucified among them." That we have here nothing more than an expressive delineation of the dying Christ and the need for him to die for men, in order to move the hearers, just as we find commonly done in a modern sermon in order to turn souls to Christ, or at the most, according to Robertson, a scenic or pictorial representation of the crucified God after the fashion of the ancient mysteries, and not an historical statement, it is surely unnecessary to prove. "If I set forth anything before the eyes of anyone," says Kurt Delbrück, "there can be no question of a supernatural and ideal being" (p. 15). In that case Delbrück

---

[1] J. Weiss, *Christus, die Anfänge des Dogmas*, *Relg. Volksbücher*, 1909, p. 62.   [2] *L'origine de tous les cultes*, 1794, ix, 13 *ff*.

must regard the paintings of the Last Judgment and Hell by Michael Angelo and Rubens as reproductions of concrete realities, or take the ghost of Hamlet's father to be a real personality. But the most remarkable deduction from this phrase in *Galatians* is drawn by J. Weiss in his work against Wrede, *Paulus und Jesus* (1909), when he says in regard to the "cross of Christ": "As he [Paul] utters these words, he has before his mind not merely the concrete image of the crucified but all the accompanying circumstances, which must have been known to him. Crucifixion is a Roman punishment; he must therefore have known that the higher Roman authority, the procurator, was involved (!). And as, on the other hand, he doubtless (!) regarded the Jews as bearing the guilt of the death (there is no proof!), he must have had some idea of the course of the trial. Indeed, the figure of the crucified must (!) have been before his mind in more than mere outline; it must have had colour, expression, vivid features—otherwise he could not have 'set it forth evidently' [in the Greek text, "before the eyes"] to the Galatians. The expression undeniably (!) implies a living, expressive, pictorial description of the event, not merely an impressive communication of the fact" (p. 11). That is what I should call "exegesis." I will permit myself one question: whether the representation of the suffering just man in *Isaiah* (c. liii) would not suffice to enable one to "set before the eyes" the terrible death of the servant of God?

Perhaps someone will quote "the twelve" to whom Paul refers (1 *Cor.* xv, 5) as a proof that Paul knew some particular facts about the life of the historical Jesus. Since the work of Holsten,[1] however, it has been an open secret in the theological world that "the twelve" is a later interpolation in the original text. The theologian Brandt also regards "the twelve" as "a very unsafe

---

[1] *Das Evangelium des Paulus*, 1880, p. 224 *ff.*

part of the Pauline text," and believes it to be a "later addition";[1] and Seufert is convinced that it is possibly a "very early (?) gloss" which was inserted in the text in order to support with the authority of the apostle Paul the later idea of twelve apostles.[2]

(b) *The Appearances of the Risen Christ.*—Generally speaking, Paul's whole account of the appearances of the risen Christ, as we find it in 1 *Cor.* xv, is not of a character to afford any evidence of the historicity of Jesus. Historical theology professes to attach much importance to this account. It sees in it some confirmation of the theory that in the resurrection we have merely "visions" on the part of the Saviour's disciples. In fact it regards it as the earliest account of the resurrection that we have, and having great authority because, in their opinion, Paul relies directly on the testimony of the "primitive community" for the truth of his statement. That, they say, is what we must understand when the apostle writes: "I delivered unto you first of all *that which I also received,* how that Christ died for our sins according to the Scriptures, and that he was buried, and that he rose again the third day according to the Scriptures," etc. But does not the phrase "according to the Scriptures" point rather to the fact that there is no question here of an historical reminiscence, but a belief based on writings—namely, *Isaiah* liii, and possibly also *Jonah* ii, 1, and *Hosea* vi, 2?[3] The story of Jonah itself seems to have been originally only an historical embodiment of the myth of the dead, buried, and risen Saviour; in fact, Jesus refers to the prophet Jonah in this sense (*Matt.* xii, 40).

---

[1] *Die evangel. Geschichte und der Ursprung des Christentums,* 1903, pp. 14, 418, and 421.

[2] *Der Ursprung und die Bedeutung des Apostolatus in der christl. Kirche der ersten drei Jahrhunderte,* 1887, pp. 46 and 157.

[3] "After two days will he revive us: in the third day he will raise us up, and we shall live in his sight"—a passage relating to the people of Israel, but which may have been taken by Paul to refer to the Messiah. Compare Hausrath, *Jesus u. d. neutestamentl. Schriftsteller,* i, p. 103, 1908.

And even if the apostle was assured by the "primitive community" of the truth of these writings, what does it prove as regards the historicity of the person seen in such visions? It has been said that his enumeration of the appearances of Jesus has a documentary and "catalogue-like" character. But where do we find in this "catalogue" the women to whom, according to *Matthew* (xxviii, 9) and *Mark* (xvi, 9), the risen Jesus first appeared? And how can Paul say that Jesus appeared to the whole of the twelve apostles, as there were only eleven after the death of Judas, as *Luke* (xxiv, 33) assumes? And how does James come into the matter, since, according to the gospels, Jesus is supposed to have had no relations with his brother, and they do not speak of any such appearance to him? If some of the more exalted religious folk saw visions and believed they perceived the bodily presence of the "servant of God," does that give any proof of historicity?

Naturally, Weiss says, and for proof he refers us to the vision of Paul, of which he says: "The appearance must have shown him features in the heavenly figure by which he recognised Jesus of Nazareth, or—as I should say in accordance with 2 *Cor.* v, 16—recognised once more" (p. 108). Yet *Acts* says nothing about Paul perceiving a definite form; it speaks only of a flash of light which fell upon the apostle from above, and a voice which he believed he heard.[1] That is enough to ruin the deduction which Weiss makes in his book against Wrede (p. ix)—that Paul must have had a personal knowledge of Jesus. We should have just as much right to regard the pagan gods, Serapis or Asclepios, which were believed to appear to their devotees in a state of ecstasy, as historical personalities because the devotees regarded them as such. Weiss himself assumes, in fact, that the transfiguration of Jesus is based upon a statement of

---

[1] ix. 5 : xxvi. 14.

Peter. Jesus is supposed to have appeared to his disciples in the company of Moses and Elias. But how did Peter know that the two were Moses and Elias? He had no personal knowledge of them.

Von Soden, however, believes that the visions mentioned in 1 *Cor.* xv show that the figure which appeared to the disciples must have had quite definite and recognisable features, by which it could be known as that of Jesus. But Paul does not say that Jesus appeared to them in bodily form. If the appearance of a light to him was enough to point to Jesus, may it not have been the same with the others, as they all hourly expected the coming of the Saviour? Von Soden quotes the "more than 500 brethren," who must all have seen him at some time, and of whom many still lived (1 *Cor.* xv, 6). It seems that he has never heard of apparitions of the Virgin Mary, which have been seen simultaneously by many of the faithful, though not one of them had the least personal acquaintance with her. He also thinks that the apparition to the five hundred may be brought into line with the Pentecostal occurrence in *Acts*. Unfortunately, this Pentecostal phenomenon was quite certainly not an historical event; the account of the outpouring of the Holy Spirit is quite understood from *Joel* ii, 28, where we read: "And it shall come to pass that I will pour out my spirit upon all flesh; and your sons and your daughters shall prophesy, your old men shall dream dreams, and your young men shall see visions. And also upon the servants and upon the handmaids in those days will I pour out my spirit. And I will show wonders in the heavens and in the earth," etc. But even if the Pentecostal phenomenon had ever really taken place, it would not help the opinion of Herr von Soden, because it would only follow that the five hundred saw an appearance of light, not a definite figure of Jesus. That is more probable, it is true, than that a definite form was seen simultaneously by five hundred men. For that reason we might regard the account in *Acts* as earlier than, if not the source of, the narrative of Paul. That would mean that the episode of the five hundred is not given in its original form in Paul, and we should then have all the more reason to regard the whole reference to the appearances of the risen Jesus in the fifteenth chapter of 1 *Corinthians* as an interpolation. The effort to put Paul's vision of Christ on a footing with those of the other apostles suggests that the whole thing is a fictitious account inserted in the interest of the apostle of the Gentiles, or, rather, of a common preaching of the apostle of the Jews and Paul.[1]

At any rate, the proof that Paul owes his account of the apparition of the risen Christ to the primitive community does not help at all, as there is no more guarantee of the historical reality of the figure seen in a vision by a number than by an individual. It merely shows the failure of theologians to find any support for their belief in an historical Jesus in 1 *Cor.* xv.

(c) *The Account of the Last Supper.*—Now we come to 1 *Cor.* xi, 23. Here we find the familiar words: " For I have received from the Lord that which also I delivered unto you, that the Lord Jesus the same night in which he was betrayed took bread," etc. This passage, J. Weiss assures us, is "fatal" to the whole theory of Drews, "because in it we not only have the words of the Lord quoted, but a perfectly definite event in the life of Jesus is described in all its details, which show a full knowledge of the story of the passion: the night, the betrayal, and the supper before the arrest " (p. 105). Certainly ; unless the words in question were not written by Paul, but are a later interpolation in the text. I was not the first to suggest this. The theologians Straatman[2] and Bruins[3] rejected Paul's account of the Last Supper, and concluded that it

---

[1] *Cf.* W. B. Smith, *Ecce Deus* (1911), p. 155 *ff*.
[2] *Kritische Studien*, 1863, pp. 38–63.
[3] *Theol. Tijdschr.*, xxvi, pp. 397–403.

does not fit the context. Steck[1] describes it as modified for liturgical use, and Völter[2] regards the whole eleventh chapter of the first Epistle to the Corinthians as an interpolation. Van Manen also has questioned the passage relating to the Last Supper in Paul, on account of its lack of connection with the preceding passage, and has said that it gives one the impression of being a collection of sayings from various sources for the purpose of displacing the love-feasts of the community, on account of the unseemly things that happened, and replacing them by the festival of the Last Supper.[3] To these we may add Schläger, the translator of van Manen's *Römerbrief*, who has raised objections to the passage;[4] and Smith also has recently declared the passage to be an interpolation. It is not therefore foolish to speak about an interpolation in 1 *Cor.* xi, 23.

Historical theology generally regards the passage in *Corinthians* as the earliest version we have of the words used at the institution of the Supper. But a particularly striking reason that prevents us from seeing in Paul the oldest tradition of the words at the Last Supper is their obviously liturgical form and the meaning which the apostle puts on the words. It is very remarkable that Paul and Luke alone represent the Lord's Supper as instituted by Jesus in "memory" of him; Mark and Matthew know nothing of this. They have a much simpler test than the other two. Hence, Jülicher, against Weizsäcker and Harnack, rightly doubts whether the Supper was "founded" by Jesus.[5] "He did not institute or found anything; that remained for the time when he came again into his father's kingdom. He made no provision for his memory; having spoken as he did in *Matthew* (xxvi, 29), he had no idea of so long a period

[1] *Galaterbrief*, p. 172.
[2] *Theol. Tijdschr.*, xxiii, p. 322.
[3] Whittaker, work quoted, p. 168.
[4] *Theol. Tijdschr.*, 1889, Heft. I, p. 41.
[5] *Theol. Abhandlungen für C. Weizsäcker*, 1892, p. 232.

of future time" (p. 244). Paul, therefore, according to Jülicher, indicates a later stage of the tradition in regard to the first Eucharist than Mark and Matthew, and the earliest tradition does not make Jesus show the least sign that he wishes these material actions to be performed in future by his followers (p. 238). If this is so, the words of the institution of the Supper were interpolated subsequently in the text of Paul, as the liturgical use of them in the Pauline sense became established in the Church, in order to support them with the authority of the apostle, and the words, "For I have received from the Lord," serve to give further proof of their authentic character; or else the first Epistle to the Corinthians was not written by the apostle Paul, as, in spite of Jülicher, it is difficult to believe that Paul could at so early a stage give a version of the Lord's Supper that differed so much from that of the "primitive community."

Or may we believe that Paul had a more reliable account of the words of Jesus than the evangelists, and has used it in 1 *Cor.* xi, 23? If so, how came Matthew and Mark to change the original words of institution, and how could this alteration be preserved in their text and received by the Church? Even in their text the words of institution do not give an impression of history. Their mystic sense is in flagrant contradiction to what theologians so appreciatively call the "simplicity" and "straightforwardness" of the words of Jesus. "How were the disciples to understand that they eat the body of Christ who was about to be put to death, and drank his blood, though not the blood present in his body, but that about to be shed soon?" asks the theologian A. Eichhorn in his work *Das Abendmahl* (1898), and he declares that the whole story of the institution of the supper, as we have it in the Synoptics and Paul, is an *historical impossibility*. "All the difficulties disappear if we adopt the later point of view of the community."[1] The mysticism of the festive supper cannot have been instituted by Jesus, but is based on the cult of the Christian community, and was subsequently put in the mouth of its supposed founder.[2]

In that case 1 *Cor.* xi, 23, etc., is of no value as a proof of the historicity of Jesus.

Let us examine the passage more closely. "The same night in which he was betrayed"—*was* he betrayed? The thing is historically so improbable, the whole story of the betrayal is so absurd historically and psychologically, that only a few thoughtless Bible-readers can accept it with complacency. Imagine the ideal man Jesus knowing that one of his disciples is about to betray him and thus forfeit his eternal salvation, yet doing nothing to restrain the miserable man, but rather confirming him in it! Imagine a Judas demanding money from the high-priest for the betrayal of a man who walks the streets of Jerusalem daily, and whose sojourn at night could assuredly be discovered without any treachery! "For Judas to have betrayed Jesus," Kautsky says, "is much the same as if the Berlin police were to pay a spy to point out to them the man named Bebel."[3] Moreover, the Greek word *paradidonai* does not mean "betray" at all, but "give up," and is simply taken from *Isaiah* liii, 12, where it is said that the servant of God "gave himself unto death." The whole story of the betrayal is a late invention founded on that passage in the prophet, and Judas is not an historical personality, but, as Robertson believes, a representative of the Jewish people, hated by the Christians, who were believed to have caused the death of the Saviour. Further, the "night," in which the betrayal is supposed to have taken place, has no historical background. It merely serves to

---

[1] Work quoted, p. 19. See also A. Schweitzer, *Von Reimarus zu Wrede* (1906), p. 152.
[2] See Feigel, *Der Einfluss des Weissagungsbeweises und anderer Motive auf die Leidensgeschichte* (1910), p. 50.
[3] *Der Ursprung des Christentums* (1910), p. 388.

set in contrast the luminous figure of Jesus and the dark work of his betrayer.[1] Hence Paul cannot have known anything of a nocturnal betrayal on the part of Judas, and one more "proof" of the historicity of Jesus breaks down.

Theologians humorously comment on the fact that all passages are rejected as interpolations which do not square with the theory of those who deny the historicity of Christ, and say that this is a wilful procedure. It is, however, quite certain that they themselves would at once abandon the passages, and find as many arguments against their genuineness as they now do in favour of it, if this suited their general system.

This much is certain: *If 1 Cor. xi, 23, etc., is not an interpolation in the text, there are no interpolations at all in the New Testament.* We can understand how difficult it is for theologians to give up the passage on account of the very thin thread which unequivocally connects the teaching of Paul with the gospels, but we cannot think much of their perspicacity when they find no fault with the passage. In earlier verses (17–22) of the chapter Paul is not dealing with the so-called last supper, but with the love-feast, or agape, which the Christians celebrated in common. From the twenty-third verse on the apostle speaks suddenly of the supper, and then in verses 23 and 24 returns to the love-feast.

(*d*) *The "Brothers" of the Lord.*—We have now to deal with "the brothers of the Lord" (1 *Cor.* ix, 5 and *Gal.* i, 19). Here the theologians believe that they play their trump. If Jesus had had corporal brothers, he must certainly have been an historical individual, and it is untrue that Paul knew nothing of any individual human feature of Jesus. "Have we not," says 1 *Cor.* ix, 5, "power to lead about a sister, a wife, as well as other apostles, and as the brethren of the Lord, and Cephas?"

---

[1] See Feigel, work quoted, pp. 47 and 114.

THE WITNESS OF PAUL

If it could only be proved that Paul had in his mind corporal brothers of Jesus and not merely "brothers" in the sect! Weinel contests this on the ground that it is unlikely that a sect would call itself "brothers" of the God of the cult. Has he never heard of brothers of St. Vincent, brothers of Joseph, sisters of Mary, etc.; that is to say, religious brotherhoods whose members call themselves after the saint whose service they have entered, and who correspond to the heroes of the cult in the ancient mysteries? "But in the case of Paul," he replies, "we can prove that he does not give that name to Christians; he calls them 'brethren' or 'brethren *in* Christ'" (p. 109).

Now, in *Romans* (viii, 44) those who are impelled by the spirit of God are called "sons of God." Christ, as "son of God" in a special sense, is called "the firstborn among many brethren" (29), and his followers are called "heirs of God" and "co-heirs with Christ" (17), from which it follows that they must at the same time be "brothers of Christ." That is, says Weinel, a figure, not a Christian name. But why should not the followers of Jesus receive a figurative name from Paul, when the "brotherhood" of the sect is only figurative, its heads are figuratively called "fathers," and the members only figuratively their sons? In *Matthew* (xxviii, 10) Jesus himself calls his followers his "brothers," and in *Mark* (iii, 35) he says: "Whoever shall do the will of God, the same is my brother and my sister and mother." In *John* (xx, 17) he so names the disciples because they have as "father" the same God as he. In fact, in the second century Justin, in his dialogue with the Jew Trypho, speaks of the apostles as "brothers of Jesus" in the highest sense (p. 106). Why, then, should not Paul have spoken of the followers of Jesus as his "brothers"? Because he usually calls them "brothers in Christ"? But just as, on the one hand, the apostle expresses the intimate connection with Christ by the continence of the faithful (*Gal.* iii, 26–29), and also by absorption in the life-atmosphere of the Supreme, so he also speaks, on the other hand, of Christ living in the faithful and bringing them into closer relationship, or making brothers of them. If in one place he does not confine himself to one mode of expression, why should he do so in another? Those who think otherwise must have been convinced beforehand that Jesus is an historical individual in Paul, and that his brothers can *only* be brothers in the flesh. As a matter of fact, the partisans of the historicity of Jesus merely reject the figurative interpretation of the expression "brothers" because they *assume* that historicity in advance.

According to Weinel, it follows that a special group of men must be named here, because in 1 *Cor.* ix there is question of the prerogatives of the apostles, and the brothers of the Lord are associated with them as apostolic men (p. 109). But was it really a "prerogative" of the apostles to be married? Were the other members of the sect besides the apostles and the corporal brothers of Jesus forbidden to take a wife? Might not Paul just as well have wished to say that in all things he felt himself in the same position as the other members of the community, and therefore his apostolic dignity could not be contested once he had won a right to that name by his missionary work? No, says J. Weiss; the "brothers of the Lord" cannot be ordinary Christians. "Why were they named between the apostles and Cephas, and why especially were the apostles not so called?" (p. 106). On the other hand, why is Cephas mentioned after the "brothers of the Lord," seeing that he was one of the apostles? And were the Corinthians so familiar with the brothers of Jesus that Paul could appeal to them and their conjugal relations? Are we not rather to understand by the "brothers of the Lord," if they do really mean a special group of men distinct from the twelve apostles, the seventy disciples whom Jesus is said (*Luke* x) to have sent on missionary journeys? We might point to the fact that James, the "brother of the Lord," is distinct from the twelve apostles according to the apostolic constitutions, and is counted by Eusebius[1] among the seventy—a view which Hegesippus also seems to hold in Eusebius.[2] There is no answer to these questions. At the best the passage remains obscure.

Other students, who do not need the "brothers of Jesus" in support of their belief in an historical Jesus, have dropped 1 *Cor.* ix, 5 altogether, and declared that it is meaningless or is an interpolation. Schläger, for instance, considers it spurious because, in his research, all passages in the first Epistle to the Corinthians, with one single exception (iv, 4), which speak of Christ as "the Lord" have proved to be interpolations. "Missionary journeys of the brothers of Jesus," he says, "are not known to us from any other source, and are in themselves improbable." That is undoubtedly correct. Imagine Simon, Jude, or Joseph (Joses) going out with the announcement that their brother Jesus was the long-expected Messiah, and would soon come again in the clouds of heaven! Steck also is surprised to hear of missionary journeys on the part of the brothers of the Lord, "who, as patriotic Jews, are not easy to imagine away from Palestine," and he is reminded of *Gal.* ii, 12, where it is merely said that Peter went to Antioch, without any further historical explanations.[3] And Bruno Bauer exclaims: "What an idea that Peter and the twelve apostles should be known to the Corinthians as travelling about! It was not until the second century that they were known as such to everybody. And how incongruous the question is whether they have not the same right to marry as the apostles, and that Barnabas should be brought into closest intimacy with the person of Paul and represented to the Corinthians as co-ordinate with

---

[1] *Comment. Is.* xvii, 5; *Eccl. Hist.*, I, 12; II, 1; VII, 19.
[2] *Eccl. Hist.*, II, 25.   [3] *Galaterbrief*, p. 272.

Paul! As if he had gone to Corinth with the apostle of the Gentiles!" (p. 52).

The partisans of an historical Jesus naturally connect his "brothers" with *Mark* vi, 3, where James, Joses, Juda, and Simon are mentioned as sons of Mary and brothers of Jesus. But Steudel has rightly called our attention to *Mark* xv, 40, where the same Mary, who is supposed to be the mother of James and Joses, is not represented as the mother of Jesus, and, consequently, James and Joses cannot be regarded as his brothers. We have evidently to deal with two independent accounts, and there can be no hesitation in saying which was the earlier; and, therefore, the belief that Jesus had brothers in the flesh is seen to be a secondary and legendary growth.[1]

Here we also have the answer to the question about the brotherhood of James (*Gal.* i, 19). I have endeavoured to show that this also is merely brotherhood in the sect, and that the position of honour which James is supposed to have had in the community, according to *Acts* xv, 13 and *Gal.* i, 19 and ii, 9 and 12, was due to his personal qualities. "It was reserved for Drews," says von Soden, "to explain the phrase 'brothers of the Lord' in the sense that James was the best Christian, the most like to the Lord" (p. 31). The learned writer evidently forgets that Origen had said long ago that James was called the brother of the Lord, not so much on account of blood-relationship with Jesus, or because he had grown up with him, as because he was faithful and virtuous.[2] It is well known what an important part James played in the second century in the Jewish-Christian communities, as we see especially in Hegesippus (in Eusebius's *Ecclesiastical History*, II, 25), precisely on account of his piety. He was at the same time the patron of the Ebionitic

---

[1] Steudel, *Im Kampf um die Christusmythe*, pp. 95 and 114.
[2] *Contra Celsum*, I, 47.

party, which formed a garland of legends about his head. Is it so improbable that the pious brother in the sect was early elevated to the position of "brother of the Lord" in a special sense, and that the name—originally only a title of honour—was used by Paul in that sense?

On the other hand, it is not impossible that "the brother of the Lord" is a later interpolation in *Gal.* i, 19, whether because a particular group of Christians wished to bring the venerated saint as close as possible to Jesus by making him a brother in the flesh, or, as Schläger (p. 46) thinks, in order to distinguish more clearly the various individuals who were named James. As Hegesippus says: "The community distinguished the apostle James, the brother of the Lord, by the name of 'the just,' from the time of Christ to our own days, as there were several with the name James."[1] It was quite natural, when they began to regard Jesus generally as a human being, to give him human features, and convert the inner spiritual relationship to him of various distinguished brethren into a bodily relationship; at times this might be done in order to vindicate the complete reality of the incarnation of Christ against the growing Gnostic spiritualism. Lastly, can it be a mere coincidence that the three "pillars" at Jerusalem agree in name with the three privileged disciples of the Lord who are present with him at the raising of the daughter of Jairus (*Mark* v, 57; *Luke* vii, 51), follow him to the mountain of transfiguration (*Mark* ix, 2; *Luke* ix, 28), and are permitted to be the witnesses of his agony in face of approaching death in Gethsemane? Was not the "pillar" apostle James originally identical with James the son of Zebedee and brother of John, and only afterwards converted into the "brother of Jesus"?

---

[1] Eusebius. *Eccl. Hist.*, as above.

Let it not be said that it is mere " subjective arbitrariness" to find here another interpolation in Paul. No theologian doubts that the Pauline Epistles have been greatly interpolated. Which passages have been inserted later can be decided only by the general theory which one gathers from the text. And that the theory of the theologians is the only correct one, that the Jesus of the Pauline Epistles was an historical individual, has not yet been proved by anything we have found in the Epistles. What is there to prevent us, then, from interpreting in our own sense, or excluding, so singular and isolated an expression as "the brother of the Lord" in *Galatians*?

As is well known, much scandal was early occasioned in Essenian-Ebionitic circles by the statement that Mary was married to Joseph and had several children, and it was said that James was not a real brother of Jesus. Some regarded him as a step-brother—a son of Joseph by an earlier wife; others thought the "brothers of the Lord" were foster-brothers or cousins of Jesus, or attempted to explain them away as equal to the apostles. This led to an identification of James the Just, the "brother of the Lord," with James the son of Alphæus, as he is briefly called in the Synoptics and in *Acts*,[1] as we find in Jerome, for instance; others identified him with James the son of Zebedee, the brother of John; and these views have found representatives among recent theologians. In the Synoptics the "brothers" have apparently a purely symbolical significance. They serve the purpose of emphasising the distinction between spiritual and bodily relationship, and illustrating the truth that belonging to Jesus does not depend on external circumstances and the accident of birth, but simply on faith.[2] Even in *John* (vii, 5) the brothers, who do not believe in him, are opposed to the twelve and their

---

[1] *Matt.* x, 3; *Mark* iii, 18; *Luke* vi, 15; *Acts* i, 13.
[2] *Matt.* xii, 46: *Mark* iii, 31: *Luke* viii, 19.

unhesitating recognition of his Messiahship (vi, 69), which also recalls the antithesis of the Jews, who, in spite of their racial connection, would hear nothing of Jesus and his intimate followers. It is only in the later *Acts of the Apostles* (i, 14) that the brothers of Jesus appear as followers of him, although not a word is said in explanation of their sudden conversion. This does not dispose us to place very much confidence in the references of the New Testament to the brothers of Jesus, and when Weinel says in regard to James, "It is all so simple, intelligible, and straightforward that it needs a good deal of art to evade the testimony of the connection of *Gal.* i and 1 *Cor.* ix and the terminology" (p. 116), I can only reply that, in spite of all my efforts to understand James from the writings of theologians, I have never been able to get at the real nature of the man. And as I find that others have had the same experience, it does not seem to be due to any defect on my part that the James-problem seems to me *hopeless;* every attempt to throw light on the obscure problem fails.[1] To base on an isolated passage such as the reference to "the brothers of the Lord" in Paul a belief in the historical character of Jesus seems to me too "simple"; I am not modest enough to do it. I can only see in the "brothers of Jesus," as far as they are supposed to have been brothers in the flesh, and in his parents, the carpenter Joseph and Mary, mythical figures; in the case of Mary especially, because the name is customary among the saviour-gods of ancient times, and the other supposed actions of the Biblical Mary agree with those of the mothers (or sisters) of those deities.[2]

(e) *The "Words of the Lord."*—We now come to what are called the "Words of the Lord," the introduction of which into the Pauline Epistles is supposed to

---

[1] See also Steudel, *Wir Gelehrten vom Fach*, p. 69.
[2] See *The Christ-Myth* and Robertson's *Christianity and Mythology.*

prove that the apostle had some knowledge of Jesus. First there is 1 *Cor.* vii, 10: "And unto the married I command, yet not I, but *the Lord*, Let not the wife depart from her husband: but and if she depart, let her remain unmarried, or be reconciled to her husband; and let not the husband put away his wife." The latter part of this precept agrees in substance (not verbally) with *Matthew* v, 32, and xix, 9, and other parallel passages. But does that mean that it is a quotation of a saying of the historical Jesus? The prohibition to part with a wife is sound Rabbinism. In the Talmud we read: "A wife must not be dismissed except for adultery" (*Gittin*, 90); "The altar itself sheds tears over the man who sends away his wife" (*Pessach*, 113); "The man who separates from his wife is hateful to God" (*Gittin*, 90 *b*). We even read in the prophet Malachi: "Let none deal treacherously against the wife of his youth. For the Lord, the God of Israel, saith that he hateth putting away" (ii, 15). How, if the apostle had this passage in mind in his prohibition of divorce, and by the "Lord" in whose name he speaks, are we to understand "the God of Israel"? Does not Paul regard the Old Testament as the word of revelation of the "Lord," whose pointing to Christ had hitherto been hidden, but is now revealed in the eyes of the faithful?[1] And when the apostle appeals in 1 *Cor.* ix, 14, to a command of the "Lord" for the right of the apostles to live by the gospel, we may be disposed to recall *Matthew* x, 10: "The workman is worthy of his meat"; but we should have just as much right to think of *Deut.* xviii, 1, where it is written: "The priests the Levites, and all the tribe of Levi, shall have no part nor inheritance with Israel: they shall eat the offerings of the Lord made by fire, and his inheritance," and xxv, 4: "Thou shalt not muzzle the ox when he treadeth out the corn." Paul himself

[1] 2 *Cor.* iii, 14.

sometimes (1 *Cor.* ix, 9) appeals to this word of the law. In order, therefore, to explain Paul's "Words of the Lord" we have no need to suppose, as I did previously, that they are rules of the community, which are clothed with an authoritative significance by ascribing them to the patron of the religious body; it is enough to appeal to the Old Testament.

If, however, we are to understand by the "Lord" in Paul, not the "God of Israel," but Jesus, there is still no security whatever that the words in question are not interpolations. "References to the words and deeds of the life of the historical Jesus are," says Schläger, "so infrequent in the Pauline writings that, whenever they occur, we have to ask ourselves whether it is not the reflectiveness of a later period, which was accustomed to rely on the evangelical literature, that introduced the authority of Jesus into the text" (p. 36). What is to prevent us from supposing that the reverse often took place also, and that words and phrases from the Pauline Epistles were afterwards put in the mouth of the Jesus of the gospels?

Von Soden, also, finds it remarkable that the "Words of the Lord" in Paul are not found, or not found in the same form, in the gospels. That is especially true of 1 *Thessalonians* iv, 15—an Epistle which is usually regarded as genuine by historical theologians: "For this we say unto you by the word of the Lord, that we which are alive and remain unto the coming of the Lord shall not prevent them which are asleep. For the Lord himself shall descend from heaven with a shout, with the voice of the archangel, and with the trump of God; and the dead in Christ shall rise first: then we which are alive and remain shall be caught up together with them in the clouds, to meet the Lord in the air; and so shall we ever be with the Lord." The passage recalls *Mark* xiii, 26, especially in view of the subsequent warning to watch, but differs from it in important points. Here we have an excellent illustration of the way in which "Words of the Lord" came into existence. For some of the most distinguished critical representatives of historical theology (Holtzmann, for instance) are convinced that the thirteenth chapter of *Mark* is in the main an apocalyptic leaflet of the time of the Jewish War, shortly before the year 70; more probably, as Graetz believes and Lublinski has recently shown, a leaflet by a Palestinian Christian of the time of Bar-Kochba.[1] These "Words of the Lord" are merely the sayings of individuals who felt the inspiration of the Holy Ghost, and believed that their utterances during the ecstatic condition came directly from "the Lord"; and sometimes, as in the case we are discussing, they were introduced afterwards into the New Testament.[2]

Such being the state of things, it is utterly futile to claim that, because certain words and phrases of the Pauline Epistles harmonise with others in the gospels, Paul is repeating the words of the historical Jesus. The late H. Holtzmann, in his attempt to refute my statement in the *Christ Myth* that Paul seemed not to be acquainted with any sayings of Jesus, hastily put together a number of such words from the apostle's Epistles, and no doubt others will be found now that attention has been drawn to them. There is, however, as I said, no disproof whatever in this, for the simple reason that most of these words are of such a nature that we cannot say whether the gospels took them from the Pauline Epistles, or the Epistles owe them to the gospels. On the one hand, even according to theologians, the gospels are repeatedly found to contain Pauline ideas; on the other, one can very easily see how it would be to the interest of the Church to discover the ideas and words of Jesus in

---

[1] Wernle, *Die Quellen des Lebens Jesu*, 1905, p. 58; *Das werdende Dogma vom Leben Jesu*, 1910, pp. 76 and 101.
[2] Steudel, *Wir Gelehrten vom Fach*, p. 37; *Im Kampf um die Christusmythe*, p. 56.

Paul, in order to bridge over the remarkable gulf between the two. Moreover, a great part of these particular words of Jesus, especially of the more important, have nothing distinctive about them to show that they were uttered by Jesus only.

This is true, in the first place, of *Romans* ii, 1: "Wherein thou judgest another, thou condemnest thyself" (*cf.* also xiv, 4). The saying is supposed to suggest *Matthew* vii, 1: "Judge not that ye be not judged." But the resemblance is so slight and the saying so commonplace that Paul himself may have been the author of it. It is written in the Talmud (*Pirke Aboth*, i, 6): "Judge only good of thy neighbours," and (*Sanhedrim*, 100): "As a man measures, with the same standard shall he be measured." It is the same with *Romans* ii, 19. When the apostle exclaims to the law-proud Jew, "Thou art confident that thou thyself art a guide of the blind," there is no necessary connection with *Matthew* xv, 14, and xxiii, 16 and 24, where Jesus pronounces his woes over the Pharisees, as the figure is too pertinent and familiar to prove anything. In *Romans* ix, 33, Paul describes his gospel of justification by faith as "a stumbling-block and rock of offence." This at once sends theologians to *Matthew* xxi, 42, where it is written: "The stone which the builders rejected, the same is become the head of the corner." Whereas in this case Jesus himself appeals to the Scriptures, and there is no reason whatever why Paul also, when he reproduced the words, should not have in mind *Is.* viii, 14, and xxviii, 16. In *Romans* xii, 14, we find: "Bless them which persecute you; bless, and curse not." That, of course, must be based on the words of Jesus in *Matthew* v, 44: "Love your enemies, bless them that curse you, do good to them that hate you, and pray for them which despitefully use you and persecute you." It is, however, written in *Psalm* cix, 28: "Let them curse, but bless thou"; and the Talmud says: "It is better to be wronged by others than to wrong" (*Sanhedrim*, 48); "Be rather with the persecuted than the persecutors" (*Babamezia*, 93); and the oldest manuscripts of the gospels (*Sinaiticus* and *Vaticanus*) do not contain the words of Jesus at all. In the same way we dispose of *Romans* xii, 21: "Be not overcome of evil, but overcome evil with good" (*cf.* also *Wisdom*, vii, 30).

In *Romans* xiii, 7, we read: "Render therefore to all their dues: tribute to whom tribute is due, custom to whom custom"; and this is paralleled by *Matthew* xxii, 21: "Render therefore unto Cæsar the things which are Cæsar's, and unto God the things that are God's"; but we also read in the Talmud (*Shekalim* iii, 2; *Pirke Aboth* iii, 7): "Everyone is bound to discharge his obligations to God with the same conscientiousness as his obligations to men. Give unto God what belongs to him." In *Romans* xiii, 8–10, we have the precept of mutual charity: "He that loveth another hath fulfilled the law. For this, Thou shalt not commit adultery, Thou shalt not kill, Thou shalt not steal......and if there be any other commandment, it is all comprehended in this saying—namely: Thou shalt love thy neighbour as thyself. Love worketh no ill to his neighbour: therefore love is the fulfilment of the law" (*cf.* also *Galatians* v, 14). Here the source seems to be *Matthew* xxii, 40, where Jesus tells the Scribe, who asks him which is the greatest commandment in the law, that it is the love of God and one's neighbour, and adds: "On these two commandments hang all the law and the prophets." But Hillel also is said to have told a Gentile who asked him to teach the whole law while he stood on one leg: "What displeases thee, do thou not to any fellow-man; that is the whole of our teaching" (*Shabbat*, 31). In *Romans* xiv, 13, Paul warns his reader to give no scandal to his weak brother (also 1 *Cor.* viii, 7–13). Here we are referred to *Matthew* xviii, 6–9, where Jesus pronounces his woes on those who give scandal: "Whoso shall offend one of these little ones which believe in me, it were better for him that a millstone were hanged about his neck, and that he were drowned in the depth of the sea." But, apart from the fact that this prohibition of scandal is too natural and obvious for Paul to need to derive it from the words of Jesus, it is written in the Talmud: "Better were it for the evil-minded to have been born blind so that they might bring no evil into the world" (*Tanchuma*, 71), and "Whoso leads his fellow-men into sin acts far worse than if he took away his own life" (*Tanchuma*, 74).

In 1 *Cor.* xiii, 2, Paul speaks of the faith that "moves mountains." But that he was referring to *Matthew* xxi, 22: "If ye have faith, and doubt not......ye shall say unto this mountain, Be thou removed, and be thou cast into the sea; and it shall be done," seems very doubtful in view of the fact that the phrase about removing mountains was quite common among the rabbis as an expression of the power of the discourse of a teacher, and might easily be transferred to express the power of faith (*Berachoth*, 64; *Erubim*, 29). The other phrases that are quoted under this head are of no importance. If it is objected that a comparison of the parallel passages shows that the composition of the sayings of Jesus is more distinguished for "originality" than that of the words of Paul, such originality proves neither that they are earlier nor that they were uttered by Jesus. It is just as conceivable that the words of the apostle received their greater freshness and force by being afterwards fitted into the peculiar frame of the gospels as that Paul himself took them from the gospels, as Steck, for instance, is disposed to think.[1] Hence, *the concordances with the gospels in Paul prove nothing whatever as regards the historicity of Jesus*, and would not if they were more numerous than those we have quoted.

---

[1] Pp. 163-72. *Cf.* E. Hortlein, "Jesusworte bei Paulus?" in the *Prot. Monatshefte*, 1909, p. 265, and Brückner, work quoted.

2.—PAUL NO WITNESS TO THE HISTORICITY OF JESUS.

We must, therefore, acquiesce in the view of Wrede and M. Brückner, which is also presented in the *Christ-Myth*, that Paul *was not concerned with the earthly life of Jesus*, and his idea of Christ was *formed independently of an historical Jesus*. "Of the 'life' of Jesus," says Wrede, "one single event was of importance to him: the end of life, the death. For him, however, even this is not the moral action of a man; indeed, *it is not an historical fact at all for him*, but a superhistorical fact, an event of the supersensual world."[1] Wrede therefore doubts whether the "disciple of Jesus" properly applies to Paul, if it is meant to express his historical relation to Jesus. "We need not repeat it: the life-work and living figure of Jesus are not reflected in the Pauline theology. There can be no doubt about this fact. He of whom Paul professed himself the disciple and servant was not the historical human being Jesus, but another."

This admission on the part of so distinguished an expert as Wrede is naturally very unwelcome to liberal theologians. It has brought into play a large number of theological pens, eager to weaken Wrede's remarks, represent them as exaggerations, and make them harmless. "Attempts at reconciliation," J. Weiss rightly calls these efforts in his work *Paulus und Jesus*, in which he emphatically opposes Wrede, and endeavours to find better arguments to prove the close connection between Paul and Jesus. Jülicher also has published a volume in the "Religionsgeschichtlichen Volksbücher," entitled *Paulus und Jesus* (1907), to correct the heresy of Wrede. In this he has endeavoured, with more rhetoric than force, to explain the agreement and the difference between Jesus and his apostles, and to prove that Paul was not indifferent to the personality of Jesus. "The 'Lord,' the supreme

---

[1] *Paulus*, pp. 85 and 95.

master, was not shown to him by the apostles, but by God alone; but what the Lord had once taught, commanded, and instituted on earth could [*sic*] be learned by Paul only from men. The friendly co-operation of Paul with other Evangelists, such as Barnabas and Mark, who assuredly did not possess such remarkable exclusiveness, makes it impossible that the gospel-story should have remained substantially unknown to Paul." Who can fail to recognise here the method which the liberal theologian regards as the only "scientific" method—namely, to assume precisely what has to be proved—the connection of Paul and the "primitive community" with an historical Jesus? It is, of course, more than improbable that, if Peter and Barnabas and all the others knew any details about Jesus, Paul should not have heard them. But the only *fact* in the matter is that the apostle's letters show no trace whatever of such knowledge. *What is the value of an argument which tries to prove the historicity of the gospels by means of the Pauline Epistles, and the historical character of the Pauline references to Jesus by similar references in the gospels?* We ask: Is there anything in the Pauline Epistles which compels us to infer from them the existence of an historical Jesus? Did the writer of these Epistles know anything in detail of the events which the gospels describe as historical? We cannot be put off with the assurance: Yes, he *must* have known of them; that is to say, *if* things fell out precisely as the New Testament writings say that they did—which is the thing to be proved.[1]

---

[1] In his pamphlet *Hat Jesus gelebt?* Jülicher seems to deny that there is any difficulty here at all, and appeals from those who deny Jesus to the "judicious historian," who must, of course, be a theologian. It is true that he generally agrees with Wrede: "The nucleus of the gospel is for Paul the *superhistorical* element in the appearance and fate of Jesus and the *superhuman* in it." "But," he asks, "ought one to expect in him a lively interest in the details of the *historical* greatness and the *human* personality of Jesus?" Then we have the pronouncement of the "judicious historian." "One can only explain the appeal of those who deny Jesus to Paul and his successors as witnesses against the historicity of Jesus by their complete inability to get from their own minds into that of a man

We do not, of course, mean that Paul ought to have taken *all* his ideas from the words of Jesus. But we ought to find the influence of the historical Jesus somewhere in the thoughts and words of Paul, especially as he often treats of things which are prominent in the teaching of Jesus. But that he never appeals to any distinctive acts of "the Lord," that he never quotes the sayings of Jesus in the gospels as such, and never applies them, even where the words and conduct of Jesus would be most useful for strengthening his own views and deductions—for we must ignore what has been said in refutation of this statement—all this is for us a certain proof that Paul knew nothing of Jesus. We should like to have it explained how a man who has the authority of "the Lord" on his side in a heated conflict with his opponents (on the question of the law, for instance), and for whom the mere mention of it would suffice to silence his opponents, instead of doing so, uses the most complicated arguments from the Scriptures and the most determined dialectic, when he might have acted so much more simply. Why, for instance (*Gal.* iii, 31), does he not recall that Jesus also had discussed the Jewish laws about food, in order to convince Peter that he is wrong in avoiding the tables of the Gentiles? Why does he not mention that the Jews crucified Jesus on the Passover, the chief solemnity, and had thus themselves shown that the law was not absolutely valid? He has not himself

who lived 1,900 years ago—that is to say, the inability to think, judge, and reason *historically*." We reply: It is only the complete inability to put themselves in the frame of mind of a man who is convinced that God's son, the second God, wandered on earth in human form and died on the cross—only the complete obsession of theologians in the ancient way of thinking, which will not permit them to see the wood for the trees, and suffers them to say that such a man had no interest in the earthly life of the God. Steudel has said all that need be said on the matter on the occasion of the Berlin debate, and it is unnecessary to return to it. "When Paul says," Jülicher continues, "that Jesus, after a poor human life, is taken from the circle of disciples to heaven by the death of a criminal, having given [?] them instructions in regard to the new Church, has he given up the *personality of Jesus* in favour of a mystic figure?" Who will gauge the depths of that sentence?

THE WITNESS OF PAUL

seen the personal conduct of Jesus, like the disciples at Jerusalem. He knew his deeds and words only at second hand, and may therefore not have had them sufficiently vivid in his mind to quote them frequently. But certain leading features and fundamental principles of the life of Jesus such as the above, which affected his own propaganda, he ought to have known and used. If he knew of an historical Jesus, it remains the most insoluble of problems why he made no use of the knowledge.

Let us not be told that Paul's letters are "occasional papers," and the apostle had no opportunity to speak more fully about Jesus. This phrase of Deissmann, "occasional papers," is one of those with which theologians conceal from themselves and others the difficulty of the problem. These letters, swarming with dogmatic discussions of the most subtle character, are merely occasional papers, so that the apostle could not be expected to betray any acquaintance with the historical Jesus! It is the same sort of science as that which, in order to get out of a difficulty, would persuade us that Paul had spoken a good deal of Jesus in his oral discourses, and so did not return to the subject in his letters. This sort of "psychology" does not impose on us, and we find it nothing less than pitiful when Weinel sorrowfully confesses: "I myself once regarded the question in this false light" (namely, that there is little or nothing about Jesus in Paul); and then adds: "What Paul says about Jesus and his words is little when measured by the standard of a gospel, and little also if it is thought that a Paul ought to base all his thoughts on the words of Jesus. It is, however, not enough to find the existence of Jesus convincingly in the Pauline Epistles; the very words of Jesus are found in Paul at every important stage [!]; and there are not only quite a number of details which Paul knows and transmits [!], but all the prominent features of the preaching and nature of Jesus are preserved for us in Paul. There is, therefore, *a great deal*, if the Epistles are not approached with the old prejudice, and if we remember that they are all occasional papers and never have reason to speak expressly about Jesus" (p. 16).[1] This pronouncement is on the same high level as that of Feine, who says that Paul has "taken great pains to obtain a *clear* and *comprehensive* picture of the activity and personality of Jesus."[2]

We must, therefore, regard the effort of theologians to disprove any statement that Jesus Christ is not an historical personality in Paul as a complete failure. Any attempt to find proof of the historical existence of Jesus in the Pauline Epistles is futile from the mere fact that the gospels are used to check the contents of the Epistles, although they are supposed to have been written after the Epistles. A proof could be found in the Epistles only if they *unequivocally* pointed to the Jesus of the gospels. As this is not the case, and the relevant passages have first to be interpreted by means of the gospels and explained in the same sense as they, it is absurd to quote the Pauline utterances on Christ as evidence for the gospel Jesus, and pretend that the historicity of Jesus is proved by the apostle. Such proof runs in a vicious circle, and is no proof at all. The frantic efforts of theologians to discover the historical Jesus in the Pauline Epistles merely show, if they show anything, the impossibility of quoting Paul as a witness to the historicity of Jesus.

3.—THE QUESTION OF GENUINENESS.

The Pauline Christ is a metaphysical principle, and his incarnation only one *in idea*, an imaginary element of his religious system. The man Jesus is in Paul the idealised suffering servant of God of *Isaiah* and the just man of *Wisdom* an intermediate stage of metaphysical evolution, not an historical personality. When we admit this,

---

[1] See, on this, Krieck, *Die neueste Orthodoxie und das Christusproblem*, 1910, p. 47.   [2] *Jesus Christus und Paulus*, 1902, p. 229.

we remove the chief obstacle that has hitherto prevented
theologians from studying seriously the question of the
spuriousness of the Pauline Epistles. What they have said
on the subject up to the present shows anything but an
unprejudiced inquiry into the matter. Historical theology
has need of genuine Pauline Epistles, in order to base on
them its belief in an historical Jesus, and therefore they
must not be spurious. But how are they going to prove
that they are genuine? There are no non-Christian
witnesses. The silence of Philo and Josephus about an
apostle who is supposed to have thrown the Jews into
excitement over the whole earth (*Acts* xxiv, 5), to have
been persecuted by them with the direst hatred, and to
have been dragged into court more than once, involving
the highest Jewish and Roman authorities, has not yet
been explained by our opponents. What about Christian
witnesses? There are " enough of them," says J. Weiss.
Unfortunately, what the theologians bring forward—such
as the letter of Clement to the Corinthians, on which
Weiss relies—have long been shown to be unreliable by
the Dutch, especially by Loman,[1] Van Manen, and Steck.[2]
There is no proof of the existence of Pauline Epistles
before Justin, and it remains an open question whether
Justin had any knowledge of such Epistles. Papias also is
silent about Paul's Epistles, even at a point where he would
have been bound to mention them if he had known them.[3]
It is also a matter for reflection that as early as the second
century there were heretical sects, such as the Severians,
who declared that all the Epistles of Paul were spurious.

(*a*) *Emotional Arguments for the Genuineness.*—We
can, therefore, only seek to prove the genuineness of the
Pauline Epistles by internal arguments, by philological
considerations or analysis of their style. But how we can
in this way establish that the Epistles really were written

---

[1] *Quæstiones Paulinæ.*   [2] *Galaterbrief*, p. 287.
[3] Eusebius. *Eccl. Hist.*, III. 40.

by the apostle Paul, and belong to the middle of the first century, seeing that we have no independent specimens of Paul's writing, it is difficult to say. When a philologist like Wilamowitz infers the genuineness of the Epistles from their vivid and personal style, and says, categorically, "This style is Paul, and no one else,"[1] we merely have one more proof of the dependence of our whole science on theology. How does the philologist know the character and personality of Paul if not from the Epistles issued under his name? He therefore finds the test of genuineness in the Epistles themselves; and when he discovers that the Epistles naturally meet this test, he thinks that he has established their genuineness. "A standard is used," says Van Manen, "which has been taken from the Epistle or Epistles whose genuineness is in question, and students proceed as if the picture of the apostle of the Gentiles which they owe to tradition, to descriptions by third persons, or to their own research, was obtained apart from the Epistle or Epistles to which it is applied. They exclaim: Paul to the life! They recognise one feature after another. But what have they really proved? They have merely hoaxed themselves."[2]

But what about the "powerful personality," the "uninventible originality," the "soul" that lives in the Epistles? When our opponents can find no other argument, they have naturally to rely on the originality, the uniqueness, the impossibility of inventing the style of the Epistles. On this point we find von Soden, Jülicher, Weiss, and all the rest in full agreement. "Then the general impression made by the Epistles," exclaims J. Weiss, ecstatically—we almost see him with his eyes raised to heaven and his hand laid on the text of Paul—"this richness of tones and shades, this extraordinary originality—any man who cannot feel it convicts himself of great uncultivation of literary taste and judgment" (p. 100).

---

[1] *Kultur der Gegenw.*, I, p. 159.   [2] *Römerbrief*, p. 185.

But who in the world contests a word of this? What we contest is the deducing of the apostle Paul from these features of the Epistles. No matter how "personal" the style of the Epistles may be, it does not give us the least assurance that the Epistles were written by the man whose name appears at the head of each. Nor does it follow from the "distinctiveness of the style" that they could not have been produced by a school or a group. Is not the style of the Johannine literature even more distinctive? Or must the Homeric poems have been composed by a single Homer because they all have the same style? As a matter of fact, moreover, the Epistles do not accord with each other, nor is there complete harmony within the limits of a single Epistle.[1] As to the originality, van Manen observed: "To be original in any form, in any language or age, is just as possible, provided that the man has the necessary ability, for one who covers himself with the mask of some distinguished person as for one who writes in his own name and person, for the pseudonymous writer just as well as for the candid writer" (p. 188). On the principles of our opponents, Nietzsche's work, *Thus Spake Zarathustra*, must have been written by the ancient Persian religious founder, because it is so personal, so original, so rich in tones and shades. On the same principles, the fourth gospel was evidently written by the apostle John; and, as a matter of fact, up to the middle of the last century theologians affected to perceive in it the very heart-beat of the disciple whom Jesus loved. "Which," as van Manen says, "ought to make us more cautious, and raise the question whether we are not at times too ready to identify an old and long-standing opinion with the fresh and unadulterated impression which the work, the Epistle, would make on an impartial reader. It is at least certain that as yet no one has succeeded in defining the 'personal' element in such a

---

[1] Compare Steck, p. 363.

way that any moderate group would agree in the description. A satisfactory portrait of Paul is one of the things that are yet no more than pious wishes" (p. 189).

Jülicher says, in reference to the "sharp variation of tone, the moods, the allusions to things known only to the people to whom the Epistle is addressed, and the outbreaks of almost sinister anger in the Pauline Epistles" (p. 25), that no man could put himself in the frame of mind of another in this way. In that he merely shows that a modern professor of theology sitting at his desk is incapable of doing it, not that an impassioned Gnostic of the second century, in the thick of the fight against legal Judaism and ardently seeking to vindicate his conception of the gospel, could not have "invented" these things. We need not, therefore, regard him as a "forger" who "works with incredible fineness and creates the most extraordinary monuments of a great enthusiasm" (p. 26). He need only put into words his own feelings and thoughts, and, as was not uncommon at the time, place on the work the name of the apostle Paul, with whom he feels a spiritual affinity, or whom he has chosen for some other reason; and what seems to Jülicher impossible is done.

(b) *Arguments for Genuineness from the Times.*—The defenders of the genuineness of the Pauline Epistles would be in an evil plight if they had no other arguments than the æsthetic considerations we have just examined. They have others, however. According to von Soden, no one has ever given an intelligible theory of the origin of these Epistles in the second century. "They deal with far too many things, and with the most lively interest, which no one in Christendom regarded seriously in the second century, as we learn from other and reliable documents" (p. 29). Jülicher also says: "They fit no other period but the years between 50 and 64." Others, however, especially the Dutch experts, are of the contrary opinion. They have, amongst other things, pointed to the rich inner life of the communities to which the apostle directs his Epistles, and to the complex organisation and ecclesiastical institutions, which are hardly consistent with the view that these were newly founded and quite young communities; they rather indicate that they had been in existence for a long time. Van Manen in particular has described the condition of the Roman community as one that we cannot conceive in the year 59, in which the Epistle to the Romans is supposed to have been addressed to it (p. 155); and Steck has shown the same in regard to the Corinthian community (p. 265).[1] Such institutions as the vicarious baptism for the dead (1 *Cor.* xv, 29) and the ascetic law of marriage (1 *Cor.* vii) rather point to the second century, with its Gnostic influence, than to the middle of the first; unless we admit that the Jesus-cult is much older than our theologians are disposed to think, and Gnosticism is the root of the whole of Christianity. The divisions and parties of the Corinthian community, also, which the apostle is eager to conciliate, and the nature of which no one has yet succeeded in explaining, give the impression that they "are merely described schematically under names which were familiar from apostolic times, and the general aim of the warning against ecclesiastical splits was such as the later period everywhere made necessary."[2] It has been said that the gift of tongues which is mentioned in 1 *Cor.* xii–xiv had "quite disappeared" in the second century, and this is advanced as a proof that the Pauline Epistles must have been written in the first century.[3] But the "ecstatic or Methodistic" phenomenon

---

[1] Besides van Manen (p. 14), William B. Smith has, in an article in the *Journal of Biblical Literature* (1910), which even Harnack appreciates, shown that *Romans* i, 7 originally read, "To all that are beloved of God," instead of "To all that be in Rome, beloved of God, called to be saints," so that the Epistle of Paul was not addressed to the Romans, but was a theological message to all Christians in general: a view that Zahn has adopted in the third edition of his *Einleitung in den Römerbrief*. (See Harnack in *Preuschen's Zeitschr.*, 1902, p. 83.)
[2] Steck, work quoted, p. 72.
[3] Otto Schmiedel, *Die Hauptprobleme der Leben-Jesu-Forschung*, p. 14.

of tongues is so general, and recurs so constantly in periods of religious excitement, being even found among certain religious sects and institutions of our own time, that the silence in regard to it of the rest of the literature of the second century gives us no right to conclude that the Pauline Epistles are genuine. We know the gift of tongues from the Epistles, which are assumed to belong to the first century. But how can anyone say that these Epistles must belong to the first century because there is question in them of the gift of tongues? The question of circumcision, also, was by no means unimportant in the second century, as Clemen says;[1] so much is clear from the *Dialogue* of Justin with the Jew Trypho (cap. 47). The question is there raised whether the Judæo-Christians who cling to the law can be saved, and the reply is that there is no reason why they should not be, provided they do not press the law on the Gentile Christians under the pretext that they otherwise could not be saved, and do not refuse to live with the Gentile Christians. That indicates that about the middle of the second century the two parties in Christendom still faced each other much as we find them doing in the Epistle to the Galatians.[2]

As is well known, the attitude of the Christian towards the law and his relation to Judaism is a central preoccupation of the Pauline system. Now, during the whole of the first century, at least until the destruction of Jerusalem, there was no opposition between Jews and Christians in regard to the law. They lived in friendliness with each other, visited each other, intermarried, and claimed each other's help—in sickness, for instance. So, amongst many others, Chwolson tells us—and he has carefully investigated the matter—in his work on *The Last Passover*. In the year 62, according to the account

---

[1] *Paulus, sein Leben und sein Wirken*, I, p. 11, 1904.
[2] Steck, p. 380.

of Josephus, the high priest Hannas had James executed, and this displeased the Pharisees. According to *Acts* (xv, 5), some of the Pharisees joined the sect. Indeed, about the year 58, the scribes among the Pharisees stood up for Paul, and acknowledged that they found no wrong in him (*Acts* xxiii, 9). *Acts*, in fact, knows nothing of a fundamental difference between Paul and the rest of the apostles in regard to their attitude towards Judaism, and even the account of his travels—the part of *Acts* which has the strongest claim to be regarded as genuine—is silent as to any difference of mind between Paul and the first disciples of Jesus, and does not betray by a single syllable that Paul has promulgated a gospel far in advance of that of the original apostles and surpassing theirs both in the richness of its contents and the depth of its thoughts. Compare with this the vigour with which the Pauline Epistles assail the Mosaic law, the profound opposition between the ideas of Paul in the Epistles and those of the Jews, especially of the Pharisees, his rejection and fresh interpretation of the older Jewish idea of the Messiah, his glorification of the crucified and risen Jesus at the cost of all that was dear to the religious feeling of the Jews; and then reflect whether such a system was more likely to develop in the first century, a few years after the death of Jesus, or in the second century—whether it does not fit any period rather than the years between 50 and 64!

As a matter of fact, it was, as the Jews affirm, and as Lublinski and others have shown, the destruction of Jerusalem that brought about the breach between Jews and Christians. It was only when, after the fall of the holy city, the Jewish priestly organisation and religious life were put out of joint, and the Jews, in order to maintain the purity and strength of their vanquished faith, stood aloof, and sought in an increased service of the law some compensation for the loss of the temple, that the Christians, with their more liberal idea of worship, their inner morality fostered by the prophets, and their stronger sense of penitence on account of their expectation of a speedy end of the world, began to separate from the other Jews, from whom they had as yet not been essentially distinct, and realise that they were a special religious community in opposition to Judaism. This separation increased to deadly enmity and irreconcilable hatred when, about the end of the first century, the section of the Christians opposed to the law got the upper hand, when the Christians went on to deny the validity of the law and its indispensability for religious salvation; when, in the last decisive struggles of the Jews against the Romans, the Christians took the side of the latter, and, abandoning their national hopes of the restoration of Jerusalem and the political recovery of Israel, endeavoured to prevent the rebuilding of the temple, and thus openly separated from their compatriots. The Jews now refused to have any intercourse with the Christians; they cursed and burned their Scriptures, and expelled them from the communities. The Christians avenged this conduct by branding the Jews as obdurate. They reproached them with cutting themselves off from the promise, and contrasted themselves as the chosen of heaven with their former compatriots as outcasts of God and damned. This is the very idea that pervades the Pauline Epistles. Such ideas as those set forth in *Romans* ix to xi, representing that the Jews, in spite of the promises made to their fathers, will have no part in the blessings of Christianity, had no foundation whatever in the time about the year 59. The question why the Jews were excluded from salvation could not arise and be answered until they were actually outside Christianity. Yet at the time when the Epistle to the Romans is usually supposed to have been written the mission to the Gentiles had only just fully developed, and at least those of the Jews who lived in the dispersion had as yet had no opportunity of learning the gospel. How, then, could Israel be at that time described as "broken off from the trunk" (*Romans* xi, 17–21)? How could anyone talk of a "fall" of the Jews, which is to be visited by "the sternness of God"? This, as van Manen observes, presupposes the fall of Jerusalem, "the first important fact after the death of Jesus in which the Christians might see a punishment" (p. 159).

The Christian tendency that most strenuously opposed Judaism was Gnosticism. Its roots go back, as Friedländer[1] and others have shown, into the period of the origin of Christianity. But it is not until the second century that we encounter it as a fully-developed religious-philosophical theory or a theosophy. Now Paulinism has the closest affinity to Gnosticism, as Holsten, Pfleiderer, Weizsäcker, and others have shown. In both the idea of faith changes into the idea of knowledge; this knowledge is based on divine revelation: the salvation of the soul depends on the recognition of certain facts of revelation. In both we find a thoroughly dualistic system, in which God and the world, law and grace, death and life, spirit and flesh, etc., are set in the sharpest contrast, and the tendency to mysticism and asceticism goes hand in hand with the striving after a speculative interpretation of the facts of religious experience. Besides their idea of God, and their Christology and doctrine of redemption, they have in common a large number of ideas, such as gnosis, grace, pleroma, ectroma, life, light, etc. They agree, also, not only in their easy disdain of history, but also in their hostility to Judaism and their depreciation—indeed, rejection—of the law. In one case the connection between Gnosticism and Paul is so evident that it may be cited as a proof that Paul knew nothing of an historical Jesus; it is the passage in 1 *Cor.* ii, 6, where the apostle speaks of the "princes of this world," who knew not what they did when they

---

[1] *Der vorchristliche Gnosticismus*, 1898.

"crucified the Lord of glory." It was long ago recognised by van Manen and others that by these "princes" we must understand, not the Jewish or Roman authorities, nor any terrestrial powers whatever, but the "enemies of this world," the demons—higher powers, which do indeed rule the earth for a time, but will "pass away" before the coming triumph of the saviour-God.[1] That is precisely the Gnostic idea of the death of the Redeemer, and it is here put forward by Paul; from that we may infer that he did not conceive the life of Jesus as an historical event, but a general metaphysical drama, in which heaven and earth struggle for the mastery.

It is well known that prominent Gnostics like Basilides, Valentine, and especially Marcion, appeal confidently to Paul. Marcion's liking for Paul won him the name of "apostle of the heretics." All this may be explained in the sense that the Gnosticism of the second century had a source in Paul, and appropriated his ideas in the exposition of their own doctrines. But it is just as possible that both Paulinism and Gnosticism belong to the same age, and are only different branches from the same root. This seems to me the more probable when we reflect how well the ground must have been prepared for the apostle's letters if they were to be understood in the communities. Such difficult dogmatic disquisitions as those in the Epistle to the Romans imply a long period of evolution, during which the apostle's ideas must have been much discussed in the communities. They suggest a familiarity with Paulinism which is hardly credible, especially in distant Rome, at the time when the Epistle is usually supposed to have been written. "Paulinism," says van Manen, "seems to be a generally familiar and much-discussed phenomenon. It has its supporters and its opponents, its catchwords and stereotyped phrases, its own language, which needs no explanation because the readers are

---

[1] *Römerbrief*, p. 124.

assumed to understand it" (p. 141). Without any explanation the apostle uses a number of expressions which would have been understood at once in Gnostic circles of the second century, but could not possibly have been understood in the middle of the first century, a few decades after the death of Jesus, in letters to newly-founded communities.

But it is particularly remarkable that Paul himself should have attained so detailed and systematic a knowledge of Gnostic ideas so soon after the tragedy of Golgotha. One has only to recall the fundamental points of the Pauline system to see that van Manen is right in saying that "a long time must have elapsed since the appearance of the first disciples before a new tendency of this character could arise. We have here more than a simple triumph over the repugnance to the cross, by which pious Jews were enabled to accept the ideal of a suffering Messiah, to hail Jesus of Nazareth as the Messiah promised to their fathers, and to join the new brotherhood. We have here *a complete breach with Judaism*, a new and substantially complete system, needing only to be elaborated in detail and accommodated to the needs of a later generation, a thorough reform of the prevailing system, assuredly the fruit of a deep experience of life and a long period of earnest thought." This reform is supposed, according to the prevailing view, to have taken place a few years after the death of Jesus, to have been brought about by a man who, himself a Jew and pupil of the Jewish scholars, is supposed to have lived wholly in Judaism until that time, and to have arisen in circumstances which would hinder rather than further it! That seems to be quite unintelligible from the psychological point of view. "It is simply inconceivable," says van Manen, "that Paul the Jew, who persecuted the community on conviction, brought about so extraordinary a revolution in the faith of this community almost immediately after he accepted it. It is not conceivable that this conscientious zealot for Israel's God, Israel's laws, morals, and customs, should perceive so suddenly, when he has overcome his repugnance to the cross, that this God was not the most-high, but must make way for the father, whom neither Jews nor Gentiles had known before the coming of Christ [?]; that this Christ was not the one promised to their fathers, the Messiah, but a supernatural being, God's own son, who merely assumed for a time the appearance of a man like ourselves; and that the law, with all its prescriptions and promises, could and should be thrust aside as without value or significance. We must not forget that all this is new in the Pauline gospel, and has no relation to the 'faith' of the first disciples, who were still full-blooded Jews in their Messianic expectations. Let us try to realise what it means for a serious-minded and pious Jew, like the convert Paul, to abandon the God of his fathers and bow down to one who had hitherto been unknown. Consider the dependence of the pious Jew on the law and the morals and customs it prescribes. Imagine what is required to make a man accept as a supernatural being, as God's own son, one whom he had shortly before regarded as an impostor, and who had died on the cross as a criminal a few years before, even if he now acknowledges his innocence and his high character as an anointed of God. A belief in the resurrection and transfigured life of Jesus could not accomplish this, any more than it led the first disciples to deify the master, because it was believed that Enoch, Moses, and Elias also had been taken up into heaven; they had not on that account ceased to have a human character in the minds of believers. In this we can clearly discern the influence of ideas of a non-Jewish origin, the ideas of oriental *gnosis*, which in turn had come into contact with Greek philosophy and pagan notions of divinity. *We have here no case of ordinary 'deification,'* for which a pious imagination might supply the material. Had not

Christianity come into contact with *gnosis* through
'Paul,' had it remained permanently under the lead of
the Jewish mind, the monotheism of Israel would have
warned it against deifying its 'founder,' just as in the
days of their fathers Moses, the founder of the religion
of Israel, was saved from deification."[1]

What efforts the historical critics have made to render
more or less intelligible the sudden revulsion of Paul
after the Damascus vision! But neither the resources
of the Hegelian dialectic, as used by Baur and, in a
certain sense, Pfleiderer, nor those of modern psychology,
employed by Jülicher, Weiss, and others, have enabled
the prevailing theory to give even plausibility to their
idea of the origin of the Pauline Christology, and to fill
with psychological and historical considerations the gap,
the reality of which J. Weiss does not deny,[2] between the
doctrine of Paul and that of the so-called disciples of
Jesus. That the light which Paul saw, and the words
he heard, led him to condemn the whole of his previous
thought, life, faith, and hope, and converted him into a
"new creature," is hardly credible. Such an event
would be so "unique" in the history of the world that
any man who admits it has no need to deny other
"miracles" in the New Testament, or regard any of its
statements as incredible. It has recently been suggested
that the historical Jesus himself may have been concerned
in the conversion; we hear of the "strong impression"
that Jesus must have made on Paul, and Kölbing[3] and
J. Weiss speak of "a spiritual action of the person of
Jesus"—some even suggest a meeting somewhere of the
two. Such a theory finds no support whatever in *Acts*
or the Pauline Epistles; indeed, as I said before, it would

---

[1] Work quoted, p. 136. As to the impossibility of the historical Jesus being deified by Paul and the great difference between this sort of deification and the deification of other outstanding personalities, such as the Emperor, etc., see Lublinski, *Das werdende Dogma*, p. 49.

[2] *Paulus und Jesus*, pp. 3 and 72.

[3] *Die geistige Einwirkung der Person Jesu auf Paulus*, 1906.

make the apostle untruthful, as he says repeatedly and emphatically that he received his gospel only by an inner revelation (*Gal.* i). Theologians also see in the "Damascus miracle" another proof of the "all-surpassing greatness and significance" of their Jesus, and try to realise the "ineffaceable impression" which Paul must have had of Jesus, in order in this way to find some justification of their cult of Jesus. The event, however, is not made more plausible in this way, because the difficulty precisely is how it was possible for a monotheistic mind, a zealous Jew, to apotheosise a man who had died not long before, not a personage of remote antiquity such as Moses, Elias, or Enoch. And the difficulty is not removed by supposing that the apostle had somewhere or other met the crucified Jesus. *Paul had never known Jesus personally. The Christianity that was linked with Paul in its later development cannot be traced to a personal action of Jesus on the apostle.* That is unequivocally shown by the documents, the *Acts of the Apostles* and the Epistles. Any man who denies this is reading into the documents something that they do not contain; in fact, they say just the contrary. Whoever reads this into them is simply introducing into the documents a conception of Jesus which he has obtained elsewhere, interpreting them in a sense that they do not justify, and cannot complain if his opponents regard his claim to be "methodical" and "unprejudiced" as a ridiculous hallucination and presumption.

(c) *The Spuriousness of the Pauline Epistles.*—If Paul refers in his Epistles to an historical Jesus, these Epistles, bearing his name, cannot possibly have been written by the apostle who was changed from Saul to Paul by the Damascus vision. For it is inconceivable that an historical individual should, so soon after his death, be elevated by the apostle to the dignity of a second God, a co-worker in the creation and redemption of the world.

If the Epistles really were written by Paul, the Jesus Christ who is a central figure in them cannot be an historical personality. The way in which the supposed Jew Paul speaks of him is contrary to all psychological and historical experience. *Either the Pauline Epistles are genuine, and in that case Jesus is not an historical personality; or he is an historical personality, and in that case the Pauline Epistles are not genuine, but written at a much later period.* This later period would have no difficulty in raising to the sphere of deity a man of former times who was known to it only by a vague tradition. And if the Epistles do not come from Paul, they belong to a totally different circle from that of the converted Jew, and are rather, as Steck says, the work of a whole school of anti-legal Gnostics of the first quarter of the second century, who aimed at detaching Christianity from its maternal Jewish stock, and making it an independent religion; *in that case their references to Jesus have no historical value, and cannot be quoted as evidence of the historical Jesus.*

Let it not be objected that the Pauline Epistles bear unmistakably the stamp of Jewish authorship, and in their Rabbinical cast of thought and argument point to the Paul of *Acts*. For, apart from the fact that this would afford no proof that Paul was the author, since the Gnostic author of the second century might be a Pharisaic Rabbi converted into an apostle by some "tremendous experience," the Jewish character of the author of the Epistles and his relation to Rabbinism are by no means so certain as believers in Paul suggest; indeed, here again it seems as if most of them know nothing of the Rabbinical cast of mind and method of argument except from the Epistles themselves. Jewish scholars, who can appreciate the point, by no means recognise the contents of the Epistles as of their own spirit; they emphatically deny that their author could have been a pupil of the Rabbis. There is serious ground for reflection in the fact that, as Kautzsch pointed out in 1869 and Steck has confirmed (p. 212), the writer of the Epistles does not quote the Hebrew text of the Scriptures, but the Greek Septuagint translation, with all its faults, and that on this account he makes statements which a glance at the Hebrew text would have shown him at once to be incorrect.[1] That would be unintelligible on the part of a rigorous Jew and pupil of the Rabbis, because the translation of the Old Testament into a foreign language was regarded by the strict Jews of Palestine as a sin against the law, a profanation of the holy word.

Did Paul know Hebrew at all? The question seems to be absurd if the author of the Epistles really was the pupil of Gamaliel and had been a zealot for the Mosaic law. Yet the Epistles give no trace of an acquaintance with Hebrew. In spite of the assurance of the writer that he was born a Jew, he seems to be Greek in everything. He thinks as a Greek, speaks as a Greek, uses Greek books; and whatever there is in him that can only be explained—we are told—by Judaism is much closer, as van Manen says, to the Alexandrian or Hellenistic Judaism of Philo and *Wisdom*, which he often uses, than to the ideas of the Old Testament, and need by no means have been taken from the Hebrew Bible.

Further, this supposed pupil of the Rabbis interprets the law in a way that, as we are told by Jewish experts, is anything but Rabbinical. While the Rabbis leave the literal meaning of the scripture untouched even in their allegorical interpretations, the apostle is extremely arbitrary in this respect; he turns the meaning of the words inside out, and changes a plain meaning into the very opposite, as Eschelbacher shows (among others) in the case of *Gal.* iv, 21 (p. 546). The author of the

---

[1] For further details see Eschelbacher, " Zur Geschichte und Charakteristik der Paulinischen Briefe," in the *Monatsschrift für Geschichte u. Wissenschaft d. Judentums*, 51 Jahrg., Neue Folge, 15 Jahrg., 1907, pp. 411 and 542.

Pauline Epistles has neither an accurate knowledge of the text of the scriptures nor an interest in, or understanding of, its contents. He twists the plain course of the text to his purposes at the moment, and grossly offends against both the letter and the spirit of the passages in a way that no man who had passed through the schools would ever venture to do. "The interpretations of scripture in the Pauline Epistles," says Eschelbacher, "cannot, either in substance or form, be brought into any relation whatever either with those of the Palestinian experts, or with those of the Judæo-Hellenistic religious philosophers, or with those of their time or of the following period. There is nothing analogous to them in the whole of Jewish literature. This is found only in the Christian writings of the second century, such as the *Epistle to the Hebrews*, the *Epistle of Barnabas*, the writings of Justin, etc." (p. 550). "There is no question whatever of a thorough knowledge of scripture, or scholarly acquaintance with what was taught in the Jewish schools in Palestine or elsewhere, in the Pauline Epistles" (p. 668).

When we survey all that has been urged, especially by the Dutch, against the genuineness of the Pauline Epistles, particularly the contradiction between *Acts* and the Epistles,[1] we cannot resist the impression that the obstinacy with which historical theology clings to the Pauline authorship, and declares every attack on it to be "beneath discussion," is really due rather to a very intelligible prejudice than to the merits of the case. In the eyes of these theologians Paul is the weightiest witness to the historicity of Jesus on whom their "science" can rely, hence nothing can be "scientific" which tends to discredit the testimony of their witness. We who are convinced that, even if the Pauline Epistles were genuine, they would not prove the existence of an

---

[1] See Schläger, *Der Paulus der Apg. und der Paulus der Briefe*, in the periodical *Die Tat*, 2 Jahrg., 1910, Heft 8.

historical Jesus, and that they probably refer to another Jesus altogether, are only moderately interested in the question who was the author of the Epistles. It is immaterial to us whether there was one author, or whether, as the Dutch have tried to show, several co-operated in producing them; whether they are original, or are merely elaborations of older letters; whether in substance they go back to an apostle Paul who preached the gospel to the Gentiles about the middle of the first century, founded communities, and was to some extent opposed to the "original apostles" at Jerusalem, or whether they are altogether products of the first quarter of the second century, and the figure of the apostle is a piece of fiction.

It is possible that, as Steck and van Manen believe, there really was a Paul, a man who, though he may have taken up a somewhat exceptional position in regard to the other apostles, can scarcely have been so decisively opposed to them as the Epistles represent, and whose features we have described, somewhat didactically, in *Acts*. This Paul, however, was in that case " a Jew by birth, who had to a slight extent turned his back on Judaism. He preaches circumcision—that is to say, fidelity to the rites and customs of Judaism, fidelity to the law in spite of his acceptance of the faith and expectations of the disciples of Jesus."[1] There was thus no direct connection between him and the author of the letters which bear his name; they show a quite different spirit. But there was an indirect connection in the sense that Paulinism, as an attempt to detach Christianity from Judaism, making it a world-religion, and at the same time spiritualising and deepening its contents, may have had a grateful recollection of the man who first gave wide publicity to the ideas of the new religion. But it is equally possible that the name of Paul is only a general

---

[1] Van Manen, *Römerbrief*, p. 206.

title for a number of letter-writers, who invented the character in order to give an air of authority to a religious system that went beyond the original Christianity. It would not be possible to ascribe so peculiar and novel a system as Paulinism to an immediate disciple of "the Lord," to whose supposed historical personality the other followers of the new religion appealed. But some sort of connection with the "historical" Jesus was needed in order to displace the older Christianity with its Judaic leanings, and to base the hostility to Judaism on a "revelation" that came from Jesus himself. Thus arose the character of the once pious Jew Paul, who rages against the Christians, and is then converted by a vision, and, as a zealot against the law, founds a purely spiritual Christianity, making it easier by his own example for the Jews to abandon the law.

However this may be, the Pauline Epistles, we need not repeat, give no support whatever to the belief in an historical Jesus. This also, as we said, puts an end to religious interest in the historicity of Paul, and profane historians and philologists may be left in peace to reconstruct, out of *Acts* and the so-called Epistles of Paul, a picture of the real sequence of events which accompanied the rise of Christianity.

THE WITNESS OF THE GOSPELS

THE evidential value of profane writers and the Pauline Epistles in regard to the existence of an historical Jesus has proved illusory. The genuineness of the Pauline Epistles is not at all established. Even if, however, they were really written by the apostle in the fifties and sixties of the first century, they would give no testimony to the historical human being Jesus. That the apostle has such a person in mind, and not a heavenly being, a saviour-god Jesus, who has become man, cannot be deduced from the Epistles, but is read into them, so that the existence of an historical Jesus is merely *assumed*. Now, this assumption is based on the gospels, and, therefore, the Pauline Epistles cannot in their turn serve to prove the existence of the Jesus of the gospels.

There is no other source of the belief in an historical Jesus but the gospels. The credibility of the historical documents of Christianity finds no support outside themselves. For an historian that is a lamentable situation. Even Weiss feels that he must make some excuse in quoting the gospels as witnesses, as sceptics may object that a witness can hardly testify in his own favour. He consoles himself by pointing to the grandeur and beauty of the gospels as some assurance of their truth, forgetting that truth only vindicates itself, and not its authors. However much we may esteem the contents of the gospels, this appreciation does not throw the least light on the historicity of the statements made in them. However much the figure of Jesus, as it is set forth in the acts and words of the gospel narrative, may move and enchain the sentiments of the reader, it cannot be deduced from these sentiments that an historical personality was the model of the character. Otherwise we should have to describe Homer's heroes, Shakespeare's Hamlet, and Goethe's Faust as historical personalities because they are so vividly portrayed, and make such a "strong impression" on sensitive souls. The attempt to prove the historicity of Jesus is *hopeless* if there are no other historical sources for it than the gospels, even if the gospel tradition is so close to the historical facts that we may be dealing with historical reminiscences. We see, therefore, how important it is for those who maintain the historicity of Jesus to have other witnesses besides the gospels, and we understand the frantic efforts of theological "historians" to retain the evidence of profane historians and of Paul, however slender and disputable it be. The importance of the inquiry into the evangelical documents is thus set in its true light. It is not merely a question of establishing the historical credibility of the gospel narratives in detail, but of securing in general a firm historical ground in which tradition may anchor. To obtain some assurance of the historical character of the gospels is a matter of life and death to the historical faith of the Christian. Hence it is that every straw is eagerly welcomed, and in this matter the theological "historians" betray a contentedness and liberality that would not be tolerated in any branch of profane history.

1.—THE SOURCES OF THE GOSPELS.

Such a straw, in regard to the belief in the historicity of the gospels, is the often-quoted testimony of Papias. It is, as is known, one of the "safest" (though by no means unquestioned) results of the modern discussion of the life of Jesus that the gospel of Mark is the oldest of the surviving four. As compared with the other gospels, it shows the "greatest freshness" and "vividness," the most impressive "picturesqueness," and such an abundance of trivial details that it gives one the impression of "directly suggesting the narrative of an eye-witness." It is, therefore, a happy coincidence, theologians assure us,[1] that Papias, bishop of Hierapolis about the year 150, makes a statement about Mark, the author of the gospel, which admirably agrees with that impression. He says: "Mark was Peter's interpreter, and he carefully wrote down all that he remembered. He did not, however, adhere to the order followed by Christ in his discourses and actions. He had himself never heard the Lord or been among his followers. But he afterwards met Peter, as I said, and Peter instructed his hearers as opportunity offered, though he did not give the words of the Lord in their proper order. Hence Mark did no wrong in writing things as they were in his memory. He was concerned only to omit nothing that he had heard, or to admit no untruth in his work."

In this way the origin of the oldest gospel seems to go back very near to the time of Jesus, and its historical character seems to be accredited. The only question is how far we can rely on the statement of the Bishop of Hierapolis. Now Papias appeals to the priest John [Presbyter Johannes] as his authority. Who is the priest John, and whence did he obtain his knowledge? According to Jerome and Irenæus, he was identical with John the Evangelist. Papias himself, however, denies this when he assures us that he himself never saw or heard the holy apostles, but owed his knowledge to their friends, the elders. Hence Papias received his information as to the origin of the gospel from John, John from Mark, and Mark received his information about Jesus from Peter, who in turn only said what he knew about Jesus. Seeing that, in addition, the writings of Papias have been lost, and we know of him only from Eusebius

---

[1] Wernle, *Die synoptische Frage*, 1899, p. 204.

(of the fourth century), that is clearly too complicated a piece of evidence to merit an unreserved acceptance. We do not, moreover, learn from Papias whether Peter gathered from his own intercourse with Jesus what he told to Mark, or, if he did not, whence this original witness derived his knowledge of the Saviour. It does not follow from the words of Papias that Peter was a personal disciple of Jesus, however emphatically Eusebius may regard him as such, and however Papias may have thought so. The good bishop was not at all the kind of man to have a clear idea of such a thing. According to Eusebius and Irenæus, he was very "narrow-minded," and the other things which he gathered from the elders in the way of parables and teachings of Jesus and deeds of the apostles, in order to have as much information as possible about Jesus and his followers, are so disputable and miraculous that even Eusebius is obliged to relegate them to the province of fable.[1]

There is another matter that we learn in regard to the bishop from Eusebius (ii, 15), and this also is supposed to help to prove the connection of the gospel of Mark with the historical Jesus. Papias is reported as saying that, when Peter came to Rome and overcame the wizard Simon in their conflict, his hearers turned to Mark, who accompanied Peter, in their zeal for the gospel, and begged him to let them have a written memorial of the teaching that had been orally delivered to them, and he did so. The apostle, he says, learned this by a revelation of the Holy Spirit (!), rejoiced at their zeal, and directed that the writing should be used in the churches. "Why," asks Lublinsky, "had Peter to learn from the Holy Spirit that his constant companion had written a gospel, instead of from Mark himself, who ought first to have asked his master to look over so sacred and important a work? It would be impossible,

[1] *Eccl. Hist.*, iii. 40.

moreover, for the apostle to confirm and commend a work which was not written in the proper order of the Saviour's life. Such carelessness is even more difficult to believe when we reflect that the Jews are said to have already taken up an attitude of hostility to the Christians, and would certainly fasten at once upon any untruth or inaccuracy on the Christian side. There were still too many witnesses of events alive for any one to dare even to correct the matter a little" (p. 62).

There is, in fact, much to be said for Lublinski's conjecture that there is question of a gospel belonging to the first half of the second century, to which it was sought to give some canonical prestige by tracing it to Peter and the Holy Ghost, and that the story of Peter's pedagogical activity was invented to cover the disconnectedness of its material. To trace it directly to the apostle, as the first gospel was ascribed to Matthew and the fourth to John, was impossible for some reason. It was, therefore, inscribed with the name of Mark, of whom it was said in the so-called first Epistle of Peter: "The Church that is at Babylon saluteth you, and so doth Marcus my son," just as the third was ascribed to the physician Luke, and thus brought into relation with the apostle Paul.[1]

In any case, it is impossible to prove the connection of the gospels with the historical Jesus from these two references of Papias, as they are preserved by Eusebius. Even if the notice in Papias were better accredited than it is, his statement need not have arisen independently of the literary character of the gospel of Mark. It is said to agree perfectly with that character. But we do not know whether the gospel was not precisely ascribed to Mark, and thus connected with Peter, because at the time of its appearance this accidentally concordant character of the gospel

---

[1] See Gfrörer, *Die heilige Sage*, I, 3–23, 1838; also Lützelberger, *Die kirkliche Tradition über den Apostel Johannes*, 1842, pp. 76–93.

impressed its readers, if it had not been expressly written in the Petrine sense.

Besides the reference to the origin of the gospel of Mark, we have in Eusebius also one to the origin of the gospel of Matthew; a reference to which the greatest importance is attached by historical theology, and of which the author is again Papias. "Matthew," he said, "wrote the words of the Lord in Hebrew, and others translated them as well as they could" (iii, 40). Theologians at once assume that these "words of the Lord" are sayings of the historical Jesus; and it is possible that Papias meant this, though he does not mention the name Jesus, and we have in early Christian literature (such as the Teaching of the Twelve Apostles and the Epistle of James) words of the Lord which are not quoted as words of Jesus, but are clearly sayings of earlier prophetic teachers, the so-called apostles. The expression "words of the Lord" often means the sayings of prominent religious personalities which were attributed to the direct influence of the Holy Ghost; even quotations from the Old Testament are called "words of the Lord"—that is to say, of the God of Israel.[1] Moreover, the identity of the Matthew who is said by Papias to have written the words of the Lord with the evangelist Matthew is not certain, as the latter drew from Greek sources, and the tax-gatherer whom Jesus calls (*Mark* ii, 14), and in whom we are supposed to have the author of the gospel, was not named Matthew, but Levi, son of Alphæus, and seems not to have been identified with the apostle Matthew until a later period.[2] That is what theologians call "a sound tradition"! We cannot avoid the suspicion that these supposed sayings of Jesus, the "words of the Lord" of Papias, which Matthew is said to have collected, were not the words of a single definite individual

---

[1] *Matt.* x, 20; *Mark* xiii, 11. Also compare *Revelation* xii, 10: "The witness of Jesus is the spirit of prophecy."
[2] Wernle, work quoted, p. 229.

or an historical Jesus, but were merely placed in his mouth afterwards.[1] In that case this second passage of Papias referring to Matthew is just as incapable of showing an historical connection of the gospels with the life of an historical Jesus. We learn nothing from it except that there were "words of the Lord" in the second century in several different versions, and that these differences were understood to be due to different translations of a common source, the author of which was believed to have been a certain Matthew, whose name appeared among the so-called disciples of Jesus.

It is on this "sound tradition" that modern critical theologians base their hypothesis of two sources. It supposes that the gospel of Mark, or an earlier version of it, the so-called "Primitive Mark," is one source of our three Synoptic gospels; it describes the actions of Jesus. The other source is the discourses or sayings-source, the document which Papias ascribes to Matthew, the so-called "Primitive Matthew." Our actual Matthew and Luke have independently taken their account of the actions of Jesus from the primitive gospel of Mark, and have taken the words of Jesus from the other source, and combined the two. Each of them, however, has his "private property," something that is not found in the words-source or the primitive Mark, but is probably due to oral tradition. In working out this hypothesis theologians differ considerably from each other. Some say that there were stories of the life of Jesus also in the primitive Matthew and discourses of Jesus in the primitive Mark. Others think that besides the primitive Matthew and Mark there was a primitive form of Luke; according to Arnold Meyer, this may have been older than the actual Mark, and contained, besides the stories of the birth and childhood of Jesus, the parables and stories

---

[1] Steudel, *Wir Gelehrten vom Fach!* p. 37; *Im Kampf um die Christusmythe*, p. 56.

which tended to glorify poverty and depreciate wealth. We thus get an "Ebionite Gospel," or gospel of "the Poor," which is believed to have been especially used by Luke. Recently, if we may so interpret a passage in Weiss (p. 155), the gospel of John, which has been almost entirely excluded from the discussion of the sources of the life of Jesus for more than half a century, seems to be returning to the group of sources. That would be another instance that "everything happens over again," as Nietzsche said. The game of combining the various possibilities seems to be an essential part of the theological discussion of the sources. At all events, the continued work of theologians has so complicated the problem of the sources of the life of Jesus that it is hardly possible to speak any longer of a "two-sources hypothesis," and speak freely of it.

Whatever may be said from the philological point of view as to the value of the two-sources hypothesis, of which German critical theologians are so proud, it has, as the above considerations have shown, no value as far as the historicity of Jesus is concerned. It would not have even if the exact contents of the sources were known to us, as Weinel seems to think, and if the reconstruction of the sources in Harnack's German translation, which is by no means generally admitted, were something more than a mere hypothetical attempt, and Wernle's corresponding analyses were not sheer and uncertain conjectures. No matter how much the method of the historical theologians is improved in the future, it can do no more. That in the gospels we really have to do with the "tradition of a personality"—namely, the historical Jesus—cannot be shown even by the acutest philological criticism and the most perfect command of technical apparatus. The attempt of historical theologians to reach the historical nucleus of the gospels by purely philological means is *hopeless*, and must remain hopeless, because the gospel tradition *floats in the air;* the belief in its historical value is not confirmed by a single external witness who has the least claim to confidence.

2.—THE WITNESS OF TRADITION.

On what general ground do theologians affirm that the gospels contain history? On no other ground than that such is the general view. "We are asked," Weinel exclaims, "to prove that Jesus was an historical personage; in other words, we are to sacrifice an historical tradition of centuries, against which as a whole......not a single objection was brought until Bruno Bauer in 1841, and Albert Kalthoff in 1902" (p. 10). He says that it is a "depreciation of tradition" to call in question the historicity of the gospel narratives (p. 10). Weinel seems never to have heard of the Gnostics, whose resistance to the growing tradition of an historical Jesus gave so much trouble to the Church in the second century. He does not seem to know that it was not Bruno Bauer and Kalthoff who first questioned or denied the historicity of Jesus, but philosophers who lived a hundred years before Bauer, Bolingbroke and the English Deists. We have heard of the saying of Pope Leo X. at the beginning of the sixteenth century about the "fairy-tale of Christ." Even so enlightened a ruler as Frederick the Great does not seem to have been entirely convinced of the historicity of Jesus. He speaks of "the comedy" of the life and death and ascension of Christ, and says: "If the Church can err in regard to facts, I see reason to doubt if there is a Scripture and a Jesus Christ."[1] Has Weinel never heard of Dupuis and Volney, who advanced an astral-myth explanation of the gospel "history" in the last decade of the eighteenth century?

As a matter of fact, the existence of Jesus has been assailed from the moment when historical inquiry began

[1] *Friedrichs des Gr. Gedanken über Religion*, 1893, pp. 87 and 92.

to oppose itself to the prevailing ecclesiastical ways of thinking—that is to say, from the eighteenth century. That is quite natural, as no one had hitherto believed in a purely historical Jesus, and the dogmatic Christ of tradition gave little occasion to contest his historical reality; he might be accepted or rejected, but not on historical grounds. "Precisely because liberal theology has," says Ernst Krieck, "constructed its Jesus in opposition to the whole of Christian tradition, we have a right to ask it for proof; precisely because, as Weinel admits (p. 22), documents are wanting in regard to their Jesus such as are generally used to prove the reality of historical personages, the demand for proof is not so absurd as Weinel represents it to be."[1]

It is a complete perversion of the facts when Weinel and his colleagues claim that tradition is on their side. The tradition of the first eighteen centuries of Christianity knows only a god-man, not the man Christ. Lublinski rightly calls attention to the fact that "in the early centuries the blood of Christian martyrs was chiefly shed because the unyielding and angry primitive Christians regarded the cult of the emperors as the horror of horrors, since it meant adoring a man. They, however, worshipped their Christ and died for him because they considered him, not a man, but a god-man. Who is nearer to tradition, the one who makes an earthly man of Jesus, or the one who is content to say that he was from the start a mythical being, a symbol—in a word, the God-man?"[2] It is precisely one of the objections raised by orthodox against liberal Christians that they are in opposition to the whole of Christian tradition! What early Christian writings are there, apart from the gospels, that show the existence of an historical Jesus? There is not one single early Christian document that speaks, not of the god-man Jesus Christ, but unequivocally of

---

[1] *Die neueste Orthodoxie u. d. Christusproblem*, p. 47.
[2] *Das werdende Dogma*, p. 82.

the mere man Jesus which modern liberal theology conceives him to have been. Weinel appeals to the apocryphal gospels, the writings of the "apostolic fathers," the apologists of the second century (Justin, for instance); they all show just the contrary of what he states (p. 103). It is precisely one of the strongest arguments of those who deny the historicity of Jesus that neither *Acts* nor *Revelation* nor the Epistles, nor the apologists, etc., relate the slenderest fact that can confidently be referred to a purely historical Jesus. As regards the apologists, in particular, they know, says Professor W. B. Smith in his *Ecce Deus*, "nothing whatever about the miraculous pure human life in Galilee and Judæa. Not a single event is mentioned, not a single proof, not a single explanation, or exhortation, or counsel—not a single motive have they drawn from the incomparable life which is supposed to have fascinated the disciples and even the bloodthirsty Saul. The modern preacher, even the modern critic, at a distance of 1900 years, fills all the vessels of his discourse at this pure and inexhaustible source of the personality and life of Jesus. But the early apologists, who lived under the Antonines and before the settlement of the canon of the New Testament, know nothing of this source in their debates with kings and emperors, with philosophers and representatives of their own group. They do not draw a single drop of the water; they rarely mention it, even remotely. It would almost seem that, if it existed at all, it was confined to an esoteric, not exoteric, source. We do, it is true, find a few scanty references to certain teachings which are 'known,' but they are all of a more or less metempirical character, such as the mystery in 1 *Tim.* iii, 16. We find no knowledge of such a human life as that which modern and orthodox theologians make the basis of their New Testament theory."

To base the historicity of Jesus on tradition is merely to make tradition the decisive factor in the question because it is tradition. "History," says Weinel (p. 22), "depends on tradition." But when tradition is so isolated as it is in the case of the gospels, we have every right to ask whether there are any historical facts whatever at the base of it. Even Weinel admits that the historicity of a tradition cannot be shown by "some simple logic." Such proof can only be given "by means of documents." There are, however, none for the life of Jesus. It has been said that Socrates and Plato might be struck out of history just as easily as Jesus, since there are spurious works among those that bear the name of Plato, and it is impossible to prove that the others are genuine. But we are assured of the existence of Socrates, not only by Plato and Xenophon, but by the comedian Aristophanes, and there is not the slightest ground to doubt his historical existence. And the historical existence of Plato is accredited, not merely by the works ascribed to him, but in other ways, as well as that of any personality in history. We should not even have ground to doubt his historicity if all the works of the philosopher were spurious. As to the existence of Luther, Frederick the Great, Goethe, or Bismarck, we have not only documents from their own hand, the genuineness of which is not open to question, but masses of evidence on the part of contemporaries.[1] All this is wanting in the case of Jesus. He has not left behind a single line. He has, as Jülicher says, "written in the sand," and there is not a single reliable document to enable us to trust the gospels, from which alone we learn something about his life. It is, therefore, just as permissible to doubt as to admit the existence of such a person; and it is an unhappy indication of the superficiality and loose thinking of our time that even leaders of science have not hesitated to bring into the field to prove the historicity of Jesus this foolish reference to historical personalities.[2]

---

[1] See Jülicher, p. 14.
[2] Steudel, *Wir Gelehrten vom Fach*, p. 6; Lublinski, *Das werdende Dogma*, p. 47.

3.—THE METHODS OF HISTORICAL CRITICISM.

(a) *The Methodical Principles of Theological History.*—
From what we have seen we perceive that critics are convinced of the historicity of the gospels *a priori*, before investigating the subject. All they have to do, therefore, is to seek the "historical nucleus" in tradition. How is that done? "The Christian element," says Weinel, "must be stripped from the figure of Jesus before he can be discovered. But this means only the Christian element in a certain sense. Jesus was not a Jew, but something new; the Christian element must be removed from him in the sense of thoughts, ideas, and tendencies which could only be entertained by a later community" (p. 28). Or, as we read in another passage: "The only standard by which the historical critic can discriminate between the genuine and the spurious is to set aside as spurious those features of tradition which could not be due to the interest of Jesus, but only to the interest of the community" (p. 30).

Notice how much is assumed in all this: that Jesus was an historical personage, that he was not a Jew, that he was "something new," and, especially—"the interest of Jesus." How is it that Weinel knows the interest of Jesus so well before beginning his inquiry that he thinks he can determine by this test what is spurious in tradition and what is not? Let us be candid. Is it not a question of the "interest" of historical theology and the Church rather than of Jesus? The gospels, it seems, are to be understood from "the soul of Jesus," not from the soul of their authors! I should have thought that in a strict historical inquiry the "interest" and the "soul" of Jesus could only be gathered in the course of the inquiry. The theological "historian," however, assumes from the start precisely what he is supposed to prove and deduce—the existence and the knowledge of the innermost nature of the man Jesus. Not only does Weinel do this, but Clemen also formulates, for use in the religious-historical interpretation of the New Testament, the famous "methodological principle"—that a religious-historical interpretation is impossible when it leads to untenable consequences (namely, the denial of the historicity of Jesus or of the genuineness of the Pauline Epistles) or starts from such premises.[1] J. Weiss says this even more plainly when he acknowledges that in all his inquiries he starts with the *assumption* "that the gospel story in general has an historical root, that it has grown out of the soil of the life of Jesus, goes back to eye-witnesses of his life, and comes so near to him that we may count upon historical reminiscences" (p. 125). It is little wonder that they find themselves "scientifically" compelled to cling to the historicity of Jesus, and regard the so-called historical method which they use as the only correct method, because it seems to establish this historicity. The truth is that it is not a result, but a presupposition of their method; the method is arranged in advance so as to confirm the presupposition, and it is not in virtue of the method that the inquiry ends in a conviction of the existence of a definite Jesus, but because this was the goal kept in mind from the start.

This, however, is not all that we have to say in regard to the theological method of inquiring into the historicity of Jesus. There is a further principle, that all that seems possible to the theological critic in the gospel narratives may at once be set down as *actual*. Thus Weinel would regard a tradition as valid as long as "it is not clearly seen to be impossible." But are there not plenty of things in traditions which are possible, yet may not in the least be actual? The story of Tell is possible, the story of the seven kings of Rome, or of Semiramis or Sardanapalus; and as long as independent documents did not exist, they were held to be real histories. Indeed, on this criterion of "possibility" we might prove that

[1] *Die religionsgeschichtl. Erklärung des N. T.*, 1909, p. 10.

Hercules was an historical personage, and endeavour to extract an "historical nucleus" out of the shell of legend. Why may there not have been a man of that name who strangled a lion, dragged a wild boar, caught a hind alive, slew a dangerous serpent, cleaned out a stable, and performed other heroic deeds, finally sacrificing himself on the pyre? That the hydra had more than one head, and that when one was cut off two new ones grew in its place, is, of course, due to later imagination; possibly it originated in a "vision" on the part of Hercules. Do we not know that he was a heavy drinker? Well, in a state of intoxication things are often seen doubled, or even trebled. Thus it would be possible to give an "historical" interpretation of the myth of Hercules on the above principle. The principle, however, overlooks the fact that, though everything that is actual is at the same time possible, the laws of logic forbid us to draw an inference in the opposite direction, from possibility to actuality. Yet it is simply on such a deduction, apart from considerations of "the interest of Jesus," that all theological constructions of the life of Jesus are based. The stories in the gospels are first examined to see if they are possible, and they are then treated as historical realities, the historicity of which is supposed to have been proved by showing that they are possible.

(b) *The Method of J. Weiss.*—J. Weiss is a master in the application of this wonderful method. His way of interpreting the miracles of Jesus must not be passed in silence.

Weiss starts from the general character of the age in which the miracles are supposed to have been performed, its credulity and thirst for miracles, an age "for which saviour and physician are almost the same thing." It is true that he grants that the sudden and remarkable cures wrought by Jesus cannot be controlled in their further course. "We do not hear of a single patient who tells anything of his subsequent history" (p. 119), which is

at least very curious, and does not say much for their
gratitude. He thinks, however, that "many [!] a one
will acknowledge" that Jesus was much occupied with
healing the sick. We have, it is true, "not a very good
idea" of the way it was done. We can only imagine the
manner in which Jesus acted. It is, however, "a quite
unreasonable scepticism to say that these scenes, because
of the difficulty of imagining them, and the healing work
of Jesus in general, should be relegated to the province of
legend. That Jesus was regarded and sought as a healer
of the sick *we are bound to assume*, as the popular side of
the great impression which he made on men," which in
turn is simply assumed in this paragraph. "The one [!]
possible explanation is that he was full of the belief that
he was allied to divine force; his confidence in God's
miraculous aid, his 'enthusiasm' in this regard, must [!]
have been strong and sincere, and it must [!] have been
based on real experience" (p. 117).

Take, for instance, the possessed in the synagogue at
Capernaum. Weiss thinks he can explain his delivery by
the enthusiastic messianic character of the preaching of
Jesus, "by which the patient, identifying himself with
the demon within him, feels that he is personally
threatened, yet at the same time attracted; and thus a
paroxysm is provoked, and it is followed by tranquillity.
In this," he exclaims, "how have we passed the bounds
of historical interpretation? What is there improbable
in the episode?" Jesus imposed silence on the demon
"by virtue of the divine spirit which he felt in himself."
If any one ventures to differ from him, Weiss bitterly
retorts: "Any man who says that these religious ideas
and emotions are inconceivable had better keep his hand
off matters of religious history; he has no equipment to
deal with them" (p. 121). Then there is the healing of
Peter's mother-in-law. "I have," says Weiss, "no
experience in such matters [What a pity! What a lot
he might have taught us had he been able to experiment

on his own mother-in-law!]; but I do not see that what is described here is impossible" (p. 122).[1] It is true that one may regard the curing of such a patient by suggestive influence as "quite possible, and even probable." But what sort of "science" it is to reduce the whole contents of the gospels to mere possibilities of this sort we must be permitted to hold our own opinion.

Perhaps the "method" by which critical theologians prove the existence of their Jesus cannot be better studied than in the case of Weiss's *Das älteste Evangelium*. Weiss tries to prove that the author of our gospel of Mark is merely incorporating an already existing tradition. "*Not without certain assumptions*," he admits, "do we set about the inquiry. We have been prepared by the tradition of the early Church, especially by the evidence of Papias [!], to find that in the gospel which has come down to us under the name of Mark we shall find an echo of the statements of Peter. Hence [!] we approach our subject with the particular question how far the reminiscences of Peter form the groundwork" (p. 120). "My aim is, I candidly admit, to trace the text of Mark in its general lines [!] to an earlier tradition. As far as it is possible [!], I endeavour to trace it to Peter's way of looking at things, and understand it as historically as possible. *I am, therefore, a partisan of my author*—that I grant to a certain extent" (p. 122). Now let us listen.

"Now, after that John was put in prison, Jesus came into Galilee preaching the gospel of the kingdom of God" (*Mark* i, 14). "Thus Peter *may* have begun his account" (p. 136). Then there is the account of the calling of the early disciples. Here we detect a certain amount of literary manipulation; the story reminds us too strikingly of the calling of Elisha by Elijah (1 *Kings* xix, 19). It is not certain that the phrase "fishers of men" was uttered

---

[1] In his work, *Das älteste Evangelium* (1903), Weiss tells us that it was "probably a case of malarial fever," and refers us to Eulenburg's *Real-Encyclopädie der ges. Heilkunde*, p. 146.

on this occasion. But it *may* have been spoken on another occasion, and the whole account may spring from a reminiscence of that "unforgettable moment" in which the word of Jesus induced Peter to follow him. The technical phrase "casting of nets" is, Weiss assures us, significant; he seems to think it improbable that any but a fisherman should use this very unfamiliar phrase, or know anything about so unusual an occupation. In this case we *may* have the first part of those narratives of Peter which Mark is said by Papias to have used. Now for the Sabbath in Capernaum, the healing of the possessed in the synagogue and of Peter's mother-in-law, the healings in the evening, the flight in the morning. How excellent a local and chronological connection there is between the stories! How vividly the details are told! How the agitation of all concerned is felt in the account! From all this the "sole scientific method, the one prudent and critical view," deduces that (we tremble with curiosity) here we have an "excellent tradition"—in fact, the recollections of Peter —because (we must complete the argument) no other man could have invented these things, or at least not have told them in that way.

In the second chapter we have the strange story of the palsied man who could not reach Jesus on account of the crowd, so that they had to remove the roof of the house and let him down to the healer within. As the scene is Capernaum, and there is "mention of a house," it is natural, according to Weiss, to suppose that it was Peter's house! Another of Peter's reminiscences, therefore. Does the parable of the sower belong to the same category? "*We should like to believe it, on account of the graphic introduction* [!]. The reminiscence recalls a very clearly-described locality [the fact is that Jesus is supposed to have spoken the parable from a boat at the shore], and the time of it also is determined by iv, 35 ["And the same day, when the even was come"]. It was *a perfectly definite* [?] *day* on which these things took place" (p. 178). The boat (iv, 1) was, of course, Peter's boat, though this is not said in the text.

Into the story of the daughter of Jairus the healing of the woman with an issue of blood is rather artistically woven. This artistic combination *cannot* be a literary device, but depends on a real historical reminiscence. "It was unforgettable that so curious an event should take place on the way to the house of Jairus" (p. 180). Then there is the calming of the tempest. The story is so improbable, and so strongly suggests *Jonah* i, 3 and 5, that most critics since Strauss have regarded it as a mere legend, and one is disposed to ask, with Weiss: "If Peter could tell things of that kind, what use is he to us?" Nevertheless, why should we not once more see a real episode at the base of it, and suppose that the evangelist afterwards gave it the first touches of miraculous quality? In the same way, the story of the Gadarene possessed is supposed to be based on "a sound tradition" (tradition is always "sound" when it fits the theological scheme). Observe how the writer's acquaintance with the locality is assumed. What a graphic description! Mountains running down to the shore and falling precipitously into the sea!¹ "This description could only originate among those who were familiar with these features of the country." Mark *could not* have so described it unless tradition had enabled him; hence the story *must* be true, and Peter must be the teller of it. And then the description of the possessed man! The symptoms are totally different from those of the possessed in the synagogue; it is "epileptoid hysteria" (this also the "historian" seems to have found in Eulenburg's *Real-Encyclopädie*). The account, moreover, must have been given by the patient himself after his restoration or by the other people; hence —once more we have a "sound tradition." The only defect of the evangelist's description is that he is too much

---

¹ *Mark* v. 11 and 13.

interested in the swine, too little in the man. "The story is interesting in any case, and if any man takes offence at it he may be told that it was narrated precisely on that account" (p. 189).

So much for the "historian" Weiss. After these specimens of his critical exegesis we may refrain from following him further along this path, although there is much in his work that ought not to be suffered to pass into oblivion; his interpretation, for instance, of the confession of Peter at Cæsarea Philippi—the locality is "drawn to the life," the detail is "thoroughly concrete"; it has, as Herr von Soden would say, "the very smell of the soil of Palestine," so that we are compelled to admit its historical reality—and his conception of the transfiguration of Moses, which must, of course, have been a "visionary experience on the part of Peter."

We may add, to the credit of science, that the effort of Weiss to reconstruct the fundamental form of Mark's narrative by means of exegetic analysis, and prove that Peter and his friends were responsible for it, has met with the most violent resistance even among his own colleagues. Wellhausen finds the tradition of Mark as regards Galilee and the Galilean narratives to be of such a nature that it cannot be referred to the primitive disciples. "Is it possible," he asks, "that Peter was the authority for the sudden vocation of the four fishers of men?—that he told of the walking on the sea, the driving of the evil spirit into the swine, the healing of the woman with an issue of blood by the virtue of his garments, and of the deaf and blind by means of spittle? And why does he not tell us more, and in greater detail, about the intercourse of the master with his disciples? It does not seem likely that the narrative tradition in *Mark* originated among the companions of Jesus?"[1] Otto Schmiedel also finds himself compelled to put more than

---

[1] *Einl. in die drei ersten Evangelien*, 1905, p. 52.

one note of interrogation after the statements of Weiss, and observes: "*We do not know with so much confidence (in spite of Papias) that Peter was Mark's authority.*"[1] In fact, the whole method is in the air, and it is quite hopeless to attempt to deduce the historicity of the gospel narratives from their character.

4.—THE "UNIQUENESS" AND "UNINVENTIBILITY" OF THE GOSPEL PORTRAIT OF JESUS.

In the absence of any objective criterion it is necessary for the theologian to rely upon *subjective feeling* and seek in this the irrefragable proof of the historicity of the gospel Jesus. Here we have especially to meet the emphatic claim that the portrait of Jesus is "unique" and "could not have been invented."

As to the uniqueness, the phrase is so obviously used for the purpose of raising the personality of Jesus above all other men, in spite of its purely human and historical character, and to provide some compensation for the loss of belief in his divinity, that we need not linger over it. Even a theologian like Paul W. Schmiedel acknowledges: "For my part I never claim that Jesus was unique; it either means nothing at all, since every man is unique, or it may seem to affirm too much."[2] And the historian Seeck observes that every man has his like, and therefore there are no unique personalities in the sense in which theologians use the word here.[3] Faust, Hamlet, Lear, and Caliban, and their like, are unique; are they therefore historical personalities?

The great point, however, is that the figure of Jesus, as it is described in the gospels, "could not have been invented." This is repeated incessantly, not only in popular discussions, but even by experts such as von

---

[1] *Die Hauptprobleme der Leben-Jesu-Forschung*, 2 Aufl., 1906, p. 62.
[2] *Die Person Christi im Streite der Meinungen der Gegenwart*, 1906, p. 29.
[3] *Geschichte des Untergangs der antiken Welt*, iii, p. 183.

Soden, Jülicher, Weiss, and even Harnack. How much truth there is in it has been shown by Steudel in his work against von Soden. It would not be easy to find a more ridiculous phrase or a feebler argument. In no other historical inquiry whatever would such an argument be admitted as proof of the historicity of a certain person or event. None but a theological historian would venture to use such an argument, and it is lamentable that he should find any support on the side of profane historians. As if one could settle *a priori* the limits of the human faculty of invention! As if the figure of Jesus in the gospels stood really apart from comparison with any others! If religious-historical inquiry has told us anything, it has shown that this is the reverse of the truth. The Saviour of the gospels is paralleled by other redeeming divinities, whom he resembles so closely at times as to be identical with them. His fate is entirely related to that of Attis, Adonis, Dionysos, Osiris, Marduch, etc. Indeed, in many and important points we recognise a human personality in the saviours of the non-Judaic religions, and the more research advances in that field the clearer it becomes that the separate features of the figure of Jesus have their counterpart, partly in ancient mythology, partly and especially in the Old Testament, and thus it is absurd to say that they could not be invented. So fine a story as that of the disciples at Emmaus (*Luke* xxiv, 13), which treats of the risen, not the living, Christ, and therefore must certainly be unhistorical according to the critical theologians, could be "invented."[1] The story of the adulterous woman also, which is found only in *John* (viii, 1), is allowed to be a later invention.[2] Even the pleasant story of the two sisters, Mary and Martha (*Luke* x, 38), is, as Smith has shown in his *Ecce Deus*, a mere allegory of the relations of paganism and Judaism to the cult of Jesus, the former

---

[1] Cf. Niemojewski, *Warum eilten die Jünger nach Emmaus?* (1911).
[2] Compare Robertson's *Christianity and Mythology*, p. 457.

receiving him with joy, the latter occupying herself much with customs and ceremonies and claiming the same service from her "sister."[1] If these three stories—three of the pearls of the gospels—were invented, what is there that could not be invented?

However, one has the feeling that the theological historians are not really very much in earnest with this argument. They use it only at times as a rhetorical auxiliary, and on account of the impression which it is apt to make on the thoughtless mass of people. Even Weiss seems to be not quite at home with it (p. 15), and Schmiedel expressly acknowledges that the statement that the figure of Jesus in the gospels could not be invented " is not a valid argument in its general form." " We must," he says, " restrict it to certain passages in which it is indisputably valid. I count nine such passages, and, in order to emphasise their importance, give them a special name : I call them the main pillars of a really scientific life of Jesus."[2]

5.—SCHMIEDEL'S "MAIN PILLARS."

We have now reached a point where the man who denies the historicity of Jesus is to be definitively put to shame: the "granite," the "historical bedrock," which, according to the theological critics, will resist every attempt to rob the gospel narratives of their fundamentally historical character. Nine main pillars of a really scientific life of Jesus! The same number as in a game of skittles. Here we have the last solid ground on which the structure of the liberal conception of Jesus rests. Beneath the roof that rests on these nine pillars

---

[1] Moreover, the circumstance that Martha ("mistress") worried also finds expression in the name of the place, Bethany, where, according to John, the episode is supposed to have taken place. In Aramaic it means "The house of her who worries."

[2] *Die Person Jesu im Streite der Meinungen der Gegenwart.* See also Schmiedel's work, *Das vierte Evangelium gegenüber den drei ersten,* p. 16.

the critic may confidently relax from the strain of his usual historical efforts. As long as the pillars stand there is no danger of the collapse of the Christian historical belief. But what if these also are fragile—if the "granite" is mere plaster or stucco, if the nine main pillars are merely wings to hide the emptiness and nakedness of the theological way of writing history? What if they are "jerry-built houses," intended only for show? As a matter of fact, the pillars will stand only as long as one refrains from putting them to a serious test, and is content to admire their "really scientific" appearance; it would hardly take a Samson to bring Schmiedel's whole nine pillars with a crash to the ground. For they are based entirely on the assumption that it is the aim of the gospels to represent the historical human Jesus as a divine being; they fall of themselves the moment one assumes that, as the "Christ-myth" maintains, they seek, on the contrary, to describe as a real man one who was originally a god.

Schmiedel's nine pillars have of late years, on account of the great part they have played in the discussion of the Jesus-problem, been subjected to a close scrutiny by more than one writer. Hertlein endeavoured to upset them in 1906, and more recently Robertson (*Christianity and Mythology*), Lublinski (*Das werdende Dogma*, p. 93), Steudel (*Im Kampf um die C.M.*, p. 88), and W. B. Smith (most fully of all, in his *Ecce Deus*) have dealt with them, and shown that they are entirely untenable. I might therefore refrain from returning to the subject were it not that so much stress is still laid by theological "historians" on Schmiedel's nine pillars; and a fresh discussion, at least of the more important of them, is needed.

First, then, what is the nucleus of Schmiedel's argument? When, he says, one learns about "an historical person merely from a book *that is pervaded with reverence for its hero*, as the gospels are in regard to Jesus, he regards most confidently those passages in the book as authoritative which are not in harmony with this reverence; he says to himself that, in view of the author's mood, they could not have been invented by him—indeed, could not have been chosen by him from the material at his disposal if they had not been forced on him as absolutely true."

There is, for instance, the statement in *Mark* (iii, 21) that the relatives of Jesus, his mother and brothers, went forth to seize him, saying that he was mad. That, says Schmiedel, cannot have been invented by one who reverenced Jesus, because he would lower his hero in the eyes of his readers; it is the less conceivable when we reflect that the other evangelists say nothing of such language being used by the relatives of Jesus, clearly because they felt it to be out of harmony with their conception of Jesus. Hence in this passage of *Mark* we have the echo of a real historical reminiscence. But in the gospel of *John,* which is generally admitted to carry the glorification of Jesus to its highest point, we find the depreciatory circumstance that even his brothers did not believe in him (vii, 5); and in x, 20, the evangelist makes the Jews say: "He hath a devil, and is mad." In the book of *Wisdom* (v, 4) we read how the godless spoke of the just man: "His life we held for a folly." In *Zechariah* (xiii, 3) it is written: "And it shall come to pass [in the days of the saving of Jerusalem from the attack of its enemies] that, when any shall yet prophesy, then his father and his mother that begat him shall say unto him: Thou shalt not live, for thou speakest lies in the name of the Lord; and his father and his mother that begat him shall thrust him through when he prophesieth." And to those who ask him about the wounds on his hands he will reply: "Those with which I was wounded in the house of my friends." In *Psalms* (lxix, 8) it is likewise said: "I am become a stranger unto my brethren, and an alien unto my mother's children." Now, no one doubts that the figure of Jesus in the gospels is in many respects determined by passages in the Old Testament. How can one doubt that what Schmiedel thinks "could not be invented" originated in that source?

Moreover, Schleiermacher has pointed out, and Strauss confirmed the fact, that the word of the Pharisees, "He hath Beelzebub" (*Mark* iii, 22), which has quite a different context in *Matthew* (ix, 34, and xii, 24) and *Luke* (xi, 15), gave the evangelist an opportunity to put it, in its meaning, also in the mouths of the relatives of Jesus, in order to explain his slighting reply when their coming was announced to him.[1] It has, however, clearly only the symbolical meaning that real relationship with Jesus is purely spiritual, not bodily, and it is neither "beyond the range of invention" nor contradictory to the divine reverence for Jesus. In fine, the conduct of the Saviour's relatives in the gospels need not be taken at all as a depreciation of Jesus, so that there is no need to regard it as historical on that account. "As if," Steudel says, "a romancer depreciates his hero by representing him as misunderstood by those about him."[2] As if it might not just as well have been his aim to bring out the surpassing importance of Jesus by representing him as too great to be understood by his relatives, and even being regarded by them as mad. When people refuse to recognise an "historical sense" in those of us who deny the historicity of Jesus because we find such an argument as this trivial, we must on our part refuse the "æsthetic sense" to Schmiedel and his followers because they so little understand the poetical fineness of that passage in *Mark* as to find it out of harmony with the general portrait of Jesus in the gospels.

We turn to the second pillar. In *Mark* x, 18, Jesus declines to be called a "good" master—"Why callest thou me good? There is none good but one, that is

---

[1] Strauss, *Leben Jesu*, I, 692.
[2] *Im Kampfe um die Christusmythe*, p. 89.

God." How little such an expression could be invented by the followers of Jesus who wrote the gospels, says Schmiedel, we learn from Matthew. In his gospel (xix, 16) the rich man says: "Good master, what good thing shall I do that I may have eternal life? And he said unto him, Why asketh thou me about the good? One is good."[1] Logically, Jesus ought to have said: "One thing is the good." But as Matthew had the words of Mark before him, and sought to avoid their offensiveness, he changed the words.[2] Unfortunately, it is not at all certain that in this case Mark has the original text. The oldest manuscripts read like Matthew, and leave out the "good" at the beginning of the usual text, so that the text of Mark may be a later form of the altered text of Matthew. This oldest text, however, is not at all as illogical as Schmiedel represents. In the Hebrew version of the reply of Jesus the masculine and neuter are both the same: it may be either "one person" or "one thing." "Let us assume (with Resch) that the reply ran: One thing is good—keep the commandments. First this was translated into the masculine gender in Greek: One is good. Afterwards the explanatory note was added, and later admitted to the text—namely, God. 'One is good, God,' seemed to be in opposition to the person of Jesus. Hence the question, Why askest thou me about the good? had to be changed into, Why callest thou me good? The connection was now broken, and it had to be restored by adding, 'But if thou wilt enter into life,' and so the original question was resumed." This is the literary-critical hypothesis put forward by Pott as regards the historical evolution of the text.[3] However that may be, in such a condition of things no

---

[1] [The English translation of the Bible has the same answer in Matthew and Mark. I find that there are different versions of the Greek text of Matthew xix, 16.—J. M.]

[2] *Das vierte Evangelium*, p. 19.

[3] *Der Text des Neuen Testaments nach seiner geschichtlichen Entwicklung*, 1906, p. 63. Also see Robertson's *Christianity and Mythology*.

one has a right to say that the correct answer of Jesus is in Mark, and that Matthew gives a tendentious modification of the original text, and to make a "main pillar" out of such material as this. Psychologically, it is just as improbable that the innocent and customary address "good master" provoked Jesus to disclaim the epithet as that the question as to doing good should have prompted him to say that God is good. Moreover, the answer "God alone is good" suggests Plato just as forcibly as the form "The good is one" suggests Euclid of Megara. Hence it is impossible to say that these words of Jesus "could not be invented." For the rest, until Schmiedel no one had noticed anything particularly offensive in the passage of Mark. Justin, for instance, finds in the reply of Jesus a proof of the Saviour's lowliness and modesty in disclaiming the appellation "good"; while other apostolic fathers, in the opposite sense to Schmiedel, saw in the words of Jesus a proof of his divinity, making Jesus apply to himself the words, "God alone is good," as if he wished to say: "That man rightly calls me good, for I am God."

Equally ambiguous is the value of the third main pillar. It consists in this, that Jesus could perform no miracle in Nazareth, on account of the unbelief of his countrymen (*Mark* vi, 5). But it is maintained that the symbolical character of this passage is obvious. Is not the glorification of the power of faith a leading tendency of the gospel of Mark? "For verily I say unto you, That whosoever shall say unto this mountain, Be thou removed, and be thou cast into the sea; and shall not doubt in his heart, but shall believe that those things which he saith shall come to pass; he shall have whatsoever he saith. Therefore I say unto you, What things soever ye desire, when ye pray, believe that ye receive them, and ye shall have them" (xi, 23 and 24). The man who believes shall receive help (x, 52). Shortly before, in the fifth chapter, the evangelist has described how the woman with an issue of blood was healed owing to her faith in Jesus; and Jesus said to Jairus, whose daughter had died: "Be not afraid, only believe." As a complement to this we have the description of the unbelief of the people of Nazareth and the failure of the wished-for miracles. Can anyone seriously doubt that the story has been "invented" to illustrate the fundamental idea of the gospel, that faith is necessary for miracles? Moreover, the sojourn of Jesus in Nazareth clearly reminds the evangelist of the familiar saying of the time, that a prophet is nowhere of less account than in his own country and among his own people. He therefore puts the proverb in the mouth of Jesus, and then illustrates it by making him refrain from performing miracles in his country. It is, in any case, impossible to find anything here inconsistent with the evangelist's reverence for Jesus. The thing that the impartial reader would be inclined to regard as beyond the range of invention is that anyone should be scandalised at the passage, and from this scandal endeavour to deduce the historicity of Jesus.

A fourth pillar, according to Schmiedel, is Jesus's cry of despair on the cross: "My God, my God, why hast thou forsaken me?" The words, however, are found at the beginning of the twenty-second psalm, which gives various details of the crucifixion—the just man hanging on the stake, the perforated hands and feet, the mocking crowd, the soldiers gambling for the clothes—everything takes place as described in the psalm. Is it possible to believe that the words were really spoken by Jesus? Yes, says Schmiedel; and Harnack agrees. If the story of Jesus is recounted in such a way that the sacred words of the Old Testament seem to be fulfilled in it, this was only done when it served "the interest of Jesus"; but this interest would have been injured if the words of the psalm had been put in the mouth of the dying Jesus. As if the gospels had been composed in much the same way as a modern writer would sit down at his desk to write a large book, and contained one consistent idea, with the various parts carefully controlled and all contradictions avoided. As if the gospels did not swarm with contradictions and "discordances" in their description of the character and experiences of Jesus, which afford another proof that there is no question in them of a single definite person and of historical recollections, but a mere collection of details taken from very different sources, the choice of which was determined, not with a view to avoiding contradictions, but with a view to making the figure of the Saviour as vivid and attractive as possible in the sense of the Messianic expectations.

Lublinski has admirably shown that in an attempt to give sensuous embodiment to a symbol, such as the supposed historical Jesus is in our opinion, the result is inevitably an irrational organism which is sure to present many "contradictions" to our intellect.[1] "The one aim of the author of the primitive gospel," says Steudel, "was to give an expressive elaboration of the *idea*; and, as he wished to describe Jesus as the 'suffering servant' of Psalm xxii, he could not hesitate for a moment to put in his mouth as a prayer the quotation in question. Whether the figure which he built up was consistent or not gave very little concern to the author."[2]

Even the theologian Spitta says that it is a "modern notion that a later dogmatic could not possibly have put into the mouth of Jesus the despairing cry of *Matt.* xxvii, 46, and *Mark* xv, 34. Dogmatics has had nothing to do with it; it was the primitive Christian tradition which saw in the twenty-second psalm a prediction of the death and resurrection of Jesus. It is a curious illusion to suppose that gospels of the Christological views which Matthew and Mark represent would not suffer Jesus to end his life with a cry of despair of God and his mission.

---

[1] *Das werd. Dogma*, p. 93.
[2] *Im Kampf um die Christusmythe*, p. 117.

That may apply to certain constructions of the life of Jesus, but it is not inconsistent with the feeling of the gospel writers. That, in view of the undoubted influence of the Old Testament doctrine of the sufferings of the just one on the suffering figure of Jesus and of the central significance of the death of Jesus in the Pauline dogmatic, the later manipulations of the evangelical tradition would not be disposed to weaken the sufferings and death of Jesus, should not need emphasising."[1]

Only if it were proved that there is question of a real history in the gospels could one admit that the evangelist would have avoided weaving into the life-story of his Jesus such details from the Old Testament as did not accord with his main idea of the personality of Jesus. If the historicity of Jesus were *established by other arguments* we should be justified in deducing from the presence of these details the fact of an historical tradition which the author was bound to reproduce. But to seek a proof of the historicity of the gospel narrative from mere contradictions, real or apparent, is not science nor the method "which every historian follows in non-theological matters"; it is simply the method of arguing in a vicious circle which is peculiar to theological "history," the thing that has to be proved being taken for granted. To go back to our earlier illustration from Heracles, we could prove the historicity of the Greek hero on that method. In the account of him there are many details that do not accord with the otherwise splendid figure of this strongest of all Greek heroes. He is supposed to have become insane at times, and to have murdered his own children when in that condition; he is said to have taken refuge with a Thracian woman in his struggle with the Meropes, and concealed himself in female clothing; in fact, he is supposed to have been altogether unmanly and weak in face of Omphale, winding

[1] *Zur Geschichte und Literatur des Urchristentums*, iii, 2, 1907, p. 204. *Cf.* Feigel, *Der Einfluss des Weissagungsbeweises, u.s.w.*, 63–69.

her wool and running round her in her garments. We might call these "main pillars of a really scientific life of Heracles"!

Hence it is sheer self-deception for Schmiedel to imagine that he has "established" the existence of an historical Jesus beyond a shadow of doubt. His main pillars are "ingenious discoveries of a theologian, masterpieces of apologetic hairsplitting" (Steudel); they are "small matters which one must examine with a microscope in order to give them the character of granite which they are supposed to have as central columns of the liberal Jesus" (Krieck).

Yet the four we have discussed are the only ones among them which even seem to have any importance. This cannot be said of the other five. When Jesus confesses, in regard to the day and hour of the end of the world, that "no man knoweth, no, not the angels which are in heaven, neither the Son, but the Father" (*Mark* xiii, 32), we can only say that omniscience is not expected of him, as the evangelist describes him as a mere man, with human qualities and human limitations. Moreover, the uncertainty in point of time of the end of the world is one of the normal features of every apocalyptic. Hence the ignorance of Jesus on that point is so natural that the evangelist himself prudently refrains from any chronological statement. Lastly, Smith points out how one may infer the divine character of the Son from his being placed after the angels in the words of Jesus.

And when Matthew (xi, 5) makes the Saviour say: "The blind receive their sight, and the lame walk, the lepers are cleansed, the deaf hear, the dead are raised up, and the poor have the gospel preached to them," to what extent can we see in this a contradiction of the idea which the evangelist had of Jesus? Schmiedel takes the words spiritually: the spiritually blind shall see, the spiritually lame walk, etc., because Jesus, he thinks, "could not have more seriously destroyed the effect of his words than by making a series of miracles, which rises as high as the awakening of the dead, close with something so simple and common as preaching to the poor." Yet we read in *Isaiah* (xxxv, 5), in relation to the promised coming of the Lord: "Then the eyes of the blind shall be opened, and the ears of the deaf shall be unstopped. Then shall the lame man leap as an hart, and the tongue of the dumb sing." And in *Isaiah* lxi, 1, it is said: "The spirit of the Lord God is upon me: because the Lord hath anointed me to preach good tidings unto the meek; he hath sent me to bind up the broken-hearted, to proclaim liberty to the captives, and the opening of the prison to them that are bound [sight to the blind]; to proclaim the acceptable year of the Lord and the day of vengeance of our God; to comfort all that mourn."[1] Clearly, the "pillar" is merely made up of these two passages, and therefore the saying of Jesus has no claim to historicity.

Of the rest of the "main pillars" it is better to say nothing. Those who are interested may consult Schmiedel and the works we have quoted. For my part, I have tried in vain to see in them any sort of argument for an historical Jesus. A man has to be a theologian to appreciate arguments of this kind. We may assume that real historians shrug their shoulders at Schmiedel's "nine main pillars," if they have gone so far as to look into the matter. Schmiedel's "nine main pillars" are excellent companions to the three "pillar-apostles" of the Epistle to the Galatians. At a distance they look very fine; when you come closer to them they dissolve into atoms. Schmiedel thinks that in virtue of his "pillars" he "knows" that the person of Jesus cannot be relegated to the world of fable. He also "knows" that "Jesus was a man in the full sense of the word, and

---

[1] See also *Isaiah* xlii. 7.

that in him the divine, which is, of course, not on that account denied, must be sought only as it can be found in a man."[1] We leave him with this "knowledge"; for our part, we decline to settle in a house that rests on these "nine main pillars of a really scientific life of Jesus."[2] Schmiedel has the support of his colleague Weiss in his search for "indubitable historical features" in the evangelical figure of Jesus. "The power of Jesus," Weiss says, "rests on the spirit that was given to him in baptism; we see how this spirit wrestles with the spirits" (*Mark* i, 25; iii, 11; v, 6, 8; xxv, etc.). Then follows the list of Schmiedel's chief pillars, and the "historian" continues: "We see [!] how the dogmatic conception of the evangelist was unable to absorb the human-historical figure" (p. 133). Surely we have here a tenth main pillar![3]

This, then, is, as regards the historicity of Jesus, the "solid" fruit of that penetrating "analytical work on the gospels which is called historical exegesis," which has been going on for more than a century. We quite understand that "there are many who are indifferent to this inquiry into the inner structure of a document, and

---

[1] *Die Person Jesu*, p. 9.

[2] Observe the play of colour in the phrase "a man in the full sense of the word," in whom, nevertheless, "the divine is not denied," though it "must be sought only as it can be found in a man." (See also his *Das vierte Evangelium*, p. 17, where it is said that, while we acknowledge that there was something divine in Jesus, he thought and lived in a way which we must regard as really human. To what triviality is this "God-manhood" reduced in our liberal theologians!) Is Jesus a God-man in the Christian sense or is he not? We might ask these theologians in the words of Elijah: "How long halt ye between two opinions?" (1 *Kings* xviii, 21).

[3] Some may see a sort of main pillar in the words of Jesus (*Mark* xiii, 30): "This generation shall not pass till all these things be done." Because, they may say, if a prophecy of this kind, which was not confirmed by the course of events, could remain in the gospels, it must have been uttered by Jesus. But is it not possible that the saying of Jesus is part of the Jewish apocalyptic which is embodied in the chapter of *Mark* quoted? In that case it is no more historical than *Matt.* x, 23, *Mark* ix, 1, and *Luke* ix, 27, which are merely due to modifications of *Mark* xiii, 30. The saying cannot be a "main pillar" because it contradicts the first "pillar" (*Mark* xiii, 32), according to which Jesus declined to tell the time of the end of the world.

declare in warning tones that the work of theologians is hopeless, though they themselves will do nothing" (Weiss, p. 134).

6.—THE METHOD OF "THE CHRIST-MYTH."

(a) *The Literary Character of the Gospels.*—Differently from the method of the theological historian, *The Christ-Myth* starts with the conviction that the gospels are, on the confession of the theologians themselves, works of edification, not of history, or tendentious works of a dogmatic-metaphysical character; that is to say, it is not so much their aim to describe the real life of Jesus as to put before the minds of their readers a Jesus that will be likely to "influence their religious feelings, inflame their hope, and awaken their faith." Even Weiss admits "how impossible it is to take the gospel of Mark forthwith, without close inquiry, as a primitive source. We cannot trace the inner movement, or even the course of external events, from the successive pieces in Mark. The form and tone which Mark gives to the various parts of his narrative are often more dogmatic than historical; he himself is not a chronicler, but a witness to the gospel of Christ, the son of God" (p. 153). In the conception of Mark the death of Jesus is, as Weiss observes, "the real aim and content of his life (!); it is seen in advance, and everything works up to it, so that the entire gospel is really a story of the Passion stretching backwards" (p. 132). Moreover, the chronological frame in which Mark encloses the details of the life of Jesus is "neither historical nor chronological, but didactic. Galilee is the life, and Jerusalem is the death; the passage from Nazareth to Golgotha is the unavailing work among Israel and the prospect of the believing heathens of the future; that the actions of Jesus in Israel did not bring salvation to that people, but that salvation is found in the mystery of his death for those who acknowledge and believe—those are the great ideas which he spreads like a net over his variegated material" (p. 136).

Even when the evangelist offers us ostensible history, we do not feel confident about what he describes. "Chronology is his weak point." "He has no idea of the duration of the activity of Jesus" [in the year 64!]. For him to make Jesus, the pious Jew, come to Jerusalem for the first time at the Passover is, according to Weiss, "a really childish idea." He gives nothing in chronological order. We never find a date that might serve to fix any event in point of time. And it is not much better with his indications of places. It is true that he knows the names of a few places, and often represents a situation as known to his readers; but his indications are generally so superficial and vague (a house, a mountain, a solitary place, and so on) that the historian can make no more of them than he could of the stage-directions of a play. "His geographical notions are," says Weiss, "confined to a few large divisions—Galilee, Peræa, Judæa, the 'sea' of Galilee, etc. But it is clear, from, for instance, the section that deals with the two miraculous meals, that he has no idea of the localities. To represent Jesus moving about the sea, suddenly appearing in the region of Tyre and Sidon, and then to the east of the sea again, shows that the writer has no idea of the topography of the country" (p. 137). "The topographical ideas of the evangelist are confused," we read in his *Das älteste Evangelium.* "He does not take the least interest in such things; he is indifferent to time and place" (p. 235). Weiss naturally complains of this vagueness as to time and place which is so conspicuous in this evangelist (p. 151). Wellhausen speaks in the same way, and even more disdainfully, of the author of the oldest gospel.[1]

But the other two synoptics are no better in this

[1] *Einleitung*, p. 51. Compare also the *Commentar zu den vie Evangelien* of P. van Dyk (S. E. Verus), Leipzig, 1902, Kap. 8 and 9.

respect. At least we might have expected more of Luke, who expressly describes himself as an "historian" in the foreword to his gospel. Unfortunately, it is not so. The phrases "In those days," "At that time," "On a Sabbath day," "After eight days," "At the same hour," etc., are just as common with him; and when he does seem to give definite indications of time—for instance, "In the days of King Herod," "At the time of the enumeration under the governor Cyrenius," "When Lysanias the tetrarch was at Abilene, and every man had to be numbered"—we find him historically inaccurate in every case. Herod had died four years before the beginning of the present era. Cyrenius was not governor until the years 7–11 A.D. Lysanias had been dead thirty-four years at the time when Jesus was born. Annas and Caiaphas could not be high-priests together, as there was only one high-priest at a time. The description of the Pharisees is wrong in Luke and all the other evangelists. The trial which ended in the condemnation of Jesus does not correspond at all to Jewish usage at the time.[1] Nothing is known by any historian of a friendship between Herod and Pilate, such as Luke (xxiii, 12) describes. It is true that we know that Pilate was procurator in Judæa in the fifteenth year of the Emperor Tiberius (28). But the character of Pilate, as described in Luke and the other evangelists, is entirely opposed to all that we know of the man; and it is not certain that we have not here an astral myth, in which the *Homo pilatus* (the javelin-man Orion) played a part, converted into history on the strength of a similarity of name with the Roman procurator Pilate, and that the whole story was not on this account placed in the time of the first two Roman emperors. It can be detached from that period without suffering any essential change. In essence it is independent of time, as myths are. This is

---

[1] Brandt, *Die evangel. Geschichte;* Steudel, *Im Kampf um die Christusmythe*, pp. 42 and 53.

strikingly confirmed by the statement of St. Augustine[1]
that Jesus died on March 25 under the consulate of the
two Gemini (29). The death of Christ falls, according to
the calculations of Niemojewski, on March 25 (during
the vernal equinox), when the new moon dies in the
constellation of the Heavenly Twins—in Latin, Gemini.[2]
There are many other details in the gospels which point
to the fact that astral relations are at the root of the
supposed historical events which they describe.

In any case, the narrative of the gospels is not of a
nature to exclude the possibility that dogmatic and
metaphysical material, which originated in a totally
different province, was afterwards worked into an historical scheme, and that this was done at a time when
the real features of Palestine in the days of Jesus were
very superficially known to the author, and by one who
had not an accurate knowledge of the geographical and
chronological conditions. From this we know what to
think when von Soden and others speak of the "graphic
miniature painting" and "smell of the soil of Palestine"
in the gospel narratives, and when Jülicher assures us
that Jesus is "a human personality that could not possibly
have been in any other time and place than those in
which he is put in the gospels," and emphasises his being
"rooted in Jewish soil." It is much the same as if a man
were to say that Romeo and Juliet were real characters
which could not have existed elsewhere but in Verona,
in medieval Italy, where Shakespeare places them.
Augustine is nearer the truth when he confesses: "Were
it not for the authority of the Church, I should put no
faith in the gospels."

We may dispense ourselves from considering more
closely the much-praised "pictorial character" of the
gospels and examining the proof of the historicity of
Jesus that is based on it. The description in the gospels

---

[1] *De civitate Dei*, xviii, 54.
[2] Niemojewski, *Gott Jesus*, pp. 131, 371, 382, 384.

may be pictorial, but it is not more so than any description which aims at giving a sensible form to a certain idea by artificial means. If we admitted this as an argument for the Biblical Jesus, we should have to accept the characters and situations of many novels, dramas, and other works of fiction as historical realities. Moreover, the vividness of the gospels is only found in situations and sensations, not in depicting characters; the character of Jesus by no means merits that description, on account of the contradictions it includes, and there is no consistent and progressive treatment in the gospels. In this respect Lublinski has very well described the style of the gospels as an "impressionist lyrical *al fresco* style": " Great stress is laid on certain scenes, while all the rest lies in a darkly-coloured background. That kind of description would be curious and incongruous, in fact unprecedented, if there were question of a biography. But as the aim is to represent a god in his superhuman splendour, no happier style could have been chosen. The god must not come too close to ourselves, otherwise he loses his altitude, yet not be too far from us, otherwise he would not have assumed human form for the redemption of sinners. The best course is to bring him out in some of his actions and situations with sudden and magical power, and then allow him to sink back again. Thus we get the transfiguration scene, the scene on Golgotha, the entry into Jerusalem, the arrest, the crucifixion, and the resurrection. We hear strong, angry words and others full of tenderness and pity, which similarly break upon us suddenly and unexpectedly in seemingly indifferent passages. At other times lofty moral sentiments are pronounced, and these in turn have to retire behind the glamour of mystic words spoken at the last supper or after the resurrection and apocalyptic visions. These details are not given in logical order and in the quiet course of a sustained narrative, but with a certain suddenness; just as, when one is travelling in a mountainous district, every turn of the road presents new aspects and wonders of the landscape. But the character that produces these effects, now humanly approaching us and now fading into the mystical distance, would not be found a definite personality if his psychology and conduct were considered from the biographical point of view. As a symbol and god-man, however, he could not have been better described."[1]

(b) *The Mythical Character of the Gospels.*—We have further to consider the resemblance of the figure of Jesus to the saviour-gods of pagan peoples, which theologians do not contest, and the resemblance of the Christian doctrine of redemption and details of the cult to those of the mystical cults in ancient times.[2] We can quite understand when the theologians, under the lead of Harnack, regard the relevant research in comparative religion with great distrust and concern, and that in this respect they warn us to proceed with extreme " prudence."[3] But all that they have said as yet against the possible

---

[1] *Das werdende Dogma*, p. 39.
[2] See Arnold Meyer, *Inwiefern sind die neutestamentl. Vorstellungen von ausserbiblischen Religionen beeinflusst*, 1910.
[3] How theologians go to work may be seen in a pamphlet by Harnack on Christmas, in which it is said that the Christmas-story is "not a mythology, but a lofty legend, comprising historical and religious facts and experiences in very fine images." One is tempted to ask the distinguished writer what there is in the story that is not mythical. Is it the child-bearing of "Mary" at "Bethlehem" at the time of the great "census"? Or the shepherds on the fields, to whom an angel announces the birth of the Saviour, and their veneration of the "son of David"? Or the story of the announcement of the birth of the Baptist? Or the massacre of the children? Or the presentation of the child in the temple? Or—but Harnack at last tells us : the story of the star and the wise men from the east ! "Here we have an ancient myth reproduced and applied to Jesus Christ, but "—he at once soothes his readers—"how rich the story is ! At that time many ancient religions were pressing from the east into the Roman Empire; they were, to some extent, deeper and richer than the Græco-Roman, and therefore had many followers. Our story shows us the wise men from the east—that is to say, those oriental religions [!]—bowing down before the wonderful star that had arisen over Bethlehem, and bringing gifts to the new-born child. And so it actually came to pass ! History has fulfilled and confirmed the myth in a wonderful way [sic]. The oriental religions brought gifts to the Christian, and then paled before its light." Thus speaks "Dr. Adolf Harnack, ordinary Professor at the University of Berlin." We now know how to give a "really scientific" interpretation of myths.

derivation of the Christ-story from the pagan myths is so lame and biassed that it is difficult to keep patience in discussing such things with them. Take, for instance, the notion of a suffering and dying God. *The Christ-Myth* has shown how familiar this idea was to Judaism from its own tradition—how the notion of a suffering king and just one, offering himself for the sins of his fellows, was based on a very ancient rite in the whole early world, which has left traces even in the Old Testament. A man must be utterly devoid of psychology and be a worshipper of the letter to doubt that the idea must have had adherents among the Jews even in the days of Jesus merely because we have no direct evidence of it in writing. And what a decisive part the idea plays in the Gnostic systems! Nor can it any longer be disputed that Gnosticism was not, as was hitherto generally believed, a product of Christianity, but is *much older* than Christianity.[1] In the second century the Talmud expressly sets forth the idea of a Messiah suffering in atonement for his people. It would be surprising if, in the circumstances, the belief in a suffering and dying saviour-god had not been found among the Jews at an earlier date. As we shall see more fully, the idea had been impressed on them by Isaiah (ch. liii). The ancient Babylonian idea of a divinity coming down from heaven and soiling himself with earthly material for the purpose of saving mankind was bound to imply suffering and death, especially among a people of strong religious feelings, surrounded by the suffering and dying gods of neighbouring peoples, in the close atmosphere and mysticism of sectarian life.

Opinions may differ as to the way and the extent in which Christian ideas, especially the gospel narratives, were influenced by the analogous myths and ceremonies of non-Christian religions—whether the influence was

---

[1] See M. Brückner, *Der sterbende und auferstehende Gottheiland in den Orient-Religionen und ihr Verhältniss zum Christentum*, 1908, p. 30.

direct or indirect, and whether the analogies were merely accidental or were, as some credulous writers affirm, divinely appointed. *The Christ-Myth* refrained from taking up any definite position on this point. It was generally content to tell the facts and let them speak for themselves, in order to justify its theory that Jesus also may have been one form of the myth, and the "history" of him may have been derived from the same mythic material as that of the pagan saviour-gods. It stimulated questions, and drew attention to points which might contribute to the elucidation of obscure passages in the gospels. If it has been misunderstood and represented as saying that on all points the Christian ideas were dependent on the non-Christian world, or as speaking of a "composition" of the story of Jesus from the analogous myths of pagan religions, the author is not to blame, and does not need to be told that analogies do not of themselves prove historical connection.

This much, at least, is certain: the origin of Christianity cannot be properly understood without regard to the mythological connections of its ideas with those of other religions. In this respect research is only just in its infancy, as up to the present there has been almost nothing but purely historical and philological work done in this field, and biblical "mythology," which has had an able and far-seeing exponent in Nork, has been thrust into the background. While Mr. J. M. Robertson has led the way and made considerable advance in England in his *Christianity and Mythology*, *Pagan Christs*, and *Short History of Christianity*, the science of religion in Germany remains wholly under the influence of theology, and is mainly concerned to avoid a conflict with theology. Hence on the theological side we find men contesting the obvious affinity of the Easter-story of the gospels with the myths and ceremonies of the Attis-Adonis-Osiris religion, saying that "there is no such thing" as a burial and resurrection in the myths of Attis and Adonis, and that the difference between the death of Jesus and that of his Asiatic kindred can only be explained by the "hard fact"—the famous theological bed-rock—of the death on the cross. Weiss is unable to recognise in Mary Magdalen and the other Marys at the cross and the grave of the Saviour the Indian, Asiatic, and Egyptian mother of the gods, the Maia, Mariamma, or Maritala, as the mother of Krishna is called, the Mariana of Mariandynium (Bithynia), Mandane, the mother of the "Messiah" Cyrus (*Isaiah* xlv, 1), the "great mother" of Pessinunt,[1] the sorrowing Semiramis, Miriam, Merris, Myrrha, Maira (Mæra), and Maia,[2] the "beloved" of her son. Weiss, however, does not question that "the belief in a dead and risen Christ has, in general outline, considered from the point of view of the science of religion, a similar structure to these cult-myths, though the details are altogether different" (p. 39). As if there were any question about the details as such! Whether, for instance, the traditional number, "after three days," in the account of the resurrection has been chosen on astral grounds, and is related to the three winter months from the shortest day, when the sun dies, to the vernal equinox, when it triumphs definitively over the winter, and so the months are condensed into three days in the myth,[3] or whether the moon has furnished the data for

---

[1] See *The Christ-Myth*, pp. 53 and 78.

[2] The mother of the "world-saviour" Augustus, who is generally known as Attia, is also called Maia in Horace and on an inscription at Lyons ("Maia's winged child"), and she is supposed to have brought her son into the world in a remarkable way and under astonishing circumstances. The name was a standing name for the mothers of the saviour-gods of antiquity, and it is naive to regard it as the real name of the historical Jesus.

[3] Weiss denies that the three days could be taken from the course of the sun, as the sun is never buried for three days and three nights. But Heracles is said, according to the scholiast of Lycophron (Cassandra, 33), to have remained three days in the belly of the sea-monster, and to have escaped with the loss of his hair, which clearly points to the rays of the sun. The somewhat similar Jason also, the Greek counterpart of the biblical Joshua, whose solar nature is beyond question, is said to have been swallowed by the dragon and spat out again. The biblical Jonah, whose name means "dove," and points to the reverence of the Ninevites

the three days and three nights, as it is invisible for that
period, and, as so often happens in myths, the moon and
the sun have been blended, we need not consider here.
Possibly the number may be explained by the popular
belief in Persia and Judæa that the soul remains three
days and nights in the neighbourhood of the body, only
departing to its place on the fourth morning. Possibly,
again, the number was determined by *Hosea* vi, 2, where
we read: " After two days will he revive us; in the third
day he will raise us up." In any case, when there are
so many possible explanations, we have no convincing
reason to regard the account in the gospels as historical,
and to say with Weiss that the third day was chosen
"because something of importance [*sic*] had happened
on it " (p. 36).

There is very little force in the other objections of
theologians to the astral explanation of the day of the
death of Jesus. It is true that the day of the vernal
equinox is at least fourteen days before the Passover,
which is celebrated at the full moon after the beginning
of spring. I may recall, however, the very common
combination of sun and moon-worship in myths. Niemojewski has proved that a moon-myth is at the base of
Luke's astral system. Moreover, we may very well
suspect that, on account of the symbolism of the Paschal
lamb, the Christians have tampered with the calendar.
That the mythic-astral method "breaks down altogether"

for doves, seems also to have been originally a sun-god and related to
Heracles, or, rather, to the sun-god Perseus and Joshua. In Jaffa, from
which Jonah is supposed to have set out for Tarsis, there were still shown
in the days of Pomponius Mela certain large bones of the fish that had
tried to swallow Andromeda whom Perseus delivered (consider the similar
liberation of Hesione by Heracles); and the dove was, according to Assyrian
ideas, the wife of Ninus (that is to say, the fish), who appears in the Old
Testament, under the name of Nun, as the father of Joshua. In fact, the
connection of the Christ-form with these pagan sun-gods is clearly seen in
the ceremony performed on December 26 in the Church of Sta. Maria di
Carmine at Naples, in which the hair is cut off the figure of the crucified
with great solemnity. Compare also the three (winter) months and five
days during which Joseph is said, according to the "Testament of the
Twelve Patriarchs," to have dwelt in the under-world (*Christ-Myth*, I, 46).

in face of the time of the death of Jesus, as Weiss says, is not true at all, and before we consent to regard Sunday the 15–16 of Nisan as the day of the resurrection, "because on that day something of importance [*sic*] happened to the first disciples" (p. 38), we have to settle the chronological confusion that we find in regard to the date of the death of Jesus, which no one yet has succeeded in doing.

In fine, we may ask, as some reader of *The Christ-Myth* did, if the death and resurrection of Jesus really took place at the Jewish Easter, why was the day not fixed once for all instead of changing with the date of Easter? If Jesus of Nazareth was crucified on a certain day and " rose again on a certain day, and if the Pentecostal gathering took place in Jerusalem forty days after the resurrection, these days ought to have been fixed. It is useless to say that the festivals of the Church were only fixed at a later date. That may be true of Christmas, etc., but not of the day of the death and resurrection, which, together with Pentecost, were days of incomparable importance for Christians *from the very first*. These definite days ought to have been celebrated everywhere by Christians with great solemnity, either joyous or mournful. There could not possibly be a doubt as to which dates were to be celebrated. The fact that the Jewish calendar had movable feasts does not affect the matter; Paul ought at least to have given his Greeks and Romans a definite date to celebrate. The Church professes to know quite accurately the day on which Peter and Paul were crucified at Rome." How has it failed to fix vastly more important dates? As long as theologians can give us no satisfactory answer to this question we prefer to think that we are dealing, not with history, but with a myth to which an historical form was afterwards given.

Critical theologians have hitherto affirmed the historicity of the gospel narratives, but they have landed in

THE WITNESS OF THE GOSPELS 167

insuperable difficulties and insoluble contradictions; so poor, not to say purely negative, a result amounts to a *bankruptcy of their whole method*. It seems, therefore, to be our duty to try the *mythic-symbolic method*, and to consider the gospels from the point of view that their Jesus was not an historical, but a purely mythical, personage. The literary quality of the gospels, their tendentious dogmatic-metaphysical character, their chronological and topographical vagueness, their constant absence of definite indications of space and time in regard to events, the slender traces of an apparently historical and geographical framework, the resemblance of their most important details to the myths of non-Christian religions —a resemblance that often extends to the smallest points —all this demands that we shall study the gospels from a very different point of view from that hitherto adopted.

The fundamental idea of *The Christ-Myth* is that their historical character is only a symbolic clothing of their real content.

Why this method is less sound than the historical method followed by theologians, less "scientific"—in fact, no real method at all—is, in the circumstances, not very obvious. It is quite certain, and will be questioned by no one, that the gospels contain a large amount of legendary matter, and that a good deal in them is to be understood mystically or symbolically. It is not at all equally well established that they have an historical basis. The idea is grounded solely on the feeble tradition of Papias. What is there to prevent us, therefore, or what methodological principle restrains us, from extending the mythic-symbolical interpretation to the *whole* contents of the gospels, and refusing them any kind of historical reality? In Homer's *Iliad* there is much that seems at first sight to be historical and real, yet no one has attempted to see in the *Iliad* an historical document, and to extract its "historical nucleus" by means of criticism and exegesis from the mythical and poetical shell. It is possible that *The Christ-Myth* is wrong in its analysis of the gospel story into myths; but in that case its failure will only bring out more brilliantly the historical character of the gospels, so that, instead of scolding us, the believers in an historical Jesus ought to be grateful that we have relieved them of their thankless and uncongenial task. Our opponents complain that our procedure is actuated by the secret hope that there never was an historical Jesus. The truth is that it is their own exertions which are inspired by the opposite hope. Would theologians ask us to believe that they approach the problem impartially? Must we be dubbed unscientific because we take no interest in their historical Jesus? Let us avoid pretence, and have respect for truth. To science as such it is *wholly immaterial* whether there ever was a Jesus or no. It has no advantage in approaching the question of his historicity either from the positive or the negative standpoint. It is theology alone that has an interest in regarding the positive standpoint as necessary, and in coming to an affirmative solution of the problem. This, however, is not a scientific, but a religious or ecclesiastical, interest; and therefore all their talk about their "scientific procedure" and all their disdain of their opponents' methods are interested manœuvres. It is ridiculous for theologians to tell the laity that "science" has "proved" the historicity of Jesus, and "historical research" has established the "fact" of his existence. We cannot repeat too often: *The science of history has up to the present taken no notice of the problem*. Theology is not science, and, strictly speaking, does not merit the name of science at all, because, in spite of its formal scientific procedure, it rests, in the long run, on faith.

7.—THE MYTHIC-SYMBOLIC INTERPRETATION OF THE GOSPELS.

(a) *The Suffering and Exaltation of the Messiah.*—The mythic-symbolic interpretation of the gospels sees in *Isaiah* liii the germ-cell of the story of Jesus, the starting-point of all that is related of him, the solid nucleus round which all the rest has crystallised.

The prophet deals with the "servant of Jahveh," who voluntarily submits to suffering in order to expiate the sin and guilt of the people :—

> He is despised and *rejected of men, a man of sorrows*, and acquainted with grief; and we hid as it were our faces from him; he was *despised*, and we esteemed him not.
> Surely he hath borne our griefs *and carried our sorrows;* yet we did esteem him stricken, smitten of God, and afflicted.
> But he was *wounded for our transgressions*, he was bruised for our iniquities; *the chastisement of our peace was upon him*, and *with his stripes we are healed*.
> All we like sheep have gone astray; we have turned every one to his own way; and *the Lord hath laid on him the iniquity of us all*.
> He was *oppressed*, and he was afflicted, yet *he opened not his mouth;* he is brought as a *lamb* to the slaughter, and as a *sheep* before her shearers is *dumb*, so he openeth not his mouth.
> He was taken from prison and from *judgment;* and who shall declare his generation? for he was cut off out of the land of the living, for the transgression of my people was he stricken.
> And *he made his grave with the wicked, and with the rich* [evildoers] *in his death;* because *he had done no violence, neither was any deceit in his mouth*.
> Yet it pleased the Lord to bruise him; he hath put him to grief; when thou shalt make his soul *an offering for sin*, he shall see his seed, he shall prolong his days, and the pleasure of the Lord shall prosper in his hand.
> He shall see of the travail of his soul, and shall be satisfied; by his knowledge *shall my righteous servant justify many; for he shall bear their iniquities*.
> Therefore will I divide him a portion with the great,

and he shall divide the spoil with the strong; because he hath poured out his soul unto death; *and he was numbered with the transgressors; and he bare the sin of many, and made intercession for the transgressors.*

The general belief is that there is here question of the sufferings of Israel in the interest of the whole of mankind. According to Gunkel and Gressmann, however, the idea of the suffering just man is joined to an allusion to the god who expiates the sins of men by his voluntary death. Certainly we detect in it all the essential features of the suffering Christ, sacrificing himself for mankind and expiating their sins. That the early Christians felt this we see in *Mark* ix, 12, and xv, 28; *Matt.* viii, 17 and xxvi, 23; 1 *Peter* ii, 21; and *Acts* viii, 28–35, where the words of the prophet are expressly applied to Jesus.

Isaiah liii speaks of the "griefs" of the just one. But Plato, who also has described, in his *Republic*, the persecutions and sufferings that befall the just man, makes him be *scourged, tortured, cast in prison*, and finally *pilloried* ("crucified");[1] and in *Wisdom* the godless deliberate about condemning the just to a "shameful death." According to *Deuteronomy* (xxi, 23), there was no more shameful death than "to hang on a tree" (in Greek *xylon* and *stauros*, in Latin *crux*); so that this naturally occurred as the true manner of the just one's death. Then the particular motive of the death was furnished by the passage in *Wisdom* and the idea of Plato. He died as a victim of the unjust, the godless, who say:—

> Let us overpower the poor just man......*Let us set snares for the just, because he is a burden to us, and opposes our deeds, and represents to us the commands of the law. He boasts that he has a true knowledge of God, and calls himself the servant of God. He has become unto us a*

---

[1] Apollonius refers to the passage of Plato's *Republic* (II, 361) in his Apology: "For one of the Greek philosophers also says: The just man will be martyred, spat upon, and at last crucified." The passage seems even to have been in the mind of James when he says: "Ye have condemned and killed the just, and he doth not resist you"; and we read in Justin: "Ye have beaten the just" (*Dial.* xvi).

living reproach, on account of our desires. He is a burden unto us, when we do but look on him, because *his ways and his conduct are different from those of all others. Us he regards as insincere*, and he holds himself from intercourse with us, as from impurities. *But he praises the eternity of the just, and boasts that God is his father.* Let us see if *his words* be true, and wait for the manner of his going forth. For if the just is a son of God, God will take care of him, and save him from the hands of his enemies. Let us *put him to the proof* with *insults and evil treatment*, so that we may know his *meekness* and prove his *steadfastness*. Let us condemn him to a shameful death; for, *according to his words, he will have protection*. Such things said they in their madness, for their wickedness dazed them, and they recognised not the mysteries of God.

These words suggest the cry of the martyred and reviled in the twenty-second psalm, whose torments also recall the death "on the tree":—

My God, my God, why hast thou forsaken me ?......O my God, I cry in the daytime, but thou hearest not......I am ......*a reproach of men and despised of the people. All they that see me laugh me to scorn; they shoot out the lip, they shake the head, saying: He trusted in the Lord that he would deliver him; let him deliver him, seeing he delighted in him*......I am poured out like water, and all my bones are out of joint......*My strength* [palate] *is dried up like a potsherd;* and *my tongue cleaveth to my jaws*...... For dogs have compassed me, the assembly of the wicked have enclosed me; *they pierced my hands and my feet* [like the lion are my hands and my feet]. I may tell all my bones; they look and stare upon me. *They part my garments among them, and cast lots upon my vesture.*

It is further said in the book of *Wisdom :*—

The souls of the just are in the hand of God, and no torment can touch them. *Only according to the folly of the unwise do they seem to be dead*, and their going in is counted a misfortune, and their going forth from us for a destruction; but they are at peace. For if they have been punished in the eyes of men, *their hope was full of the faith in immortality.* And after they have *borne a brief torture*, they will receive great rewards; for God has but tried them, and *has found them worthy of him.* Like gold in the crucible has he *tried* them, and *like the gift of a whole offering has he accepted them.* And at the time of their home-coming they will *shine bright*, and will *pass like sparks in the reed.* They shall *judge the heathen* and *rule over the peoples*, and the Lord shall be their *king* for ever. *They who trust in him shall know the truth, and the faithful will remain with him in love.* For grace and mercy shall be the part of his elect. But the godless shall be *punished* according to their deeds, who despised the just and rebelled against the Lord.

In these words we clearly perceive the fundamental idea of the Christian mysteries. The love of the "Lord" and trust in him are for the good and just the conditions of their glorious exaltation and an eternal life with God after death : "For God has created man for immortality, and made him in the likeness of his own being. But death came into the world through the envy of the devil" (ii, 23). Hence the wicked irreclaimably fall to him, no matter how long they enjoy life on the earth. The just, on the other hand, dies young :—

He is withdrawn from the midst of sinners......In a little while he hath fulfilled much time. For his soul was pleasing to the Lord ; therefore did he hasten to take him from the wicked world......*The just will himself judge the living godless after death*, and the *early closed youth* the long old-age of the unjust......For they shall see the end of the wise, and shall not know what he hath designed concerning him, and why the Lord hath brought him to safety. They will see and understand not, but of themselves will the Lord make sport......At the reckoning of their sins they shall stand shivering, and their transgressions of the law shall appear before them as accusers. Then will the just with much confidence stand against them that have oppressed him and have slighted his needs. At sight of him they will be smitten with a terrible fear, and will be astonished at his unexpected safety. They will see ruefully to themselves, and in the anxiety of their soul will they moan : This was he who once made sport for us and for an object of contempt to us fools. *His life we counted a folly, and his end without honour.* How, then, was he numbered among the *sons of God* and hath a possession among the holy ? We have, therefore, wandered from the way of wisdom, and *the light of justice* has not illumined us, and the *sun* has not shone upon us......

But the just live in eternity, and their reward is with the Lord, and the care of them is with the most high. Therefore will they receive the kingdom of glory and the crown of beauty from the hand of the Lord.

Since the just is here described in his heavenly exaltation as accuser and judge of the godless, speaking judgment on them after their death, it would be curious if in the minds of the pious the figure of the exalted just did not instinctively blend with that of the expected Messiah. It was an essential element of that expectation that the Messiah would appear in heavenly glory, and judge Israel according to its deeds, condemning the godless and taking the good to eternal life in heaven. If this happened, it would follow that the Messiah also would suffer and die, and by his voluntary death remove the guilt of men, and obtain heavenly happiness for those who love and trust him and walk in his footsteps. It is true that *Wisdom* refers the love of the faithful to God. But we know how in the Jewish mind the figure of the Messiah tended to be identified with that of Jahveh, and the "son of God," as the just is called in *Wisdom*, is one with his father, and is in a certain sense only another name for him.

Read in the prophet Isaiah the important references to the coming lordship of the Messiah and mysterious indications of his nature: "Say ye to the righteous, that it shall be well with him; for they shall eat the fruit of their doings. Woe unto the wicked; it shall be ill with him; for the reward of his hands shall be given him" (iii, 10). That was already contained in the passage we quoted from *Wisdom* :—

Behold, my servant shall deal prudently, he shall be exalted and extolled, and be very high.

As many were astonied at thee; his visage was so marred more than any man, and his form more than the sons of men;

So shall he sprinkle many nations; the kings shall shut their mouths at him. For that which had not been told them shall they see, and that which they had not heard shall they consider.[1]

Would not that recall to readers the astonishment and fear of the godless at sight of the exalted just as described in *Wisdom*? "And he shall judge among the nations, and shall rebuke many people" (ii, 4). The prophet applied this to Jahveh, but in *Wisdom* it is said of the just, who is raised by God to heavenly glory after his humiliating death. Is it possible to doubt that the just, the "servant of God" in the fifty-third chapter of the prophet, was Jahveh himself, or rather that "son of God," in the special sense, which the Messiah was conceived to be?

Then there are the words of the prophet that the servant of God grew up before Jahveh "as a tender plant, and as a root out of dry ground" (lii, 2). Here the connection is quite obvious, for the eleventh chapter of *Isaiah*, in which the prophet describes the glory of the Messianic kingdom in especially impressive tones, began with almost the same words: "And there shall come forth a rod out of the stem of Jesse, and a branch shall grow out of its roots." Here the servant of God is also described as of the root of David, as the prophet Zechariah, too, had said: "Behold I will bring forth my servant the branch" (iii, 8; also see vi, 12), leaving no room for doubt that the Messiah is intended here. Will it now be said to be impossible that the Jews had blended the servant of God in *Isaiah* liii with the Messiah, and had seen in the passage a mysterious reference to some preceding suffering and humiliating death of the expected Saviour, and thus Israel's Saviour fell into line with the suffering, dying, and rising gods of the religions of nearer Asia?

(b) *The Character and Miracles of the Messiah.*—Of all these gods special myths were related by their

---

[1] *Isaiah* lii. 13-15.

followers. Their life-story was related, and curious things were said of their origin, character, deeds, etc., from birth to death. Did the prophet who spoke of the sufferings, death, resurrection, and exaltation of the servant of God give any indications of this character? Read the forty-second chapter:—

> Behold my servant, whom I uphold; mine elect in whom my soul delighteth; *I have put my spirit upon him; he shall bring forth judgment* to the Gentiles.
> He shall not cry, nor lift up, nor cause his voice to be heard in the street.
> *A bruised reed shall he not break, and the smoking flax shall he not quench;* he shall bring forth judgment unto truth.
> He shall not fail nor be discouraged, till he have set judgment in the earth; and the isles shall wait for his law.

Thus the servant of God is to be wise, gentle, tender, full of endless pity for the oppressed and suffering. He is indefatigable in the exercise of the office committed to him by God, and his mission is to proclaim truth and establish righteousness on earth—the kingdom of that perfect righteousness of all, which is to the prophet the condition of the fulfilment of all that God has promised to his people (ch. lviii). In agreement with this we read in ch. l, 4 :—

> The Lord God hath given me the tongue of the learned, that I should know *how to speak a word in season to him that is weary*......
> The Lord God hath opened mine ear, and *I was not rebellious, neither turned away back.*
> *I gave my back to the smiters, and my cheeks to them that plucked off the hair; I hid not my face from shame and spitting.*
> For the Lord God will help me, therefore shall I not be confounded; therefore have I set my face like a flint, and *I know that I shall not be ashamed.*

Obedience to God, his father, trust in his heavenly power, patient submission to his lot, not disturbed even by the foulest maltreatment and shame, are the essential features of the servant of God. He submits willingly to the command of God, just as the saviour-gods and redeemers of the pagan religions descended to earth at the command of their divine "fathers"; as the Babylonian Marduch was obedient to his father Ea; as Heracles, the most resolute and powerful hero, nevertheless bowed to the command of his heavenly father and undertook the heaviest labours.

Now we can also understand the words of the sixty-first chapter:—

> The spirit of the Lord God is upon me; because the Lord hath anointed me *to preach good tidings unto the meek;* he hath sent me *to bind up the broken-hearted, to proclaim liberty to the captives,* and the opening of the prison to them that are bound;
> To proclaim the acceptable year of the Lord and the day of vengeance of our God; *to comfort all that mourn.*

They seem to be the words of the servant of God himself, who reveals in them the meaning of his Messianic task. He is not sent to the rich and fortunate, but to the poor and miserable; he does not come as a powerful leader of armies, to lead his followers to victory over their enemies; but, like the saviour-gods of other peoples, he chiefly heals suffering of body and soul, and alleviates the lot of the people, as we read in ch. xxxv, 4: "Behold, your God......will come and save you. *Then the eyes of the blind shall be opened, and the ears of the deaf shall be unstopped. Then shall the lame man leap as an hart, and the tongue of the dumb sing.*" And again (xxix, 18): "And in that day shall the deaf hear the words of the book, and the eyes of the blind shall see out of obscurity and out of darkness. The meek also shall increase their joy in the Lord, and the poor among men shall rejoice in the Holy One of Israel."

To announce the gospel, the glad message of the realisation of salvation, of the fulfilment of the hopes of a happy life, is the essential activity of the servant of God during his life on earth. For so speaks God,

Jahveh, who spread out the heavens: "I, Jahveh, have called thee in righteousness, and I will take thee by the hand, and will protect thee, and make thee to *represent the covenant with the people of Israel, and a light to the nations*, as I open the eyes of the blind, deliver the prisoners from their prison, and from their captivity those that sit in darkness......And I will give my glory to none other, nor my fame to the idols."

What a mysterious indication of the real nature of the servant of God! The covenant that Jahveh made with Moses is renewed by him; he is therefore a second Moses. Nay, did not the prophet seem to intimate that Jahveh would confer on him his own glory, and does not this seem to imply his equality in nature with Jahveh? Assuredly *he was no ordinary man*, this servant of God of the prophet; and the hopes of the people for the kingdom of God would be fulfilled very differently from what they expected, if salvation was to be extended to the Gentiles as well as the Jews. But that the prophet's servant of God is really he for whom the Jewish people longed is shown by his marvellous deeds.

Thus we can explain the miracles of Jesus on which the critics have expended so much fruitless labour; they followed at once from the above passages, the moment an attempt was made to give a detailed picture of the life of the servant of God, and to embody the intimations of the prophets in impressive stories. These miracles must have been performed by Jesus simply because they were part of the character of the servant of God. They serve as evidence of his supernatural power and his mysterious relation to Jahveh, and they differ in no respect from the miracles which the pagans also ascribed to their saviour-gods, such as Asclepios, Hermes, Anubis, etc., just as the Old Testament had attributed them to Moses, Elijah, and Elisha, and as, in the common feeling of ancient times, they were expected of any outstanding man. Take Apollonius of Tyana, for instance.

The prophet speaks of the curing of the blind, deaf, lame, and dumb. Those are precisely the miracles of the gospels. It is true that he does not speak of raising the dead to life or driving out demons—feats which were related of Asclepios and Apollonius. He does, however, make the servant of God deliver captives. But if we interpret the text with deeper insight, does it not seem to mean the opening of the doors of sense and bodily life, which form the kingdom of the devil, and which Plato had described as the prison of the soul, or the unsealing of the tombs that hold the dead as prisoners? Introduced into the mental world of the doctrine of mysteries, the words of the prophet would naturally lose their original and real meaning, and become symbols of a mysterious truth hidden in them, the meaning of which would be clear only to the initiated. If Isaiah's servant of God was a saviour, a lord over natural forces chosen by God, like the pagan saviour-gods, he must, like them, have above all a dominion over the dread world of spirits and demons, by which the men of the time saw themselves surrounded and threatened everywhere, in whom they recognised the causes of disease, and for protection against whom they took refuge in the magical realm of the mysteries.[1] It would, therefore, be childish to take the miracles of Jesus at their face value, and seek to extract from the gospel narratives which describe them an "historical nucleus." Compare a story like that of the Gadarene swine (*Mark* v, 1) in the symbolical explanation which Lublinski (p. 131) gives of it with the historical conception of it in Weiss. Only complete unintelligence could attempt to deduce from the description of the locality, the presence of the swine, etc., the historical place and truth of the story; whereas there is obviously question of the nether world, of a symbolical representation of the power of the Saviour over the demons,

---

[1] Compare *Zechariah* xiii, 2: "In that day......I will cause......the unclean spirit to pass out of the land."

and the swine are introduced only as "typhonic" beasts, to suggest the scenery of the nether world.¹ A good deal of amusement has been expressed over the childish miracles which the gospels attribute to the son of God. We have, however, only to recognise that they are built on the prophet's intimations and inspired by them, and are merely symbols of the spread of faith in Jesus, as Smith has shown at length in his *Ecce Deus;* and we shall see that even in regard to the miracles the evangelical way of putting things can be justified. In this way the much-discussed question of the miracles of the gospels may be settled.

SUPPLEMENT.

As we have seen, *Isaiah* and *Wisdom* are the germ-cell of the figure of Jesus in the gospels and the Christian theory of redemption. But a third element has been at work—the figure of Job.

The canonical book of *Job* depicts for us a just man who, just like the prophet's servant of God, is tried by a conflict with Satan, by intolerable suffering and humiliation, and is afterwards raised again to his former condition. There is much in the book that directly reminds us of *Isaiah* liii and Psalm xxii; for instance, the circumstance that Job and the servant of God are both afflicted with leprosy (*Isaiah* lii, 14; liii, 4). Or read the following lament of Job :—

> They have gaped upon me with their mouth; they have smitten me upon the cheek reproachfully; they have gathered themselves together against me.

¹ That the whole story is only meant to be symbolical is recognised by some theologians, such as von Baur and Volkmar. But to what absurdities their historical point of view will lead theologians we have a charming illustration in Otto Schmiedel (p. 114). In his opinion, the possessed man is no other than Paul, and the whole thing is a piece of malicious Judæo-Christian ridicule of the apostle. Yet these are the men who reproach us with "fantastic" explanations, and ask us to respect the "method" of theologians.

God hath delivered me to the ungodly, and turned me over into the hands of the wicked.......

His archers compass me round about; he cleaveth my reins asunder, and doth not spare; he poureth out my gall upon the ground.......

My face is foul with weeping, and on my eyelids is the shadow of death.

Not for any injustice in mine hands: also my prayer is pure.......

Let my cry have no place.

Also now, behold, my witness is in heaven, and my record is on high.

My friends scorn me, but mine eye poureth out tears unto God.......

My breath is corrupt, my days are extinct, the graves are ready for me.

Are there not mockers with me? and doth not mine eye continue in their provocation? [My eye must rest on their brawls. Compare the soldiers casting dice for the garments of Jesus.]

He hath made me also a byword of the people, and aforetime I was as a tabret. [I must let my face be spat upon.]

Mine eye also is dim by reason of sorrow, and all my members are as a shadow.

Upright men shall be astonished at this, and the innocent shall stir up himself against the hypocrite.

The righteous also shall hold on his way, and he that hath clean hands shall be stronger and stronger.[1]

Job cries again (ch. xxix):—

Oh that I were as in months past, as in the days when God preserved me;

When his candle shined upon my head, and when by his light I walked through darkness.

As I was in the days of my youth......

When the Almighty was yet with me, when my children were about me......

When I went out to the gate through the city, when I prepared my seat in the street.

......and the aged arose, and stood up.

The princes refrained talking, and laid their hand on their mouth. [Compare *Isaiah* lii, 15.]

The nobles held their peace, and their tongue cleaved to the roof of their mouth.

---

[1] *Job* xvi. 10–xvii. 9. Also see **xxxix.** 1, 9–11, and 20.

THE WITNESS OF THE GOSPELS 181

> When the ear heard me, then it blessed me; and when the eye saw me, it gave witness to me.
> Because I delivered the poor that cried, and the fatherless, and him that had none to help him.
> The blessing of him that was ready to perish came upon me; and I caused the widow's heart to sing for joy.......
> I was eyes to the blind, and feet was I to the lame.
> I was a father to the poor, and the cause which I knew not I searched out.
> And I brake the jaws of the wicked, and plucked the spoil out of his teeth.......
> Unto me men gave ear, and waited, and kept silence at my counsel.
> After my words they spake not again; and my speech dropped upon them.
> I laughed on them when they despaired; they believed it not, and the light of my countenance they cast not down.
> I chose out their way, and sat chief, and dwelt as a king in the army, as one that comforteth the mourners.

These words remind us of the prophet's servant of God. But at the same time we see Jesus before us, as, surrounded by his disciples, he speaks to the people in the market-place and the streets, disputes with the Pharisees and Scribes, and silences them, strides through life helping, working miracles, consoling, healing, and encouraging, and is blessed by the crowd and by the lost and the saved.

Still greater, however, than with the canonical book of *Job* is the concordance of the gospel figure of Jesus with the popular Jewish additions to it. One of these we have in the so-called *Job's Testament*, which was first published in 1883, and again in 1897 by Montague Rhodes James and K. Kohler, and very closely studied by Spitta in its relation to the New Testament.[1] James held at first that *Job's Testament* was purely Jewish and pre-Christian, but afterwards attributed it to a Jewish convert to Christianity, as he could find no other explanation of its astonishing agreements with the New Testament, not only as regards its general contents, but at times even in

---

[1] *Zur Geschichte und Literatur des Urchristentums.* 1907, iii, 2.

words.[1] Kohler regards it as pre-Christian, an Essenian Midrasch on the book of *Job*; this is, however, denied by Spitta. Bousset, a careful man, finds a "slight Christian modification" of a Jewish work, while Spitta believes that the remarkable work has a purely Jewish character: "One of the Jewish pre-conditions of Christianity, a full knowledge of which is of great importance for an appreciation of Christianity itself, and especially of the figure of Jesus." "In this case, it seems to me," he says, "the view would be more plausible that the figure of Jesus is of pre-Christian origin than in connection with the Gilgamesch-epic or W. B. Smith's pre-Christian Jesus." He emphasises the following points: "Job and Jesus are both of royal race; both are healers of the poor and distressed; both struggle against the power of Satan, and are fruitlessly tempted by him to fall away from God; both incur suffering and contempt, even death, by the machinations of the devil; both are saved from necrotes [the state of death], attain honour on earth, and are raised to the throne at the right hand of God" (p. 198). Spitta does not fail to point out the differences between Job and Jesus; but he considers the resemblance to be so great that, in his opinion, it is enough "to explain how it could happen that the figure of Jesus was involuntarily endowed by Jewish writers with features which originally belong to the Job-legend" (p. 200). That this figure could have arisen only in connection with the figure of Job is a possibility which, of course, lies beyond the horizon of the theologian. Yet so many details of the gospel portrait of Jesus have been shown to be due to foreign influence that we can hardly say what is really supposed to be historical in it. For the rest, the Christians themselves were well aware of the resemblance of their Jesus to Job. It is proved by *James* v, 10, where we read: "Take, my brethren, the prophets who have spoken in the name of

[1] Compare, especially, the remarkable resemblance to the story of the Magi in *Matthew* ii. See Spitta, p. 192, and James, pp. 169, 199, and 204.

the Lord, for an example of suffering affliction, and of patience. Behold, we count them happy which endure. Ye have heard of the patience of Job, and have seen the end of the Lord; that the Lord is very pitiful, and of tender mercy." Here Jesus is put on a level with Job, assuming that by "the Lord" we are to understand Jesus, and not Jahveh, which seems more likely, in view of the reference to the prophets who have spoken "in the name of the Lord."[1]

(c) *John the Baptist and the Baptism of Jesus.*—Weiss rightly speaks of the gospel of Mark as "a story of the Passion prolonged backwards." This rich fullness of the earthly life of Jesus is assuredly something more than a development of Pauline principle; he humbled himself, and was obedient even to the death on the cross. From the Pauline gospel alone the evangelist could not possibly have evolved his narrative (p. 132). But no one has said that he could. What I do say is that the prophet Isaiah has supplied the chief features for the story of Jesus, and the general framework. There, and there only, do we find the real "main pillars of a truly scientific life of Jesus." Not only the sufferings, death, resurrection, and exaltation, but the description of his character and activity and miraculous power, come from the prophet's words. Even the first appearance of Jesus, in connection with the penitential preaching of John, links with the text of Isaiah. The words with which the earliest gospel opens are also the beginning of the second part of the book of the prophet, the author of which is known as the Deutero-Isaiah, and distinguished from the older prophet; he is believed to have written his work at Babylon in the last days of the captivity.

---

[1] Is *James* a Christian Epistle in the ordinary meaning of the word? The Epistle, it is true, contains sayings of Jesus, but they are not described as such, and there is no clear indication that the Epistle reflects anything but purely Jewish ideas. Perhaps it belongs to "pre-Christian Christianity," when the Jewish Jahveh, "the Lord," was worshipped under the name of Jesus. See later.

> The voice of him that crieth in the wilderness : Prepare ye the way of the Lord, make straight in the desert a highway for our God.
> Every valley shall be exalted, and every mountain and hill shall be laid low; and the crooked shall be made straight, and the rough places plain;
> And the glory of the Lord shall be revealed, and all flesh shall see it together: for the mouth of the Lord hath spoken it (xl, 3-5).

The gospel refers the words to the Baptist, the "voice of one crying in the wilderness," to whom "the word of the Lord came" (*Luke* iii, 2). But we know that, as Mark himself says, he has been influenced by the prophet Malachi, who says in his third chapter: "Behold, I will send my messenger, and he shall prepare the way before me"; that the words "in the wilderness" have been inserted by a copyist in the wrong place; in reality, they do not denote the place whence the cry came, but mean that the way is to be prepared in the wilderness. We are thus led to suspect that the figure of the "precursor" also may have grown out of the above passage in the prophet, and that the idea of a double mission of Jahveh to his people may have arisen from the passage in which Isaiah, consoling his fellows, says that Jerusalem has received "double from the hand of Jahveh" for all its sins (xl, 2). The ideas of the Baptist's message also agree with the admonishing words which the prophet earnestly addresses to Jerusalem. "There cometh one mightier than I after me," we read in *Mark* (i, 7), "the latchet of whose shoes I am not worthy to stoop down and unloose." In *Isaiah* it is said: "The Lord God will come with strong hand." The prophet then describes the power and greatness of Jahveh, before whom all the peoples and powers of the earth are nought, whose spirit is immeasurable, his power incomparable, and who says: "I have raised up one from the north, and he shall come; from the rising of the sun shall he call upon my name; and he shall come upon princes as upon mortar, and as the potter treadeth clay" (xli, 25). "Whose fan is in his hand"—so Matthew and Luke complete the words of the earliest gospel—"and he will thoroughly purge his floor, and gather his wheat into the garner; but he will burn up the chaff with unquenchable fire" (*Matthew* iii, 12; *Luke* iii, 17). In *Isaiah* Jahveh says to Israel: "Behold, I will make thee a new sharp threshing instrument, having teeth; thou shalt thresh the mountains and beat them small, and shalt make the hills as chaff. Thou shalt fan them, and the wind shall carry them away, and the whirlwind shall scatter them" (xli, 15). And in xlvii, 14, it is said of the Gentiles: "Behold, they shall be as stubble; the fire shall burn them; they shall not deliver themselves from the power of the flame."[1]

It is a language of repentance and warning that the evangelist puts in the mouth of the Baptist: "Repent ye, for the kingdom of God is at hand." The last judgment approaches. The expected Messiah is near. So in the prophet also Jahveh appears as a kind of judge who summons the nations before his chair, to prove to them the nothingness of their deities in comparison with the hero whom he has raised for the redemption of his people. "Bring forth the people *that is blind, though it hath eyes,* and *they that are deaf, although they have ears.* All ye peoples, gather yourselves together, and let the nations congregate." "Behold, ye are of nothing," he says, reviling the gods of the nations, "and your work of nought; an abomination is he that chooseth you" (xli, 24). Who is not reminded of the reproaches which John addresses to the Pharisees, scourging their stubbornness and darkness: "Generation of vipers, who hath warned you to flee from the wrath to come"?

The publicans come to John and ask: "What shall we

---

[1] See also *Isaiah* v and *Psalm* i, 22, where the just, who rejoices in the law of Jahveh, is compared with the tree by the stream, "that bringeth forth its fruit in due season," while the godless are described as "chaff," which "the wind sweeps away."

do?" And he replies: "Exact no more than that which is appointed you." The soldiers put the same question and receive the answer: "Do violence to no man, neither accuse any falsely; and be content with your wages" (*Luke* iii, 12–14). We read in *Isaiah* (xxxiii, 15): "He that walketh righteously and speaketh uprightly, he that despiseth the gain of oppressions, that shaketh his hands from holding of bribes, that stoppeth his ears from hearing of blood, and shutteth his eyes from seeing evil; he shall dwell on high; his place of defence shall be the munitions of rocks."

"Bring forth fruits worthy of repentance," the Baptist cries to the Pharisees, "and begin not to say within yourselves: We have Abraham to our father; for I say unto you that God is able of these stones to raise up children unto Abraham. And now also the axe is laid unto the root of the trees; every tree therefore which bringeth not forth good fruit is hewn down and cast into the fire" (*Luke* iii, 8 and 9). Can it be a mere coincidence that there is also question of "the seed of Abraham" in the forty-first chapter of *Isaiah*, and Israel is consoled precisely as the Pharisees are in the gospels, when they boast of their "righteousness" in having Abraham for father? And what do we read at the beginning of the fifty-first chapter of the prophet? "Hearken to me, ye that follow after righteousness, ye that seek the Lord: Look unto the rock whence ye are hewn......Look unto Abraham, your father." Isaiah also makes "the day of the Lord" humble all that are proud and lofty (ii, 12), and Ezekiel makes the proud oaks of Lebanon fall at Jahveh's command because of their haughtiness and godless nature (xxxi, 12).

Robert Eisler has, in an essay on the baptism of John,[1] drawn attention to *Micah* vii, 14, where the prophet makes Zion say to Jahveh:—

---

[1] In the *Süddeutsche Monatshefte*, 1909, Heft 12.

Feed thy people with thy rod, the flock of thine heritage, which *dwell solitarily in the wood in the midst of Carmel* the orchard.......

According to the days of thy coming out of the land of Egypt will I shew unto him marvellous things.

The nations shall see and be confounded at all their might......their ears shall be deaf.

They shall lick the dust like a serpent, they shall move out of their holes like worms of the earth; they shall be afraid of the Lord our God, and fear because of thee.

Who is a God like unto thee, that pardoneth iniquity, and passeth by the transgression of the remnant of his heritage?......

He will turn again, he will have compassion upon us; he will subdue our iniquities; and *thou wilt cast all their sins into the depth of the sea.*

Thou wilt perform the truth to Jacob, and the mercy to Abraham, which thou hast sworn unto our fathers from the days of old.

Here the situation is just the same, not only as in the fortieth and forty-first chapters of *Isaiah*, but as in the gospel account of the appearance of John. Nearly every detail of the words put in the mouth of the Baptist is found in the words of the prophet: Jahveh conceived as a pastoral inhabitant of the wilderness in Israel, about whom the people in the wilderness gather in spite of the orchards about them, the reference to the coming anger of Jahveh, the stubbornness of the "nations," the threat that they will be humbled before Jahveh in spite of all their power, the comparison of the stubborn with serpents ("generation of vipers"), the remark that the stubborn themselves do not share in the forgiveness of sins and inherit grace because they are descended from Abraham, to whom Jahveh promised these things; while, on the other hand, the penitent shall see such wonders as were done at the flight from Egypt, and especially the baptism, by which sins are cast into the sea and washed away by its waves. It was not unusual to put an expiatory meaning on the passage of the Israelites through the Red Sea, and to regard it as a kind of baptism and forgiveness of sins of the whole people, as Paul says: "All our fathers ......passed through the sea, and were all baptised unto Moses in the cloud and in the sea" (1 *Cor.* x, 1).

In *Isaiah* also the "Holy One of Israel," Jahveh, promises his people that they shall rejoice over him. "When the poor and needy seek *water*, and there is none, and the tongue faileth for thirst, I the Lord will hear them......I will open rivers in high places, and fountains in the midst of the valleys; I will make the *wilderness a pool of water*, and the *dry land* springs of water" (xli, 17). "Fear not, O Jacob, my servant......for *I will pour water upon him that is thirsty*, and floods upon the dry ground: *I will pour my spirit upon thy seed*, and *my blessing* upon thine offspring; and they shall spring up as among the grass, as willows by the water courses" (xliv, 2). The figure of the springs in the desert waste recalls the "shoots on dry land," and we have the connection between the baptism of John and the baptism of the servant of God: "Behold, I will do a new thing; now it shall spring forth; shall ye not know it? I will even make a way in the wilderness, and rivers in the desert......to give drink to my people, my chosen" (xliii, 19 and 20).

"I baptise you with water," Matthew and Luke make John say, "but one mightier than I cometh who shall baptise you with the Holy Ghost and with fire." In *Isaiah* it is written: "When thou *passest through the waters*, I will be with thee; and through the rivers, they shall not overflow thee; when thou *walkest through the fire*, thou shalt not be burned; neither shall the flame kindle upon thee" (xliii, 2); and the following verses show clearly that he also has in mind the baptism in the Red Sea, the baptism by water as distinct from the baptism by fire, since he says: "I gave Egypt for thy ransom......therefore will I give men for thee and people for thy life."

And now we read in the famous eleventh chapter of

the prophet, on "the rod of the stem of Jesse": "The spirit of the Lord shall rest upon him, the spirit of wisdom and understanding, the spirit of counsel and might, the spirit of knowledge and of the fear of the Lord" (xi, 2). These are the words which have given rise to the story of the baptism of Jesus and the descent of the Holy Ghost upon him, and we now understand why the preacher of repentance, John, threatens with a coming judgment. The "rod" of the passage is represented mainly in the character of an upright judge, of whom it is said that he will "judge the poor with righteousness, and reprove with equity for the meek of the earth; and he shall smite the earth with the rod of his mouth, and with the breath of his lips shall he slay the wicked. And righteousness shall be the girdle of his loins, and faithfulness the girdle of his reins" (xi, 4 and 5).

Thus the whole story of the appearance of John and the baptism of Jesus is built on the prophet Isaiah. This removes the difficulties which a purely historical conception of the story encounters, especially in the contradictory statement that a Jesus could submit to the baptism of John; all the countless attempts to explain this are merely play on words. What has not been written on the character of John and his relation to Jesus! It would be just as reasonable to take as the subject of a "scientific" investigation the question why Achilles remained inactive ten years before Troy, instead of going home and devoting himself to other matters. One must regard with some pain a science that, on account of its connection with ecclesiastical life, has to propose such questions and deal with them in academically approved and learned works, when it is clear from the above passages in *Isaiah* that the whole story of the baptism belongs to the province of fiction.

As yet we have not touched upon the astral features that seem to occur in the story of the baptism.

Dupuis long ago identified the John of the gospels with the Babylonian Oannes, Joannes, or Hanni, the curiously shaped creature, half fish and half man, who, according to Berosus, was the first lawgiver and inventor of letters and founder of civilisation, and who rose every morning from the waves of the Red Sea in order to instruct men as to his real spiritual nature. He believed that he could recognise him in the southern constellation of the Fishes, as this seemed to the inhabitants of Babylon to rise out of the Red Sea, and its rising and setting indicated the two yearly solstices.[1] Possibly, however, he was originally Aquarius, as this constellation is depicted as a fish-man in the old oriental sphere, and the constellation of the Fishes was afterwards detached from it.[2] In any case, it was connected with the division of the year by solstices, and was in this sense a "teacher of astronomy." We have a reminiscence of this primitive astral significance of John in the fact that we still celebrate his festival on the day of the solstice, when the constellation of the southern Fishes rises as the sun sets, and disappears as the sun rises. Also the newly baptised Christians used to be called fishes (*pisciculi* in Tertullian), and the baptismal font is still called the *piscina*, or fish-pond. Thus the fish-man has been turned in Christianity into a sort of fisher of men. To this there is an allusion in the Ambrosian choral (*hamum profundo miserat piscatus est verbum Dei*), representing John as drawing the converted out of the water with an arm of the cross; which recalls Oannes, who saved the first man from the flood, and is supposed to have endowed him with his real life as a man and spirit.

That the evangelist himself perceived this relation of John to the fishes is proved by the parable attributed to the Saviour, comparing the actual generation to children who sit in the market-place and call to each other:

---

[1] Dupuis, *L'origine de tous les cultes*, 1795, III, pp. 619 and 683.
[2] Creuzer, *Symbolik und Mythologie der alten Völker*, 1820, II, p. 78.

"We have piped unto you, and ye have not danced" (*Matthew* xi, 16; *Luke* vii, 32). For these words remind one very much of Herodotus, according to whom, when Cyrus heard the willingness of the Ionians, who had hitherto refused to obey, to submit after his victory over Crœsus, he said in a parable: "A fisherman saw fishes in the sea, and played his flute in order to bring them out upon the land. And when he saw that he had failed, he took a net, and caught a great number of fishes in it, and drew them out. And when he saw them floundering, he said to the fishes: 'You need not dance now, since you would not dance when I piped.'"

As the one who indicates the solstices and divides the year, Oannes becomes identical with the sun itself, as a rising and setting star. In this way he entered the myth-group of Joshua, Jason, and Jesus, and, indeed, corresponds to the Old Testament Caleb, as representative of the summer solstice, when the dog-star (Sirius) sets in the month of the Lion, or of the autumnal equinox, which is the division of the year equivalent to the former, when the sun descends below the celestial equator into the land of winter. Joshua (Jesus), on the other hand, represented the winter solstice, at which the days begin to grow longer, or the vernal equinox, when the sun again advances beyond the equator, and enters victoriously the "Promised Land" beyond the Jordan (or the Milky Way) of the heavenly Eridanus, the watery region of the heavens, in which the zodiacal signs of Aquarius and Pisces predominate. The evangelist expresses this by making John be born six months before Jesus (*Luke* i, 36), and disappear from the scene and be put to death at the time when Jesus enters it (*Mark* i, 14). Hence the words of John: "He must increase, but I must decrease" (iii, 30). Again, as the setting sun the Baptist resembles the Greek Hermes Psychopompos, who, at the time of the autumnal equinox, leads the constellations or souls into the nether world, the dark and sterile half of the year—symbolically represented by the "wilderness," in which the people come to John, who is there. On the other hand, Jesus, as the rising sun, resembles Hermes Necropompos, who leads back the souls at the time of the vernal equinox to the heavenly home of light, the "kingdom of heaven," their true home. Hence it is said of the Baptist in the gospel: "John came neither eating nor drinking"; but of Jesus: "The son of man came eating and drinking" (*Matthew* xi, 17). This is quite intelligible when we see the relation of the one to the winter, and of the other to the summer.

The oriental imagination, however, is not satisfied with this general idea. It affects to find the Baptist in the constellation of Orion, near which, at the time when the point of spring falls in the constellation of Taurus, the sun is found at the time of the vernal equinox. It stands in the celestial Eridanus, in the Milky Way, at Bethabara (*John* i, 28), the "place of setting"—that is to say, near the spot where the sun crosses the Milky Way in the zodiac. With one foot it emerges from Eridanus, which connects with the Milky Way, and seems to draw water from it with the right hand, at the same time raising the left as if blessing—really a very vivid astral figure of the Baptist; we have also the three stars of Orion's belt in the (leathern) girdle which the gospels give to the Baptist, and the people are seen in the constellations about Orion, and, according to Babylonian ideas, a meeting of the gods takes place at the vernal equinox when the sun has run its course through the zodiac.[1]

It is useless to oppose to this conception of John the familiar passage of Josephus (xviii, 5, 2) as proving the historicity of the Baptist. The genuineness of the passage is just as doubtful as that of the two references in Josephus

---

[1] I borrow this indication of the connection of the Baptist with the constellation Orion from Fuhrmann's work, *Der Astralmythos von Christus*. Also see, as to the astral features of the Baptist, Niemojewski (work cited, under "Joannes" in the index).

to Jesus. Not only does the way in which it interrupts the narrative plainly show it to be an interpolation, but the chronology of the Jewish historian in regard to John is in irreconcilable contradiction to that of the gospels. According to the gospels, the appearance or the death of John must have taken place in the year 28 or 29; whereas the war of Herod with the Nabatæan Aretas, the unfortunate result of which was, according to Josephus, to be regarded as a punishment for the execution of John, falls in the years 35 and 36 of the present era. Moreover, the complaints against Herod Antipas on account of his ncestuous marriage with his brother's wife, which are supposed to have occasioned the death of John, cannot have been made before then.[1] In fine, John might be an historical personality without there being any historical truth in what the gospels say of him. His connection with the story of Jesus is certainly due to astral considerations and the passages we quoted from Isaiah. We have, therefore, no reason to regard it as historical.

Space will not permit us to go more closely at this point into the astral features of the gospel narrative. Here there is a field open to future research which has as yet been touched only by a few isolated students, and from which historical theology may expect some unpleasant surprises. The examination of the gospel story from the astral-mythological point of view was begun by Dupuis, Volney, and Nork a century ago; and Niemojewski has more recently done very promising work in that field. Others will follow him, and furnish us with an entirely new key to the problems of the New Testament.[2] It will, however, always be difficult to say how far the story of Jesus is affected by astral relations and how far by the

---

[1] Compare Graetz, *Gesch. der Juden*, 1888, III, p. 278.
[2] See also Wilhelm Erbt, *Das Markusevangelium. Eine Untersuchung über die Form der Petruserinnerungen und die Geschichte der Urgemeinde*, 1911.

Old Testament, which of the two influences was the earlier, and whether the relevant passages of the Old Testament may not possibly themselves be influenced by astral considerations.

In general it may be said that astral mythology has furnished the framework or skeleton of the gospel story, and made it clear that many episodes which seem to be disconnected in the gospels owe their position to their place in the astral system. It suffices here to mention the importance of astral mythology in the interpretation of the gospels, and to show in the case of the Baptist how the two methods of interpretation work together. When the actual prejudice against astral mythology disappears, when a closer knowledge of the starry heavens than we now have places the student in a position to test these relations in detail, when it is generally recognised that astronomy and a knowledge of astrological language are at least as necessary for a correct understanding of the ancient east as philology is for critical theology, the time will have come for the last supports of the present purely historical conception of the gospels to break down, for the symbolical-mythical method to triumph completely over the present historical method, and for the "twilight of the gods" of critical theology. For the present theologians know what they are doing when they meet all such research with a disdainful smile, and declare it "unscientific." Their position in regard to it is much the same as the position of the early Church in regard to the astrological speculations of the Gnostics, which were met with the bitterest hostility, because they betrayed too much of the real origins of Christianity, and were the most dangerous obstacle to its representation as historical.

(d) *The Name of the Messiah.*—Meantime what we have seen will suffice to convince any impartial reader that, as we said, the figure of the saviour or redeemer in the gospels is really due to the prophet Isaiah, and that the character of the suffering servant of God, as described by the prophet, was in the mind of the evangelists.[1] His very name, Christus, the "anointed," can be traced to *Isaiah* (lxi, 1), where the prophet says that the spirit of the Lord rests on him, because Jahveh has "anointed" him (see also xlii, 1). It is, however, very significant that the saviour and servant of God everywhere submits to him, as if he were speaking the other's words, and Jahveh, the prophet, and the servant of God combine in one personality; just as in the gospel of Luke Jesus at once applies the word of the prophet to himself, and by its means unfolds the programme of his future work in his first public appearance in the synagogue. In the Jewish mind the "anointed" is the Messiah, which is merely the Hebrew for Christ. It is a fresh proof that the idea of a suffering Messiah was bound to begin early to build on the above passages in Isaiah, as soon as the announcement of the glad tidings was conceived as an announcement of the servant of God or of the Jahveh who was identified with him.

Now, in *Isaiah* vii, 14, the "son of the virgin" is named *Emmanuel*, and this is translated "God with us." That is also the meaning of the name *Jesus*, since in *Matthew* i, 21, the son of Mary receives this name, "that it might be fulfilled which was spoken of the Lord by the prophet, saying, Behold, a virgin shall be with child, and shall bring forth a son, and they shall call his name Emmanuel." In the Septuagint, as we know, Jesus is the Greek form of the Hebrew Jeschua, which in turn is the same as Jehoschua or Joshua. Joshua, however, means something like "Jahveh is salvation," "Jah-Help," and corresponds to the German name "Gotthilf." We read in Matthew: "And she shall bring forth a son, and thou shalt call his name Jesus; *for* he shall *save* his people from their sins." The name was fairly common among the Jews, and in this connection it is equivalent

---

[1] Also compare *Matthew* xii, 17.

among the Hellenistic Jews to the name Jason or Jasios, which again is merely a Greek version of Jesus.[1] How did it come about that the unusual name Emmanuel for the saviour of Israel was displaced by the commoner name Jesus?

Various reasons may be assigned for this. First, the fact that in the name Jesus the symbolic significance of salvation in the spiritual and bodily sense, as Isaiah attributed it to the servant of God, was perceived more clearly, especially among the dispersed Jews. Jaso (from *iasthai*, to heal) was the name of the daughter of the saver and physician Asclepios. He himself was in many places worshipped under the name of Jason. Thus we read in Strabo that temples and the cult of Jason were spread over the whole of Asia, Media, Colchis, Albania, and Iberia, and that Jason enjoyed divine honours also in Thessaly and on the Corinthian gulf, the cult of Phrixos, the ram or lamb, being associated with his (i, 2, 39). Justin tells us that nearly the whole of the west worshipped Jason and built temples to him (xlii, 3), and this is confirmed by Tacitus (*Annals*, vi, 34). Jason was also supposed to be the founder of the Lemnic festivity, which was celebrated yearly at the beginning of spring, and was believed to impart immortality to those who shared in it. Jasios (Jasion) was called Asclepios, or the "mediating god" related to him in this respect, and the conductor of souls, Hermes, at Crete and in the famous mysteries of Samothracia, which enjoyed the greatest repute about the beginning of the present era, and were frequented by high and low from all the leading countries.[2] Here again the idea of healing and saving is combined in the name, and would easily lead to the giving of the name to the saviour of the Jewish mystery-cult. Epiphanius (*Hæres.* c, xxix) clearly perceived this connection when he translated the name Jesus "healer" or "physician" (*curator*,

---

[1] Compare 2 *Macc.* iv.   [2] Preller, *Griech. Mythologie*, 1894, p. 862.

therapeutes). It is certain that this allusion to the healing activity of the servant of God and his affinity with the widely known Jason contributed not a little to the acceptance of the name of Jesus and to its apparent familiarity in ancient times.[1]

For the Jews there was the further and intimate relationship of the saviour to the Joshua of the Old Testament. As Joshua, as successor of Moses in the leadership, was believed to have conducted the Israelites from the bondage of Egypt into the "promised land," the land of their "fathers," their ancestral home, so they expected of the saviour of Israel that he would gather

---

[1] Jasius is, according to Vergil (*Æneid* iii, 168), the name of the old Italian god Janus Quirinus ("Father Jasius, from whom our race descends"). The oldest Roman bronze coinage, on one side of which there is a figure of Jasius or Janus, takes its name from this—*ass, eis, jes*. According to the *Odyssey* (xvii, 443), Jasus (Jaso) is the name of a powerful king of Cyprus, whose son Dmeter is identical with Diomedes, a name under which Jason was worshipped, with sacrifice of horses, by the Veneti on the Adriatic Sea. Under the name Ischenos, as the god was also called by the Veneti, Chronos (Saturn-Janus) was honoured every five years at Elis with the Ischenia (Chronia, Olympiada). Ischenos was supposed to have been the lover of Coronis, the mother of Asclepios (Jason). Jes Crishna was the name of the ninth incarnation of Jesnu, or Vishnu, whose animal is the fish, as in the case of Joshua, the son of the fish Nun, Ninus, a name which seems itself to have been written Nin-jes. Jes is a title of the sun. Jesse was the name of the sun-god of the southern Slavs. Jasny is in Slav the name of the bright sky, and Jas is still a proper name among the people of the Crimea and the Caucasus. The word also occurs in the name of Osiris=Jes-iris or Hes-iris (according to Hellenicus), in Hesus (the name of a Celtic god), in Isskander, as the Persians called Alexander, whom they revered as a world-saviour; and in the name of the lower-Italian people, the Jazygi, Jesygi, Jezidi, or Jesidi, which was related to the Veneti. Among the Mohammedans the word stands for "heretic." The Turks give the name to a detested nomadic race, which apparently worships Jesus Christ, though really Jes Crishna, and is distinguished in several ways both from the Mohammedans and the Christians. The mother of all these gods whose name contains Jes is a virgin (Maya, Mariamma, Maritala, Mariam, etc.); her symbol is the cross, the fish, or the lamb; her feast is the Huli (Jul), from which Cæsar took the name Julus or Julius when he was deified in the temple of Jupiter Ammon; and her history agrees in essential particulars with that of Jesus Christ. See the proofs in the important work of Alex. del Mar, *The Worship of Augustus Cæsar* (New York, 1900). In this, on a basis of thorough research, it is shown what a significance the Indian Jes had, as regards the chronological divisions, in the whole of the ancient world, especially in the reforms of the calendar under Cæsar and Augustus. Our historians and theologians ought to study this work very carefully. See also Volney's *Ruins*, p. 198.

together the dispersed Jews and lead them into the coveted land of their " fathers "—that is to say, of souls; to their heavenly home, whence the souls had originally come, and whither they return after death. He was therefore regarded as a second Joshua, and it was natural to give him the same name.

In the Epistle of Barnabas (about the year 115) Joshua is described as the "forerunner of Jesus in the flesh" (xii, 20). Justin also stresses the relationship of Jesus with the Joshua of the Old Testament, and observes that the latter, who was originally called Hosea (Auses), received the name of Joshua from Moses, not by chance, but with a view to Christ, whose predecessor in leadership he was (*Contra Tryph.*, cxiii). Eusebius traces not only the name Jesus, but also the name Christ, to Moses, saying: " The first to recognise the name Christ as one of especial veneration and repute was Moses. He appointed a man high-priest of god in the highest possible sense, and called him Christ. In this way he settled upon the dignity of the high-priesthood, which in his opinion far transcends all other human prerogatives, the name Christ, to add to its honour and splendour.[1] The same Moses, enlightened by God, also clearly knew the name Jesus, and honoured it with a great distinction. He gave the name Jesus, which had never been used before the time of Moses, to him who, he knew, would after his death—as a type and figure of Jesus—have dominion over all. Thus he gave to his successor, who had not previously been called Jesus—he was called Nave (Nun), as his parents had named him—the name Jesus, and meant by this to confer on him a distinction greater than the diadem of a king. He did this because this Jesus, the son of Nave, was a figure of our redeemer, who alone would, after Moses and the fulfilment of the symbolical service of God introduced by him, enter upon the

---

[1] This refers to *Lev.* iv, 16, where it is said in the Greek translation: *Ho hiereus, ho Christos* (the high-priest, the anointed).

dominion of the true and pure worship of God. Thus did Moses give to the two men who then stood out from the whole people in virtue and repute—namely, the high-priest and his successor as leader of the people—as their highest distinction, the name of our saviour Jesus Christ" (*Eccl. Hist.*, I, 3).

There is, however, in the Old Testament a high-priest Joshua, who plays a similar part to that of Jesus and of the successor of Moses; he also is supposed to gather the dispersed and imprisoned Jews, and lead them to their old home, Palestine, as was expected of the Messiah. We find him in *Ezra* iii, 2. According to *Zechariah* iii, the prophet sees the high-priest Joshua before the angel of Jahveh, and Satan standing at his right hand to accuse him. But the angel orders the dirty clothes to be removed from him and be replaced by festive garments, and promises him the continuance of the priesthood if he will walk in the ways of God. He calls him "a brand plucked from the burning," just as the saviour Asclepios is supposed to have been delivered from the burning womb of his mother by his father Apollo. In fact, Joshua himself is represented in the light of a saviour, when the angel speaks of him and his companions as "fore-signs of a wonderful future," and refers to his "servant the branch," who is to come, observing that Jahveh will wipe away in one day the guilt of the land. It is true that we at once learn that the "branch" is Zerubbabel, the leader of the Jews of David's race, in whom the prophet saw that "branch" which Isaiah (xi, 1) had referred to the coming Messiah. Nevertheless, in *Zech.* vi, 11, the prophet puts a crown on the head of Joshua, as well as Zerubbabel, and they are placed on a common throne. But the Greek text of the prophet was altered, as the great hopes entertained of Zerubbabel were not fulfilled; the name of Zerubbabel was struck out, the plural (vi, 12) changed into the singular, and Joshua alone was represented as crowned, and was raised to the rank of the expected Messiah.[1] Thus the two Joshuas, the successor of Moses and the high-priest, blend into one person; the name "Jesus" received a Messianic significance, and came to be used for the "branch" of the prophet Isaiah.

There was, therefore, not merely a *pre-Christian Christ*, as Gunkel admits, "a belief in the death and resurrection of Christ in Judæo-syncretist circles,"[2] but there was also a *pre-Christian Jesus*, as Jesus and Christ were only two different names for the suffering and rising servant of God, the root of David in Isaiah; and the two might be combined when one wished to express the high-priesthood or the Messianic character of Jesus. *Jesus was merely the general name of the saviour and redeemer;* and if on two critical occasions in the history of Israel a Jesus had saved the people and led it from abroad into its true home, it was natural to suppose that on the third occasion also the work would be done by a Jesus.[3] Now, if his very name thus becomes ambiguous, what is there left of the historical Jesus?[4]

(e) *The Topography of the Gospels.*

I. NAZARETH.

The historical Jesus is said to have been born in Nazareth. This, however, is, in turn, anything but

---

[1] Stade, *Gesch. des Volkes Israel*, 1888, II, p. 126, *note*; Hühn, *Die messianischen Weissagungen des israel. Volkes*, 1889, p. 62.

[2] *Zum religionsgeschichtl. Verständnis des Neuen Testaments*, 1903, p. 82.

[3] The possible connection of Jesus with the two Joshuas of the Old Testament has been discussed by Robertson and by M. Brückner in his *Der sterbende und auferstehende Gottheiland*, although the latter refrains from drawing any "particular conclusions as to the pre-Christian significance of a Joshua-Jesus" (p. 39). These relations, therefore, cannot be so foolish as they have been represented when we find them discussed by a theologian in a popular religious work intended for general circulation. The excellent Hebraist Prof. T. K. Cheyne writes in the *Hibbert Journal* (April, 1911), p. 658: "The direct evidence for the divine name Jeshua or Joshua in pre-Christian times is both scant and disputable. Yet I incline (on grounds of my own) to agree with Prof. Drews in his view of the main point in dispute." Cf. p. 662: "In my opinion Prof. Drews and his authorities are right in the main."

[4] Consider, also, the admission of Zimmern that the name "Jesus" might "very well be unhistorical," in his *Zum Streit um die Christusmythe*, p. 4.

certain. It may be a matter of chance that neither the Old Testament nor Josephus nor the Talmud mentions the place; and, except in the gospels, the name is unknown until the fourth century (Eusebius, Jerome, and Epiphanius). But the statement of Weiss, that it "cannot be denied that it was firmly believed by the Christians of the first century that Jesus came from Nazareth" (p. 21), is wholly unjustified, and is based only on the unproved assumption that the gospels already existed then in their present form. On the other hand, it is entirely inadmissible that the sect of the Nazaræans, as the followers of Jesus are first called in *Acts* (xxiv, 3), took their name from the supposed birthplace of their founder, as Nazareth played scarcely any part in the life of Jesus which was known to them. It is true that Matthew (ii, 23) says that Jesus received his epithet "the Nazaraios" from Nazareth, and he appeals to a passage in the prophets. But no such passage is to be found, quite apart from the fact that in that case he ought to be called a "Nazarethene," or else Nazareth, his supposed birthplace, ought to be called Nazara; this is, indeed, found in some of the old manuscripts, and has been affirmed, but merely in order to harmonise it with the name Nazoraios, Nazaraios, or Nazarene, which is given to Jesus in the gospels.

The fact is that the name only occurs in the latest stratum of the gospels (*Matthew* ii, 23; *Luke* iv, 16), whereas the older stratum (*Mark* vi, 1; *Matthew* xiii, 54) merely speaks of his "native town." *Mark* i, 9, is clearly only an amplification of the older reading of *Matthew* iii, 13, where it is simply said that Jesus came "from Galilee"; and *Matthew* iv, 13, and xxi, 11, are plainly interpolations, since Nazareth has not previously been mentioned. The same must be said of *Matthew* xxvi, 71, where it is written "Jesus of Nazareth," in accordance with the earlier expression of the evangelist. On the other hand, no theologian will deny that the story of the childhood in

Luke is of late date. In Mark Jesus is called "the Nazarene" in i, 24; x, 47; xiv, 67; and xvi, 6, without any statement that this indicates the place of his origin. It may, therefore, just as well have a different meaning, and may be a sect-name.

This is the view of William B. Smith. In his opinion the name can be traced to the ancient root N-Z-R, which means something like watcher, protector, guardian, saviour. Hence Jesus the Nazoræan or Nazarene was Jesus the Protector, just as Jahveh,[1] or the archangel Michael, the "angel-prince," who often takes the place of the Messiah, is known as the "protector of Israel," its spokesman with God, and its deliverer from all its cares (*Daniel* xix, 13, and xii, 1; *Gen.* xlviii, 16); the rabbinical Metatron also plays this part of protector and supporter of the Jewish people, and is regarded as the "angel of redemption," especially of the damned suffering in hell. The followers of Jesus will, therefore, have called themselves Nazoræans because they primarily conceived the expected Messiah in the sense of a Michael or Metatron, a protector; that is, at all events, more probable than that they took their name from the place Nazareth, with which they had no close connection.[2] It is not at all impossible

---

[1] *Psalm* 121. The fact that the protector is here called *schomer*, not *nozer*, has nothing to do with the matter, any more than the fact that the Palestinians of the time about the birth of Christ did not use the Hebrew *nazar* for "the protector," but the Aramaic *ne'tar*: it is well known that the language of a sect tends to preserve antique words, and we are concerned here, not with the word itself, but its meaning.

[2] Smith, *The Pre-Christian Jesus*, 1906. Also see his article on "The Real Ancestry of Jesus" in the *Open Court*, January, 1910, p. 12, and the article "The Nazarene," by Dr. P. Carus, the editor, in the same number (p. 26). Differently from the German theologians, who cannot speak disdainfully enough of Smith's hypotheses, on philological grounds, Carus admits the possibility of that origin of the name, and regards the existence of a place called Nazareth at the time of Jesus as improbable. Indeed, in his book *The Pleroma: An Essay on the Origins of Christianity* (1910), he says that it is absolutely impossible that the Nazarene could mean the man from Nazareth (p. 46). Moreover, Schmiedel has recently maintained against Weinel in the *Protestantenblatt*, 1910, Nr. 17, p. 438, that Smith's hypothesis is philologically admissible. Hence the charge of "gross ignorance of the Semitic languages" which Weinel brings against Smith is quite unjustified.

that the place Nazareth took its name from the sect of the Nazaræans, instead of the reverse, as is admitted by so distinguished a scholar as W. Nestle.[1] According to the Assyriologist Haupt (of Baltimore), Nazareth was a new name for the older Hethlon (*Ezech.* xlvii, 15), or Hittalon or Hinnathon, which means "protection," and has reference to the protected position of Nazareth among the hills. In that case it would be natural for the evangelist to choose a place called "protection" as the birthplace of the "protector."

According to *Mark* x, 47, the blind Bartimeus, hearing that "Jesus the Nazarene" is passing by, calls out to him, "Jesus, thou son of David." It is possible that we have here another indication of the original meaning of the name. In Isaiah *nazar* is the Hebrew word for the "branch," called *zemah* in Zechariah; and he is called in Isaiah "a rod from the stem of Jesse"—that is to say, a "son (descendant) of David." May it not be that the expression Nazaræan or Nazarene also contains an allusion to the "branch," as Robertson suggests?[2] If the figure of Jesus, and even his name, as we have seen, are derived from Isaiah, it is natural to assume that his secondary name "the Nazaræan" may also be traced to the same source, and that in the name of his sect there is a relation to the prophet's branch of David. "He grew up as a tender plant, a *nazar*" (*Isaiah* liii, 2); from this a later age has made him a "Nazarene" and put his birth at Nazareth.[3] This would also afford a

---

[1] *Südwestdeutsche Schulblätter*, 1910, Heft 4 and 5, p. 163. M. Brückner also says, in regard to Smith's hypothesis: "His proof that the epithet 'Nazaræan' applied to Jesus in *Matthew* ii, 23, cannot have been derived from Nazareth, but was the name of a pre-Christian Jewish sect, especially *deserves attention*" (p. 47). In Hugo Winckler we read: "From the word *necer* comes the name of the religion of those who believe in the 'saviour'—the Nazarene-Christians or Nazaræans. Nazareth as the home of Jesus is merely a confirmation of his character as saviour for the symbolising tendency" (*Ex oriente lux*, Band ii, 1906, p. 59, *note*). Cf. also Winckler, *Die babylonische Geisteskultur* (1907), p. 147.

[2] Cf. also Alfred Jeremias, *Das Alte Testament im Lichte des alten Orients*, 2 Aufl., 1906, pp. 353, 577.

[3] Possibly *nazar* also has an astral significance, as the Hyades in

simple explanation of the curious reference in *Matthew* ii, 23, to some unknown passage in the prophets, and we need not suppose that Nazareth only became the name of a place at a later date; it may have existed already, and have been chosen as the birthplace of Jesus because of its connection with *nazar*.

We are disposed to believe that the sect of the Nazoræans was originally the same as the Nasiræans, the "initiated" or "holy," who were distinguished from the rest of the Jews by their abstinence from oil and wine and the use of the razor, and by the rigour of their lives; and that the Nazoræans were those Nasiræans who conceived the expected Messiah in the sense of the *nazar* of Isaiah. In *Lamentations* (iv, 7) the "pure" are called "Nazarites" [Nazaræans], and Josephus writes Nazaraios in *Antiquities* iv, 4, 4, but Naziraios in xix, 6, 1.

It is admitted that the origin of Jesus from Nazareth is in contradiction to the belief that the Messiah was to be born in Bethlehem as a shoot from David. But it is not a contradiction between the Messianic dogma and a "hard fact of history," as Weiss says (p. 22); it is due simply to the fact that the man of the race of David is called by the prophet a "branch" (*nazar*); and, when men began to make an historical person of Jesus, they found the agreement of the word with Nazareth a very welcome opportunity to conceal the real origin of Jesus in Isaiah. The contradiction gave no more trouble to the early Christians than the circumstance that possibly there was no such place as Nazareth at the time of Jesus. There was also probably no such place as Capernaum, Emmaus, Bethesda, Nain, Gethsemane, or Golgotha. And if our opponents say that, if that were so, the story of Jesus would have betrayed its character as fiction, and a Jew would have seen the defect at once, we may remind them that the massacre of the children at Bethlehem, the

---

Taurus have the form of a branch; and Orion, in which we have already suspected the Baptist, seems to bring the "twig" (Fuhrmann).

wandering about of people to be included in the census, the astronomically impossible eclipse of the sun, which is supposed to have lasted three hours, at the death of Jesus, and many other details, did not give the evangelists the least concern. Even to-day the pious reader of the Bible is not disquieted by these things. Nor was there any fear of Jewish objection to the derivation of Jesus from Nazareth, because the process of the historicisation of the Christ-myth was only completed at a time when no historical evidence whatever of the real origin of Jesus could be adduced, since, as we have seen, the oldest gospel uses the name Nazaræan probably not to indicate the birthplace of Jesus, but as a sect-name with reference to the "protector" or "saviour" and the *nazar* of Isaiah.[1]

II. JERUSALEM.

So far, then, from the name Nazaræan, or Nazoræan, or Nazarene, being derived from the town of Nazareth, we must say that this is the *least probable* of all possible suggestions. The names of places in the gospels, in fact, afford no evidence whatever of the historicity of Jesus, since the whole topography of the life of Jesus is in its main lines borrowed from Isaiah and other prophets. So it was inevitable that, as soon as the process began to be regarded from the historical point of view, the great drama of the suffering and death of the servant of God and the associated redemption of mankind should be located in Jerusalem. As Luke says (xiii, 33—see also *Psalm* cxvi, 14–19) : "It cannot be that a prophet perish out of Jerusalem." It is the unvarying theme of the prophets that Jerusalem will be glorified by Jahveh, and become the centre of the world's history (*Isaiah* lxii, 7). In the prophet Zechariah we read of the inhabitants of the city :—

And they shall look upon me whom they have pierced,

---

[1] Compare Robertson, *Christianity and Mythology*, p. 311, and P. van Dyk's *Krit. Kommentar zu den Evangelien*, pp. 28 and 152.

and they shall mourn for him, as one mourneth for his only son, and shall be in bitterness for him, as one that is in bitterness for his firstborn.

In that day shall there be a great mourning *in Jerusalem*, as the mourning of Hadadrimmon in the valley of Megiddon.

And the land shall mourn, every family apart; the family of the house of David apart, and their wives apart (xii, 10–12).

On Jerusalem the eyes of the whole nation are bent. There will their desire be consummated. From there will salvation spread over the earth, and judgment be meted out to men (*Isaiah* ii).

"Behold, I lay in Zion for a foundation a stone, a tried stone, a precious corner-stone, a sure foundation" (*Isaiah* xxviii, 16). "And he shall be for a sanctuary, for a stone of stumbling and for a rock of offence to both the houses of Israel, for a gin and for a snare to the inhabitants of Jerusalem. And many among them shall stumble, and fall, and be broken, and be snared, and be taken" (*Isaiah* viii, 14, 15—see also xxviii, 13). So the evangelist makes Jesus say, with reference to the prophet: "The stone which the builders rejected, the same is become the head of the corner [*Psalm* cxviii, 22]...... Therefore I say unto you: The kingdom of God shall be taken from you and given to a nation bringing forth the fruits thereof. And whosoever shall fall on this stone shall be broken; but on whomsoever it shall fall, it will grind him to powder" (*Matthew* xxi, 42–44). In *Isaiah* the prophet speaks in the same vein to those who held Jahveh holy, his "disciples": "Behold, I and the children whom the Lord hath given me are for signs and for wonders in Israel from the Lord of hosts, which dwelleth in mount Zion" (viii, 18). "He that is left in Zion, and he that remaineth in Jerusalem, shall be called holy, even every one that is written among the living in Jerusalem" (iv, 3). So the Tarsic tent-maker Paul calls the Christians in Jerusalem "the saints"; and we are reminded of *Acts*, of the Pentecostal gathering, and the first Christian propaganda, when it is written :—

> As one whom his mother comforteth, so will I comfort you; and ye shall be comforted in Jerusalem......
> It shall come, that I will gather all nations and tongues; and they shall come, and see my glory.
> And I will set a sign among them, and I will send those that escape of them unto the nations, to Tarshish [!], Pul, and Lud......to the isles afar off, that have not heard my fame, neither have seen my glory; and they shall declare my glory among the Gentiles.
> And they shall bring all your brethren for an offering unto the Lord......to my holy mountain Jerusalem, saith the Lord, as the children of Israel bring an offering in a clean vessel into the house of the Lord.
> And I will also take of them for priests (*Isaiah* lxvi, 13-21).

In what does this comfort consist that Jahveh promises to his people? He himself will come as the king of Israel, and lead his own towards Jerusalem: "How beautiful upon the mountains are the feet of him that bringeth good tidings, that publisheth peace; that bringeth good tidings of good, that publisheth salvation; that saith unto Zion, Thy God reigneth"! (*Isaiah* lii, 7— compare xii, 6). "Go through, go through the gates; prepare ye the way of the people; cast up, cast up the highway; gather out the stones......Say ye to the daughter of Zion, Behold, thy salvation cometh; behold, his reward is with him, and his work before him. And they shall call them, The holy people, The redeemed of the Lord; and thou shalt be called, Sought out, A city not forsaken" (*Isaiah* lxii, 10—see also xxvi, 2). The prophet refers the words immediately to Jahveh. But we have already seen how Jahveh is constantly identified with the figure of the servant of God and redeemer. How easily might the story of the entry into Jerusalem develop from these passages!

"Rejoice greatly, O daughter of Zion; shout, O daughter of Jerusalem," says the prophet Zechariah (ix, 9), in similar words to those of Isaiah: "Behold, thy king cometh unto thee: he is just, and having salvation; lowly and riding upon an ass, and upon a colt the foal of an ass." Hence, in *Matthew* xxi, 2, Jesus bids the disciples bring him the ass and its foal that they shall find, the evangelist having in mind also the words of *Genesis* xlix, 11: "Binding his foal unto the vine, and his ass's colt unto the choice vine." And Mark (xi, 2) adds to the words of Jesus that no man had yet ridden the ass, because it is said in *Numbers* (xix, 2) that a faultless cow "upon which never came yoke" shall be brought to the priest Eleazar.[1]

The hosanna of the people and their cry, "Blessed is he that cometh in the name of the Lord" (*Matthew* xxi, 9), are taken from the 118th Psalm: "Save now, I beseech thee, O Lord ["Save now" is the meaning of the Hebrew *hoschia-na*, which the evangelist seems wrongly to have taken to be a cry of joy!]: Blessed is he that cometh in the name of the Lord" (26). The words that Jesus is supposed to have said about his followers on entering into Jerusalem, "If these should hold their peace, the stones would immediately cry out" (*Luke* xix, 40), are based on the prophet Habakkuk: "For the stone shall cry out of the wall" (ii, 11). Even the name "Gethsemane," which is nowhere else found as the name of a place, is, as Smith observes, inspired by Isaiah. The name means "oil-press," or "olive-press." It seems to refer to *Isaiah* lxiii, 2, where it is said of Jahveh: "Wherefore art thou red in thine apparel, and thy garments like him that treadeth in the press [Hebrew *gath*]?" "I have trodden the press alone," says Jahveh; "and of the people there was none with me; for I will tread them in mine anger and trample them in my fury; and their blood shall be sprinkled upon my garments, and I will stain all my raiment. For the day of vengeance is in mine heart, and the year of my redeemed is come.

---

[1] Compare *Deut.* xxi, 3.

And I looked, and there was none to help; and I wondered that there was none to uphold; therefore mine own arm brought salvation unto me." Here we have a clear relation to the abandonment of Jesus on Gethsemane and his comforting by an angel (*Luke* xxii, 43), and the reference to the blood (*Luke* xxii, 44) accords. Jahveh's vengeance on the Gentiles is transformed in the gospels into the contrary act of the self-oblation of Jesus; and whereas in Isaiah it is the wine of anger and vengeance that flows from the press, here it is the oil of healing and salvation that pours from the press (*gath*) over the peoples.

Like Gethsemane, Golgotha, "the place of skulls," is another place that we cannot verify. It is possible that the name is connected with the pillars (*golgoi*) of the western-Asiatic mother of the gods, and points to an ancient Jebusitic centre of the cult of Adonis under the name Golgos. But possibly there is an astral element, seeing that Matthew (xxvii, 33) makes the word mean "place of skulls" (from the Hebrew *gulguleth*, the skull), and suggests the skull or beaker (skull as a drinking vessel) which is found under the vernal cross in the heavens.[1]

III. GALILEE.

According to the gospels, the Saviour does not at first live in the holy city. Whence did he come? Again we find the answer in Isaiah: "I have raised up one from the north" (xli, 25). In the north is Galilee, of which it is said in the prophet: "At the first he lightly afflicted the land of Zebulun and the land of Naphtali, and afterward did more grievously afflict her by the way of the sea, beyond Jordan, in Galilee of the nations. The people that walked in darkness have seen a great light; they that dwell in the land of the shadow of death, upon

---

[1] Niemojewski, p. 420. Reflect on the familiar pictures of a cup or skull at the foot of the crucifix.

them hath the light shined " (*Isaiah* ix, 1-2). That, in point of fact, Galilee was generally regarded as the land from which the Messiah would come is confirmed by the Talmud, which says that, as the Galileans were the first to be driven into exile, they should be the first to receive consolation, in harmony with the law of compensation which governs all the divine plans.[1] Hence the following words of the prophet might be referred to the Galileans and their rejoicing : " They joy before thee according to the joy in harvest, and as men rejoice when they divide the spoil......For unto us a child is born, unto us a son is given ; and the government shall be upon his shoulder : and his name shall be called Wonderful, Counsellor, The mighty God, The everlasting Father, The Prince of Peace. Of the increase of his government and peace there shall be no end, upon the throne of David, and upon his kingdom, to order it, and to establish it with judgment and with justice from henceforth even for ever " (*Isaiah* ix, 3, 6, 7).

Hence it is the word of the prophet, not a " hard fact of history," that demands the birth of the Saviour in Galilee. Then Nazareth, with its relation to *nazar*, occurred at once as the proper birthplace of Jesus, as soon as men began to conceive the episode historically.

Astral considerations may have co-operated. Galilee, from *galil*=circle, connects with the zodiacal circle which the sun traverses; even in the prophet the Saviour is identified with the sun. The " people that walk in darkness " and that " dwell in the land of the shadow " might easily be identified with the " familiar spirits " of whom Isaiah speaks (viii, 19), in whom " there is no light," who " pass through " the land " hardly bestead and hungry ; and it shall come to pass, that when they shall be hungry, they shall fret themselves and curse their king and their God, and look upward ;

---

[1] Sohar on *Exodus*, quoted by Gfrörer, *Das Jahrhundert des Heils*, 1838, ii, p. 231.

and they shall look unto the earth, and behold trouble
and darkness, dimness of anguish, and they shall be
driven to darkness." They suggest the souls in the
nether world, the stars in their course below the celestial
equator, which "rejoice" at the birth of the "great
light" at the winter solstice and are led to their time of
brilliancy. On this view Galilee of the Gentiles (Galil-
ha-goim) coincides with the lower half, the "water-
region," of the zodiac, in which are found the aquatic
signs of the southern fish, Aquarius, the Fishes, the
Whale, and Eridanus.[1] We thus understand why "Galilee,
the way to the sea, the land by the Jordan," plays so
great a part in the story of Jesus; it was bound to be
recognised in a Messianic age. Hence this "watery
region" of the sky is the chief theatre of the Saviour's
life; hence in the gospels the "Sea of Galilee," the Sea
of Genesareth, and the many names of places in the
district. For the Greeks and Romans they had no
ulterior significance, and were mere names, but much
like the names of places in Homer or Vergil, or the
description of the voyage of the Argonaut by Apollonius
of Rhodes. It is incredible that von Soden should seek
a proof of the historicity of the gospel narrative in these
names.[2]

[1] In truth, Zebulun, according to Genesis xlix, relates to the sign of the
zodiac Capricorn and Naphtali to Aries, both of which belong to the water-
region of the zodiac, the dark part of the year. (Cf. A. Jeremias, *Das Alte
Testament im Lichte des alten Orients*, p. 398.) According to M. Müller,
galil means, in a derivative from the Coptic, the "water-wheel." A
water-wheel might (according to Fuhrmann) be traced in the constellation Orion, the spokes being represented by the four chief stars and
the axis by the stars of the belt, the wheel being set in motion by the
falling "water" of the Milky Way. In so far as Orion is the hanging
figure of the 22nd Psalm, we may note that the latter is a *galil* (Galilean),
and as the constellation Orion is, as we saw, astrally related to the *nazar*
(the Hyades), the birth of the Saviour in Nazareth might be deduced
from this. See Niemojewski, pp. 161 and 193.

[2] Work quoted, p. 21. Herr von Soden's attempt to prove the
historicity of Jesus from the "smell of the soil of Palestine" seems to me
much the same as if one were to conclude that Tell was historical because
of the many place-names in the legend. A Swiss hotel-keeper might do
that, but—a student of history!

We have already seen that the Jordan has an astral significance in the gospels, and corresponds to the celestial Eridanus (Egyptian, *iero* or *iera*=the river) or to the Milky Way. It may be the same with other supposed names of places. In regard to the most important of them all, Capernaum, Steudel has called attention to *Zech.* xiii, 1, where it is said: "In that day there shall be a fountain opened to the house of David and to the inhabitants of Jerusalem for sin and for uncleanness," and reminds us that in his *Jewish War* (iii, 10, 8) Josephus mentions a "very strong" and fertilising spring "which is called Capharnaum by the inhabitants of the district." When we read in Josephus the description of the fish-abounding Sea of Genesareth and the country about it, with its beauty and charm, its palms, nuts, figs, olives, and fruit-trees of all kinds, we feel that no other "knowledge of the locality" was needed in order to "invent" the whole regional background of the life of Jesus with the aid of these indications.

(*f*) *The Chronology of the Gospels.*—Not only is the topography of the gospels clearly based on Isaiah, but, as we have already seen, the chronological frame of the events described in them presents very serious difficulties. Many names of supposed historical persons in the gospels seem to have been originally of an astral character, and to have been later pressed into the historical scheme; such are Herod, the high-priests Annas and Caiaphas, and Pilate. There is hardly anything related about them that agrees with the facts known to us in other ways, but it agrees very well with astral features and constellations.[1]

---

[1] Niemojewski, pp. 367, 370. The high-priest Annas, who is supposed to have held office with Caiaphas, is identical in name with the prophetess Anna (Sib-Zi-Anna of the Babylonians, Anna Perenna of the Romans), and according to Niemojewski (p. 367) corresponds to the star γ in Gemini, but according to Fuhrmann to the constellation Cassiopeia which dwells "in the temple," or at the highest point of the Milky Way. Caiaphas is clearly, in that case, the constellation Cepheus, near Cassiopeia; and the two names were subsequently applied to the Jewish

The conception of the just one as "hanging" and the symbolic transformation of the martyr's stake into the mystic form of the cross as a sign of fire and life, corresponding to the constellation Orion, suggested the idea of making the servant of God and life-bringer, who dies on the cross, be put to death by the Romans, not the Jews, as the Jews killed the blasphemer by stoning. This settled the period for the story of Jesus. It can also be imagined that the figure of Augustus had some influence on this; it would be natural to oppose to the Roman lord of the world, whose reign opened a new era of history and who was greeted as saviour and redeemer of the world, the true saviour in the person of Jesus, born in his time.[1]

Then there was, perhaps, a more general reason for fixing the time of the death of Jesus. According to Luke's gospel, Jesus must have died in the year 29. As he died in the same year as John, and John, according to the indications in Josephus, died shortly before the year 36, Keim[2] and others have assigned the death of the saviour to that year. Keim recalls the general feeling of strain in the Roman Empire in the year 34, and with this he connects the appearance of the Baptist. At Rome the death of Tiberius was expected daily. The Parthians threatened from the east, and their prince Artabanes had wrested Armenia from the Romans and turned his attention to Syria. About the same time great events were announced in Egypt, which seemed to indicate the opening of a new epoch. In the year 34 it was believed that the fabulous phœnix, which came every five hundred years to Heliopolis to burn itself and rise again rejuvenated, had been seen. The phœnix was connected with the Messianic

---

high-priests on account of the similarity. The Talmud enumerates the names of the principal men who directed the sanhedrim from Antigonas (B.C. 250) until the destruction of the temple; a Caiaphas is not to be found among the number. He was high priest for eighteen years; but this also is not mentioned in the Talmud, although it gives the names of all who have been high priests for ten years or more.

[1] Compare Del Mar, *The Worship of Augustus Cæsar*.
[2] *Geschichte Jesu*, 1873.

expectation of the Jews. Just as the marvellous bird destroyed itself at the close of each world-epoch and re-created itself, so the Messiah was expected as the creator of a new world.[1] The whole world was discussing the extraordinary event at the time, and it may have contributed to the locating at that period of the death of the saviour and his glorious resurrection from the flames of the old world.

Further, the Hindoo Krishna, who, as saviour, conqueror of dragons, and "crucified," is in many respects as like Jesus as one egg is like another, was said to have predicted at his death that the fourth world-period, Kaliyuga, the iron-age, would commence thirty-six years afterwards, and men would become wicked and miserable. For the Jews the year 70, in which Jerusalem was taken and the temple, the national sanctuary and centre of the faith, destroyed, was the turning-point in the history of the world. It was the year of the great judgment on the Jews, as Isaiah had predicted, the coming of which the saviour was supposed to forecast. Reckoning backwards, this again gives the year 34 as that of the death of Jesus, and agrees with the idea that the gospels reached their present form in the first quarter of the second century, in the terrible period when the Jews and Christians began to separate, as Lublinski has so vividly shown.[2]

---

[1] We may recall that Joseph, who was believed to have been sold into Arabia, gone from there to Egypt, and married the daughter of the priest at On (Heliopolis), bore in Egypt the name Zaphnat Phanech ("biding of the phœnix"—that is to say, of the sun or year-god—in the five Epagomena or intercalary days during which the old year passes into the new). Joseph was a kind of Adonis or Tammuz; he was a foretype of the Messiah, and is called even in Apollodorus (iii, 14, 4) a "son of the Phœnix," just as Joshua is called a son of the dove (Semiramis-Mirjam), and Asclepios a son of the crow, from whose burning womb he was delivered. See Gruppe, *Griech. Mythologie*, ii, p. 144, where it is suggested that the myth of the birth of Asclepios may be a version of the legend of the phœnix. Jesus also seems originally to have had a dove for mother, as the baptism in the Jordan was, according to some, the act of birth of the saviour; and the Holy Ghost, who descended on him in fire and flame in the form of a dove, was represented in certain Gnostic sects as "the mother of Jesus" (*The Christ-Myth*).

[2] Compare A. Kniepf, *Zehn Thesen zur natürlichen Welt- und Lebens-*

Whether this is so or not, we have no certain date of the death of the saviour, and every attempt to reconcile the contradictory indications is futile.[1] These facts, however, enable us to suspect why, when the myth of the servant of God began to assume historical form, his death was fixed about the year 30 of our era. The life of Jesus may for a long time have been told unhistorically as far as any definite period of time is concerned; possibly it was originally astral, as Niemojewski believes. We can only repeat that from the chronological point of view also there is no need whatever to take the supposed historical data of the gospels seriously. That is unfortunate for those who represent them as history, as they for the most part derive their material from the gospels alone. It is quite time to listen to the learned Jews (Graetz, Joel, Chwolson, Lippe, Lublinski) who say that in point of fact it is the conditions of the second, not the first, century that have provided the framework of the gospel story in detail. The Gnostic sects, from which Christianity originated, knew at first only an astral Jesus, whose mythic "history" was composed of passages from the prophets, Isaiah, the twenty-second Psalm, and *Wisdom*. In this they were not far removed from the Pharisees, who, being "believers in fate," as we know from Josephus and the Talmud, also favoured astrological ideas.[2] It was only after the destruction of Jerusalem, when the

anschauung, 1903, p. 34. Notice also the story of Jesus, the son of Ananus, told by Josephus, which happened shortly before the destruction of Jerusalem (see further below), and may also be a reason for putting the death of the evangelical Jesus about that time.

[1] This applies also to the attempt to determine the date of the crucifixion that is made from time to time on astronomical grounds. To all such speculations we may say that eclipses, earthquakes, and other natural catastrophes are part of the standing requisites in descriptions of the birth and death of saviours, such as Krishna, Buddha, Dionysos, etc. Even at Cæsar's birth a remarkable star is supposed to have announced the event, and an earthquake is said to have taken place at his death. Much the same is related about the birth and death of Augustus, whose life, moreover, is made to resemble that of the divine saviour in many respects by contemporary writers. See Alex. del Mar, pp. 92, 99, 124, 162, and 169.

[2] Cf. E. Bischof, *Babylonisch-Astrales im Weltbilde des Talmud im Midrasch*, 1907.

Pharisees abandoned these speculations and adhered strictly to the law — indeed, expressly combated the fancies of astral mythology—and when the new faith spread to wider circles which did not understand the astral meaning of the Jesus-myth and regarded the myth as a real history, that the knowledge of the astral features was gradually lost, and people began to seek standing-ground for the story of Jesus in the real course of events.

The Gnostics of the second century, however, still held in principle the astral character of the story of the saviour, and possibly we have an echo of the increasing struggle against the narrowness and one-sidedness of the Pharisaic view by those who were "initiated" into the "mysteries" of the astral doctrine in the words of Jesus to the scribes: "Woe unto you, lawyers, for ye have taken away the key of knowledge; ye entered not in yourselves, and them that were entering in ye hindered" (*Luke* xi, 52).

(*g*) *The Pre-Christian Jesus.*—We saw that there was a pre-Christian Christ as well as a pre-Christian Jesus. In both cases Isaiah furnished the immediate occasion for the figure. There was a belief in the suffering and the death of the "servant of God," his resurrection and exaltation by God, and the spiritual and corporal redemption of men by this means, as the Jews expected of their Messiah. The servant of God, it is true, was not himself, in his human lowliness and poverty, to be the Messiah, for with the Messiah was associated the idea of a worldly conqueror triumphing over the enemies of Israel, restoring the power of David, a powerful lord of life and death, descending from heaven to judge sinners, to found a new heaven and new earth, and inaugurating a golden age for his followers (*Isaiah* lxv). But his appearance on earth was to be the *condition* for the coming of the Messiah, and his death was to be the great expiation for the guilt of men, without which the Jews could not share the glory of the Messianic kingdom (*Isaiah* lviii). The figure of the servant of God, moreover, sometimes blended with that of Jahveh himself, and it was he who was to hold the last judgment and lead his people into the coveted kingdom (*Isaiah* xiii, 7; xxv, xxvi, xxxi, etc.); at other times he seemed to be a special being, beside or below Jahveh, the "son of God," or the representative of "the just," who, according to Plato and *Wisdom*, endure much from their enemies on earth, but are raised to divine heights after death and attain eternal life. It was a view closely akin to the belief, among non-Jewish peoples, in a suffering, dying, and rising saviour-god, celebrated in secret cults and represented by various sects. It is natural to suspect that the idea of the Messiah's mission derived from Isaiah was a secret doctrine among the Jews, and had its chief representatives in peculiarly mystic circles or sects apart from the official Jewish religion.

Possibly the Nazoræans or Nazaræans, as Epiphanius calls the first Christians, were such a sect, as he observes that they existed *before* Christ, and knew nothing of Christ—that is to say, of an historical man of that name (*Hæres*, xviii, 29). It is true that he only affirms this of the Nasaræans, a Jewish sect that lived east of the Jordan, practised circumcision, observed the Sabbath and the Jewish festivals, but rejected animal food and sacrifices, and regarded the Pentateuch as a forgery,[1] and takes the greatest care to distinguish between the two sects, the Nazoræans and the Nasaræans. But it is not easy to believe that they were really distinct, and the confusion of his text at the relevant passage is due, Smith suspects (*The Pre-Christian Jesus*), merely to his attempt to obscure the real situation.

According to Epiphanius, the Nazoræans were closely related to the Jessæans; indeed, the name is said to have

---

[1] According to Nilus, a younger contemporary of Epiphanius (x, 430), they were not Christians (in the current sense), but a sort of Rechabites, living in tents, avoiding wine and other luxuries, and living an extremely simple life. This would agree with our idea of a coalescence of the Nazaræans and Nasiræans.

been originally a name of the Nazoræans. Epiphanius leaves it open whether they took their name from Jesus or from Jesse (Isai), father of David and ancestor of the Messiah. Either is possible, since the Hebrew name Joshua can be rendered either Jesus or Jessus in Greek, as is seen in the relation of Maschiach and Messiah. Possibly, however, we have in their name (Jessæans = Jesaiæans [Jessaioi]) an echo of the name of the prophet to whom they owed their particular conception of the suffering Messiah. The name Isaiah is, moreover, closely connected with the name Jesus, Jehoschua, or Joshua, and means "Jahveh salvation." "God-salvation" would, of course, be just as fitting a name for the "saviour-god" as "God-Help."

Further, the Jessæans or Jessenes must have been closely connected with the Essæans or Essenians who, like the Therapeuts of Egypt, cultivated a mystic esoteric doctrine, and cured disease and expelled devils by the magic of names. The "servant of God" in Isaiah was also a physician of the soul, a healer, and an expeller of demons. When, therefore, Epiphanius observes that the name Jesus means in Hebrew *curator* or *therapeutes* (healer or physician), it is not at all improbable that the Essæans worshipped their god under the name Jesus or Joshua.

In the gospels (*Mark* ix, 39; *Luke* ix, 49; x, 17), in *Acts* (iii, 16), and in the *Epistle of James* (v, 14), we read that the name Jesus had a miraculous power, and the Talmud also says that about the end of the first century disease was healed in the name of Jesus. According to Weiss, this is " one of the strongest proofs that he was known to Jews and Gentiles as a successful exorcist " (p. 19); and Weinel charges Smith with " a poor knowledge of the subject," because he concludes from this that the name Jesus must from the first have been the name of a god. "For," he sagely informs us, "devils were expelled in the name of Solomon, for instance, as well as in the name of God or of a god.[1] In this way they secured the mysterious power which, according to the ideas of the age, Solomon or Jesus possessed—the latter in virtue of the cures which he had actually accomplished" (p. 94). Indeed! Unfortunately, in the passage quoted from Josephus it is not said at all that the Jewish magician Eleazar exorcised demons "in the name of Solomon," but merely that he exorcised them and at the same time "remembered" the name of Solomon and pronounced the magical formulæ composed by him. From this it does not follow at all that it was the name of Solomon, and not the name of some divine being, that worked the miracles. Is Solomon supposed to have expelled demons in his own name? That would be too much like Zeus in Offenbach's operetta *Orpheus in the Underworld*, who swears "by me"! That was not even done by Jesus, who drove out devils in the name of the Holy Ghost (*Matthew* xii, 28). We read in Justin, moreover, that the Joshua of the Old Testament was only made capable of performing miracles when Moses changed his name from Hosea into that of the Christian saviour (*Numbers* xiii, 16).[2] Hence, miracles were not done in the name of Jesus because the historical Jesus had been "a successful exorcist," but the name itself was supposed to have the power of expelling demons and compelling nature, quite independently, it seems, of the miracles of the "historical" Jesus.

In this connection there seems to be more probability in the suggestion of Smith that the words of the magic-papyrus published by Wessely, "I adjure thee by the God of the Hebrews, Jesus," points to a pre-Christian use of the name Jesus in exorcisms. Weiss, it is true, says that the papyrus was "certainly" written by a pagan "who was unable to distinguish between Jews and Christians" (p. 19). Deissman also believes that the

---

[1] Josephus, *Antiq.*, viii, 2, 57.   [2] See Justin, 113, 4.

name was subsequently interpolated by a pagan, since neither a Christian nor a Jew would call Jesus the God of the Hebrews. But what if Jesus was originally the name of a god? What if there were a pre-Christian Judæo-Gnostic Jesus-god? Is it possible that Deissman has himself fallen here into the error of the "destroyers of names" whom he so much despises—those who think "nothing genuine that is not trivial," and who strike out "a great name" wherever they find it? The copyist has added "the *cathari*" (*i.e.*, "the pure") to the words quoted. No less a scholar than Albrecht Dieterich has declared that the "pure" are identical with the Essenes or Therapeuts, and pointed out that the papyrus betrays no Christian influence whatever, but belongs to Judæo-Hellenistic circles,[1] and, if this is so, the Essenes must have recognised a Jesus-god. What does Weinel, who thinks it "childish" to identify "the pure" with the Essenes, say to this? He says flatly: "Everybody knows that we have Christian influence here; that it is the Christian Jesus who is meant, and he is mistakenly represented as a God of the Hebrews" (p. 103). The truth is that theologians have hitherto thought they had proved this, because they did not consider any alternative to their own view.

Then there is the Naassene hymn, which Hippolytus has preserved for us, in which the name Jesus occurs. He "prays his father" to send him down to bring redemption to those who walk in darkness. "In possession of the seal will I go down: all æons will I traverse: all mysteries will I solve, the forms of the gods will I reveal, and what is hidden of the holy way [gnosis] will I make plain." Theologians say, in opposition to Smith, that this hymn is post-Christian. But as there were Naassenes or Ophites before the appearance of Christianity, as Mosheim (*Geschichte der Schlangen-*

---

[1] *Abraxas*, 1891, p. 143; see also his *Mithrasliturgie*, 1903, pp. 27 and 44.

brüder) and Baur (*Die christliche Gnosis*, 1835, pp. 37, 52, and 194) supposed, and Hönig has completely proved (*Die Ophiten*, 1889), it is *merely begging the question* to say that in the case of this psalm we have "Christian Naassenes," especially seeing that the psalm itself has a very ancient character and is closely related to the corresponding Babylonian forms of adjuration. On the contrary, it is difficult to resist the suspicion that the ancient Babylonian name-magic was combined at an early date with the idea of a divine healer, and Jesus (Joshua, Jason, Jasios) was a name used in exorcisms by the pre-Christian Gnostic sects. Further, the name must indicate some sort of divine being, as few will doubt who have any acquaintance with the old ideas of adjuration and magic.

Whittaker (*The Origins of Christianity*, 2nd ed., 1909, p. 27) has drawn attention to *Jude* 5, where it is written: "I will therefore put you in remembrance, though ye once knew this, how that the Lord, having saved the people out of the land of Egypt, afterwards[1] destroyed them that believed not; and the angels which kept not their first estate, but left their own habitation, he hath reserved in everlasting chains under darkness unto the judgment of the great day." So it reads in the revised text. But in the original text, as we have it in Buttmann's Greek edition of the New Testament, we read the name Jesus instead of "the Lord," and this, as we saw, is equivalent to Joshua. If we then remove the comma after "Egypt," where it is quite arbitrary and has no meaning, and put it after "a second time," we read: "that Jesus, having saved the people out of the land of Egypt a second time," and we have a strong proof that there was a pre-Christian saviour of that name known in the Judæo-Christian circles to which the Epistle is addressed. Not only does it confirm the belief

[1] [Not "afterwards," but "a second time," in the Greek text.—J.M.]

in a god Jesus in these circles, as, of course, only a god could judge the angels and put them in chains; it at the same time shows us the identity of this Jesus with the Joshua of the Old Testament, and strengthens our conviction that Joshua also, who saved the Israelites from the bondage of Egypt a second time, Moses having saved them once before, was regarded in those circles as a divine being and not as a mere hero. That "Jesus" is really the earlier reading is shown by the fourth verse, where Jesus is described as the "only Lord" of the Christians, so that it is impossible that in the very next verse the writer should call another—say, Jahveh—the Lord, especially as Jesus Christ is also expressly called the "Lord" in verses 17, 21, and 25. Hence we have in the Epistle of Jude and the changes of its original text a positive proof of an attempt to conceal the traces of a pre-Christian Jesus-god.

With this passage in the Epistle of Jude Whittaker compares one in the "Sibylline Oracles," an essentially Jewish work, in which we read: "Now a certain excellent man will come again from heaven, who spread forth his hands upon the very fruitful tree, the best of the Hebrews, who once made the sun stand still, speaking with beauteous words and pure lips." The German translation runs: "Whose hands outspread on the fruitful tree of the best of the Hebrews," and relates the "one" to Moses and the cross to *Exodus* xvii, 22. But Moses does not stretch his hands *on* the cross, but *in the form* of a cross; and it was not Joshua who made the sun stand still, but Aaron and Hur who supported his arms, Joshua in the meantime being engaged with the Amalekites. Here again the figures of Jesus and Joshua are blended, and we learn from the passage that they identified the Old Testament Joshua, not only with the "crucified" servant of God, but also with the Messiah descending from heaven.

A further proof that Jesus was the name of a god in

pre-Christian times is found in the "Teaching of the Twelve Apostles," according to Harnack and others an originally Jewish work, which was afterwards, somewhat superficially, Christianised. It says, in connection with the Last Supper: "We thank thee, our father, for the holy vine of David, thy servant, whom thou hast made known to us by thy servant Jesus......We thank thee for the life and the knowledge that thou hast given us through Jesus, thy servant......We thank thee for thy holy name, for which thou hast prepared a dwelling in our hearts, and for the knowledge and the faith and the immortality that thou hast made known to us through thy servant Jesus." How is it that the words of institution of the Last Supper in the gospels, which must have been so important and dear to Christians, are omitted and replaced by the above words? Is this Jesus of the "Teaching," who is supposed to have made known to his followers the "holy vine of David," the same as the Jesus of the gospels? This Jesus who reveals life and knowledge, and in this way communicates immortality to his followers, has a suspicious resemblance to the Jesus of the ancient Gnostics, in whose case also the knowledge (gnosis) revealed by him was the essential mark and condition of eternal life.

Then there is the so-called "Revelation" of John! Here, again, apparently, we have an originally Jewish work which was afterwards modified in a Christian sense, and no one can say confidently whether the nucleus of the revelation was composed before or after the supposed time of Jesus. There is the terrible form of the "son of man" coming in the clouds, who says: "I am the Alpha and the Omega," just as Jahveh says of himself in *Isaiah*: "I am the first and the last" (xlviii, 13). "His head and his hairs were white like wool, as white as snow; and his eyes were as a flame of fire; and his feet like unto fine brass, as if they burned in a furnace; and his voice as the sound of many waters. And he had in his right hand seven stars; and out of his mouth went a sharp two-edged sword; and his countenance was as the sun shineth in his strength" (*Rev.* i, 14-16). Then there is the lamb with seven horns and seven eyes, that is "as if slain," and the mysterious book opened with the seven seals (v, 5), and the child of the woman "clothed with the sun, and the moon under her feet, and upon her head a crown of twelve stars," who is carried to the throne of God, and of whom it is said that he will "rule all nations with a rod of iron" (xii). Or consider the rider on the white horse, with many diadems on his head, clothed in a blood-stained garment, whose name is "the word of God......and he treadeth the winepress of the fierceness and wrath of Almighty God; and he hath on his vesture and on his thigh a name written, King of Kings and Lord of Lords" (xix, 11). What have all these forms to do with the "simple" Jesus of the gospels? How could we explain the transformation of such a Jesus into these extraordinary mixtures of the grotesque and gigantic so soon after his death? Have we not rather a product of the unrestrained imagination of some religious sect or conventicle, to whom Jesus was from the start, not a man, but a supernatural, divine being, and in whose ecstatic visions mythical and prophetic elements grew into the frenzied figures which we have in *Revelation*?

In details we perceive a connection with the prophet Isaiah—in the form of the child and the lamb which is slain, in the allusion to the "root, the offspring of David, and the bright and morning star" (xxii, 16; *Isaiah* lx), in the figure of the rider who treads the winepress of the anger of judgment (*Isaiah* lxiii), in the reference to the sufferings of the saints, which by no means relates to the persecutions of the Christians, as has hitherto been believed, but rather to the sufferings of the just in *Wisdom*, in the comforting with the "fountain of life" and the eternal light of the lamb, in which the nations walk and to which the kings of the earth bring their glory (*Isaiah* lx), in the promise of the new Jerusalem, in which the treasures of the nations will be heaped up and only the just shall live, in the struggle of Jahveh with the Leviathan, and the figure of the last trumpet (*Isaiah* xxvii). The historical Jesus, who is supposed to have been the occasion of all this, is nowhere to be recognised, and could not be found at all in *Revelation*, if it were not read under the conviction that it belongs to Christian circles, and that the Jesus of whom it speaks is the one whose supposed life-story is told in the gospels. It may be an esoteric work of the "Jessæans," in the sense of the word previously explained. There is no proof that it is a Christian work and relates to the "historical" Jesus. The numerous astral-mythological allusions in the work which were indicated by Dupuis point, not to an historical, but a purely mythical Jesus.

If, therefore, Jesus had a mythic significance in pre-Christian times, it would be very surprising if he were not also worshipped in certain sects, especially in view of the part played by the similarly-named Jasios or Jason as healer and patron of physicians in the Greek mysteries. It is certain that Moses was regarded as divine, not only in the Alexandrian religious philosophy of Philo, which is closely connected with the Palestinian sects, but also in the belief of the sects themselves. Just as Philo sees in him the lawgiver and prophet, the "purest spirit," the ideal type of humanity, the mediator and reconciler with God, even a divine being, and makes him equal to the Messiah, so, on his own showing, this happened in many of the Judæo-Gnostic sects, who looked up to Moses as a kind of god, had a legend of his being taken into heaven, and on this account venerated him as the conqueror of death and the demons. Philo says that the Therapeuts held a great festival on the seventh Sabbath, the fiftieth day of the year at that time, in which, after a festive nocturnal meal, which probably had a mystic significance, the men and women were arranged in a double choir, which Philo calls an imitation of the choir which Moses and his sister Miriam arranged to sing their victory and gratitude after the passage of the Red Sea. In Philo and the Therapeuts the delivery of the Jews from the bondage of Egypt means the delivery of the soul from the bonds of sense and the passage to the kingdom of the pure spirit. But as the meal of the Therapeuts was certainly related to the Passover meal, which the Jews celebrated before the escape from Egypt, it had an historical as well as a mystic significance, like the Christian Supper. "The soul prepares in the Passover or in its imitation the Therapeutic meals for delivery from the bonds of sense; it then asks divine aid in the passage through the Red Sea which borders Egypt (or the body), and rejoices in the sacred choirs, inebriated with heavenly love and full of gratitude to the saving God, the redeemer."[1]

Now Joshua is a close relation, if not a mere duplicate, of Moses. In his case the passage of the Red Sea is paralleled by the passage of the Jordan, the river of heaven, as the Mandæans regarded it;[2] and in his case also the passage is connected with the feast of the Passover (*Joshua* v). The story of Joshua is built, point by point, on that of Moses;[3] indeed, it seems as if they are only two different forms of the same mythical figure, the lawgiver and leader of Israel—that is to say, the sun in its passage through the watery region in the spring, in combination with Oannes as determining and announcing the division of the year (see p. 190). After this, is it a strained and precarious supposition that Joshua also was originally an Ephraimitic name for the sun, an ancient Jewish sect-god, a hero of the cult in certain Gnostic circles, who were in this influenced by their heathen pastoral neighbours and their veneration of similar

---

[1] Gfrörer, *Philo und die jüdisch-alex. Theosophie*, 1835, ii, p. 295.
[2] Brandt, *Die mandäische Religion*, 1889.
[3] Jeremias, *Das alte Testament im Lichte des alten Orients*, 2 Aufl., 1906, p. 465.

mythic personalities? If Melchisedech, who is, like Moses, put by Philo on the same footing as the divine "word," the Logos and Messiah—if Noah, Henoch, Joseph, and even Cain were worshipped, is it likely that Joshua, the second Moses, was overlooked?

We now know that there was a pre-Christian Jewish Gnosticism. In his admirable work, *Der vorchristliche jüdische Gnostizismus* (1898), Friedländer has amply described it and its connection with the religious philosophy of Alexandria;[1] Gunkel has traced its relations to Persian and Babylonian ideas.[2] Must we reject outright the idea of a pre-Christian cult of Jesus because we have no *direct* evidence of it? We can, however, deduce its existence from the few extant traces on the same rules of science on which we deduce any other facts from indications and survivals in historical investigation when there is no direct evidence. It is true that we can only attain more or less confident suppositions, especially as there is question of a secret cult, the teaching of which was probably not committed to writing (Gunkel, p. 63), and because the Christian Church and Jewish synagogue have done all in their power to destroy heretical works and all traces of the real origin of Christianity.

We have ample experience of the conduct of the Roman Church in suppressing inconvenient writings. How was it likely to act when it had better means of doing so than now, when it still had unlimited power over souls, and when the difficulty of publishing works was such as to restrict their number in a way that we can now hardly appreciate; especially as there would, in any case, be few copies of these esoteric Gnostic works? All that we know of Gnosticism is derived from the biassed accounts of its ecclesiastical opponents, as the Church moved heaven and earth to destroy the works of its supporters. We can no more forget the treasures we have lost in this

[1] Also see Harnack, *Gesch. der altchristl. Literatur*, i, p. 144.
[2] *Zum religionsgesch. Verständniss*, etc.

way than we can forget its brutal destruction of our earliest literature (songs of the gods, legends of heroes, magical formulæ, etc.) in the first years of the Christian mission in Germany and during the Middle Ages; in those years we lost an invaluable treasure, torn by the hands of fanatical priests, trampled under the heavy feet of monks, and given to the flames.

And even if we reject the idea of a pre-Christian cult of Jesus, those who believe in his historical character gain nothing. It is *not true at all* that, as is constantly said in pamphlets, lectures, and journals, *The Christ-Myth* stands or falls with the existence of a pre-Christian Jesus. The mythical nature of the Christian saviour is sufficiently proved by the character of the gospels themselves and the lack of independent evidence; it is *entirely independent* of the question whether Jesus had or had not been previously worshipped. The belief in an earlier cult would merely throw a welcome light on the origin of Christianity and its connection with the surrounding Jewish and pagan world. One may venture to say that theologians have found so much in their documents, when it suited their purpose, that they will certainly be able to discover a pre-Christian Jesus whenever their theory requires one, and they are no longer prevented by their dependence on the Church from studying the subject impartially.

(h) *The Conversion of the Mythical into an Historical Jesus.*—We must now make a special inquiry into the question how the mythical Jesus—the Isaiahian (or Jessæan) saviour, the suffering, dying, and rising servant of God and just one—was converted into the historical Jesus, and see how far prophetic promises and astral-mythological speculations of the Gnostic sects co-operated in the process, and how far personal experiences and religious dispositions of the communities determined the figure of the historical Jesus and transformed an abstract scheme into a living personality. *The Christ-Myth* has been content with a few general indications in this regard. It has merely gathered together material from which one may obtain some idea of the origin of Christianity. Perhaps the time has not yet come for a fuller study of the matter, as one has first to accomplish the work of clearing a veritable Augean stable of prejudices and errors and preparing the ground for a sober construction. It is clear that the conversion of the mythical into the historical Jesus could not have taken place before the beginning of the second century, when there would be no living witnesses of the events related. The seventy or eighty years that would elapse after the supposed death of Jesus would be quite enough to permit his "history" to seem plausible, especially as the destruction of Jerusalem had so disturbed the life of the people that there was no fear of Jewish opponents proving the falseness of their assertions. At the same time, we need not postulate a deliberate deception in the conversion of the myth into history. As all the chief features of the character of Jesus had, as we saw, long been in existence, and the myth would naturally tend to take the form of narrative, as if there were question of real events in the past, the whole process might take place so gradually and unconsciously that there is no occasion to speak of "glib lying" and "thorough swindle," as some say.

The cult-legend spoke of an Immanuel or Jesus who had, according to Isaiah, sacrificed himself for the sins of the people, and would then come down from heaven in the shape of the expected Messiah and lead his followers into the kingdom they desired. As the question of the Messiah had become urgent after the destruction of Jerusalem and the collapse of all the political hopes of the Jews, and amid the sufferings of the people from the Roman oppression, the further questions were found to rise spontaneously to the lips: When did the servant of God really suffer? Where did he die? What was he like? What did he do before he was put to death by his enemies? Who were these enemies? And so on. And it was just as inevitable for the answer to be found in the indications of the prophets and of astral-mythological speculation, and thus to lead to the historicisation of the originally mythical figure of Jesus.

His death could not be placed too long before the destruction of Jerusalem for the reasons we have already seen. The Messiah must have been born in the days of Augustus, whom the pagans have regarded as the desired saviour of the world. Astral mythology furnished the name of Pilatus to pierce with his spear (*pilum*) the son of God hanging on the world-tree, the Milky Way; and Pilate had, according to Josephus, been procurator in the time of Tiberius. According to the words of the prophet, the servant of God was to be a healer of spiritual and corporal ills, a supporter of the poor and oppressed. Miracles of extraordinary kinds were to reveal his future Messianic significance, yet he was not to be understood by his own people and was to succumb to the attacks of his enemies. And who could these enemies be but the Pharisees and scribes, who had been more and more hostile to the Jewish sects after the destruction of Jerusalem?[1]

As long as their belief in the redeeming death of the servant of God was a secret belief within the sect there could be no conflict with the Pharisees; in fact, sometimes the Pharisees were united with the sectarians, both in their mystic and astrological tendencies and in

---

[1] Chowlson says that it was the Sadducees, not the Pharisees, who were the real enemies of Jesus and brought about his condemnation. That is historically not very probable, as Steudel has shown (*Im Kampf um die Christus-Mythe*, p. 45). If there is any truth in it at all, it can only be that, according to *Wisdom*, which, as we saw, contributed much to the picture of the sufferings of the just one, the impious enemies of the just might be regarded as the Sadducees, as it is written in the second chapter (verse 22): "They knew not the mysteries of God, or hoped for a reward of eternal life, and would hear nothing of a recompense for stainless souls. For God has created man for immortality, and made him in the image of his own likeness." The chief difference between the worldly-minded Sadducees and the Pharisees was that the former did not believe in immortality, or the eternal reward or punishment of men beyond the grave.

their hostility to the worldly-minded priestly nobility of the Sadducees. We saw how in Isaiah the figure of the Saviour constantly blends with that of Jahveh. As is known, the aim of the preaching of Isaiah is to confirm the people in monotheistic ideas, in belief in the one God, who says: "I am Jahveh and no other, and there is no god beside me. I am the first and the last." These words are put in the mouth of the "son of man" in *Revelation*. In *Isaiah* xlv, 15, Jahveh is called a "hidden God," a "Saviour," just as the servant of God and Saviour was supposed to grow up in obscurity, and the just to expiate sins by his death without attracting much attention or the real significance of his death being recognised. What if, after the manner of Isaiah, the belief in Jahveh were to coalesce with the belief in Jesus in the mind of the sect, and Jesus become the form in which Jahveh was worshipped as healer, expiator, and redeemer in the mystic and esoteric cults? For *the religion of Jesus was merely a religion of Jahveh of deeper mysticism, a new and special form of Jewish monotheism;* and the orthodox Jews, for whom monotheism was the sum of their faith, had on that account no occasion to put difficulties in the way of the original Christians, the Jessæans or Nazoræans, the "saints," as they were called in *Isaiah*.[1]

Weiss thinks that the early Christians, with their belief that the crucified Jesus was the Messiah, put themselves in the sharpest opposition to Judaism, and incurred hatred and persecution, and says that it is "absolutely ridiculous to think that the first Christians would have voluntarily encountered this difficulty" (p. 44). But that was not the belief of the "first Christians"; they believed that Jesus, the servant of God, the Saviour of Isaiah, who was believed to have

---

[1] This is suggested by Smith in his *Ecce Deus*, who tries to show that the original Christian movement was a protest against polytheism, a "crusade in favour of monotheism."

suffered a humiliating death among men, as Messiah, would return in glory, and realise their hope of eternal life. It may seem "bold" and "paradoxical" to imagine Jahveh sacrificing himself for his people and so entering the ranks of the pagan saviour-gods—Marduk, Adonis, Tammuz, Attis, Osiris, etc. Yet this may have been simply a revival of an older idea, that Jahveh was himself Tammuz, dying every year, mourned by the women of Jerusalem according to Ezechiel (viii, 13), rising and dying again, to enter once more into life.[1] A reluctance to connect Jahveh with finiteness may have prevented those who held this belief from identifying the Saviour strictly with the supreme God. This may have been the reason why Jesus, though essentially one with God, was nevertheless distinguished from him as a special being. It was a "stumbling-block to the Jews" that their God was related to the pagan saviour-gods; a "folly to the pagans" that the redeemer of the world should be a Jewish deity. But this seems impossible only when one, like Weiss, conceives the crucified Jesus as an historical human being. That the Christians would arbitrarily create the difficulty of representing *such a person* as the Messiah we should certainly hesitate to think. But the ground for believing in a crucified saviour need not have been in historical events at all; it may have been because the fact of the suffering and death of Jesus was revealed by the prophet Isaiah.

As long as Jesus was the object of worship of a very small body, and the belief in him was obscured by mystic confusion and mythological mists, it seemed to the orthodox Jews to be harmless. The figures of Jesus and Jahveh were blended, and the religious foundation of Judaism, monotheism, seemed not to be endangered. But when, after the destruction of Jerusalem, the orthodox Jews, deprived of their political independence,

---

[1] See H. Schneider, *Kultur und Denken der Babylonier und Juden*, 1910, p. 282.

now placed their national unity and cohesion in a unity of faith, and therefore drew up the ranks of the ecclesiastical regiment more strictly and hardened the ritual law of monotheism into a dogma, *Jesus was detached from Jahveh*, the god of the sect was opposed to the god of the official religion as an *independent* divine being, and a bitter hostility set in between the scribes and Pharisees on the one hand, who represented monotheism in its most abstract form and, in connection with it, held rigidly to the forms of the law, and the sects on the other hand, with whom the common folk sympathised as we read in the gospels. Under the fearful pressure of the uprooting of the Jewish people, and in view of the religious need of the time, which had reached its highest pitch with the loss of the temple, it seemed that the terrible time foretold by the prophets had come, and that they should look for the immediate appearance of the Messiah. The promises that had been made must now be fulfilled. This was the opportunity of the Jewish sectaries to come out of the seclusion of their mystic sects and conventicles with their "gnosis" and proclaim to the whole people their faith in Jesus.

Possibly exalted by visions, in which they believed that they saw the risen "Lord" in bodily form, the emissaries of the faith went about announcing the "glad tidings" of the coming of the Messiah and the speedy establishment of the kingdom of heaven on earth. In market-place and on the street the appeal for change of heart through faith in the Lord Jesus Christ rang out. Then the innovation became dangerous to the official Jewish religion. Weiss can only attribute to a "real Jesus," the "influence of a personality," and the experience of his life on earth, "the immense step from the vague Messianic hope to the confidence of possession, fulfilment, and the joy and gratitude for what God has given them in his servant Jesus, as we find it in the prayers of that early time" (p. 48). But this confidence of possession had long been a peculiarity of Jewish sectarianism before they gave publicity to their faith and made it the object of a popular propaganda; Paul and others may have begun this at an earlier period. If this is now done more vigorously and on a larger scale, it is not because an historical Jesus has caused it, but because the general conditions of the time inflamed the religious sentiment and made it seem a duty to the sectaries to communicate their "knowledge" (gnosis) to their compatriots and the rest of mankind and "reveal" the approach of the kingdom of heaven, and thus bring them to a change of heart. It is true that the rest of the Jews also believed in the speedy coming of the Messiah. But the belief had so often been falsified that its strength and sources threatened to become weaker. The sectaries, however, had a powerful framework for that belief in their astrally and prophetically grounded legend of Jesus, who was supposed voluntarily to have sacrificed himself and to be about to return as king and judge of his people. That was new and unfamiliar, and precisely on that account it appealed to the feeling of the time, and found credence among their Jewish compatriots the more easily as the belief gave them a weapon against the detested sanctity and pride of the Pharisees, and the concentration of the sectarians on the plain and intelligible morality of the prophets and proverbial books offered the possibility of religious salvation to all men who would endeavour to lead good lives. It may have been then that the saying of Luke was formulated: "Woe unto you, lawyers, for ye have taken away the key of knowledge [gnosis]. Ye entered not in yourselves, and them that were entering in ye hindered" (xi, 52). It means that the representatives of the official Jewish religion had abandoned their earlier predilection for astrology, and now attached the astrological speculations to the Gnostics. This made an end of the astral ground of the hope in a Messiah; there remained only the prophetical, and the original astral Jesus became more and more vague and was replaced by the historical Jesus. The more the new faith spread among the people the more the gnosis was adapted to their intelligence, and thus the supposed historicity of the Saviour was substituted for the mythical and astral character of their religious ideas.[1]

(*i*) *Jesus and the Pharisees and Scribes.*—We turn now to consider the relation of Jesus to the Pharisees. Jewish scholars like Chwolson[2] have often expressed their astonishment at the way this relation is described in the gospels. What, they ask, could be the reason for the deadly enmity between Jesus and the representatives of the official Jewish religion? Religious-moral reasons could not possibly suffice of themselves to explain it. In this respect there was not a very sharp opposition between them. "In the teaching and sayings of Jesus," says Chwolson, "there was nothing that could offend the religious feeling of anyone educated according to Pharisaic laws and acquainted with the Pharisaic—that is to say, Rabbinical—literature" (p. 88). Jesus is supposed to have preached in the synagogues, of which the Pharisees were the masters; he cannot, therefore, have infringed the law. Moreover, he is supposed to have adhered strictly to the law, since he says that he had not come to undo, but to fulfil, it (*Matthew* v, 17)—a saying that is found almost word for word in the Talmud: "Not a letter of the law will ever be destroyed," and "The laws of Noah have not been abolished, but increased" (*Cosri*, i, 83).[3] *Matthew* xxiii, 3, makes Jesus bid his disciples listen in all things to the commands of the Pharisees. This, however, seems to be based on *Ecclus.* vii, 31 : "Fear the

---

[1] In every heathen religion the dying and risen god is an astral being; the sun descending in the summer-solstice or in the autumn-equinox, and ascending in the winter-solstice or spring equinox. So Dupuis, in his monumental work *L'origine de tous les cultes* (1794), has shown in reference to Tammuz, Adonis, Attis, Osiris, Mithra, etc. Cf. also Jeremias, the work above mentioned.

[2] *Das Passahmahl*, p. 85.   [3] *Sanhedrim*, 107 ; *Bereschit rabba*, 27.

Lord, and honour the priest, and give him his part, as it is commanded from the beginning." In passing over one or other prescription, or interpreting it in an unfamiliar sense, he did nothing extraordinary. There were among the Pharisees and scribes themselves many differences in the exposition and application of the prescriptions of the law, though this never led to charges of heresy or persecution.

One of the worst of his transgressions is that he and his disciples are said to have violated the law of the Sabbath by healing the sick on that day. Even among the rabbis, however, the holiness of the Sabbath had to give way when a man's life was in question. In fact, it was obligatory to disregard the Sabbath when there was danger in the observance of it, and the man who in such a case held to the letter was regarded as a "murderer." We read in *Lev.* xviii, 5 : " Ye shall therefore keep my statutes and my judgments ; which, if a man do, he shall live in them." And in the Talmud (*Tract. Joma*, 85b) we read : " The Sabbath is given to you, not you to the Sabbath." To heal by merely stretching out one's hand over the patient, as Jesus is said to have done on the Sabbath in *Mark* iii, 5, was not forbidden by the rabbis, and therefore the Pharisees could not be "filled with madness," as they are said to have been on such an occasion in *Luke* vi, 11.

Even on the question of divorce Jesus did not take up a position opposed to that of the Pharisees. We read in *Matthew* v, 31 : " It hath been said, Whosoever shall put away his wife, let him give her a writing of divorcement; but I say unto you, That whosoever shall put away his wife, saving for the cause of fornication, causeth her to commit adultery." But it is also said in the Talmud: " Whosoever shall put away his wife, over him the altar sheddeth tears " (*Pessachim*, 113), and " Whosoever putteth away his wife is hated of God" (*Gittin*, 90b). Even the prophet Malachi had said: " Let none deal treacherously against the wife of his youth, for the Lord,

the God of Israel, saith that he hateth putting away"
(ii, 15). Divorce is permitted only when an internal
breach between the spouses has already taken place
because of the infidelity of one or other, as is said in
Isaiah in regard to the union of Jahveh and his people,
which is conceived as a marriage-bond: "Thus saith the
Lord, Where is the bill of your mother's divorcement,
whom I have put away? or which of my creditors is it to
whom I have sold you? Behold, for your iniquities have
ye sold yourselves, and for your transgressions is your
mother put away" (l, 1). In the passage quoted in
regard to divorce, Jesus merely pronounces for the stricter
opinion of the school of Gamaliel against the laxer school
of Hillel.

Not only is there no opposition between Jesus and the
Pharisees on this point, but even the fact that he is
supposed to have openly proclaimed himself the Messiah
was not calculated to turn them against him. Not only
the children of Israel, but even individual men, are called
"sons of God," and the priests and rabbis themselves
have at times called a man the Messiah and supported
him with their respect; consider Zerubbabel, and the
relation of the rabbi Akiba to Bar-Kochba.

In *Matthew* xv, 5, and *Mark* vii, 11, Jesus reproaches
the Pharisees with perverting the command to honour
one's father and mother in favour of one's duty to God.
We find, however, no trace of such a thing in Jewish
tradition, which expressly forbids any misinterpretation of
the commandments of the law. Again, in regard to the
laws regulating food, Jesus cannot possibly have acted as
he is supposed to have done in *Matthew* xv, 11, and
Mark vii, 15, because in that case it would be unintelligible for Peter to refuse to touch unclean food
(*Acts* x, 14). Moreover, Jesus is supposed to have given
him full power to bind and to loose, or to decide questions
of law according to his own judgment.

It is just as accurate for Jesus to blame the Pharisees

for making proselytes (*Matthew* xxiii, 15). If we were to take his words seriously, they were wholly absorbed in bringing men into the Jewish faith wherever they could. As a matter of fact, the Talmud expressly forbids this indiscriminate making of proselytes, and makes the entrance into Judaism dependent on righteousness of heart. Still less can there be question of the Pharisees declaring that to swear by the temple and altar was not binding, but it is binding to swear by the gold of the temple and the sacrifice on the altar (*Matthew* xxiii, 16). If Jesus meant that the sanctity clung to the temple and altar, not to the things therein, that is precisely the view of the rabbis.[1] And when Jesus says (*Matthew* xxiii, 23): "Woe unto you, scribes and Pharisees, hypocrites! for ye pay tithe of mint and anise and cummin, and have omitted the weightier matters of the law, judgment, mercy, and faith: these ought ye to have done, and not to leave the other undone," the charge falls to the ground, from the simple fact that plants that grow wild, and vegetables, were not subject to tithe.[2]

These charges are either brought by someone who was unacquainted with the real facts, or have been invented arbitrarily to confuse opponents, without any regard to historical truth. It is the same when Jesus accuses the Pharisees of the murder of prophets, and charges them with having slain Zacharias, son of Barachias, between the temple and the altar, and holds them responsible for the shedding of his innocent blood (*Matthew* xxiii, 35). Here Zechariah, the son of Jehoiada, who was stoned in the court of the temple by order of King Joash (2 *Chron.* xxiv, 21), is combined or confused with Zachariah, the son of Baruch, who was slain by the zealots in the temple for supposed treachery during the siege of Jerusalem by the Romans.[3] Indeed, the whole of the words in

---

[1] See *Nedarim*, 10*b* and 14*b*.   [2] *Menachoth*, i.
[3] Josephus, *Jewish War*, iv, 5, 4. See also on the subject K. Lippe, *Das Evangelium Matthæi vor dem Forum der Bibel und des Talmud.*

Matthew xxiii, 34: "Wherefore, behold, I send unto you prophets, and wise men, and scribes; and some of them ye shall kill and crucify, etc.," together with the subsequent prediction of the destruction of Jerusalem, are based on the prophet Jeremiah (vii, 25):—

> Since the day that your fathers came forth out of the land of Egypt unto this day I have even sent unto you all my servants the prophets, daily rising up early and sending them:
> Yet they hearkened not unto me, nor inclined their ear, but hardened their neck; they did worse than their fathers.
> Therefore thou shalt speak all these words unto them; but they will not hearken to thee; thou shalt also call unto them, but they will not answer thee......
> Cut off thine hair, O Jerusalem, and cast it away, and take up a lamentation on high places; for the Lord hath rejected and forsaken the generation of his wrath......
> And the carcases of this people shall be meat for the fowls of the heaven, and for the beasts of the earth; and none shall fray them away.
> Then will I cause to cease from the cities of Judah, and from the streets of Jerusalem, the voice of mirth and the voice of gladness, the voice of the bridegroom and the voice of the bride; for the land shall be desolate.

Many writers have insisted that the relation of Jesus to the scribes and Pharisees affords a proof of his historicity. Yet almost the very same charges which Jesus makes against the Pharisees are brought by Isaiah against the heads of the people. "*Your hands are full of blood*," the prophet says (i, 15; see also lix, 3); "Wash you, make you clean; put away the evil of your doings from before mine eyes; cease to do evil. Learn to do well, seek judgment, relieve the oppressed, judge the fatherless, plead for the widow." And Isaiah bemoans that Jerusalem, "the faithful city, full of judgment, righteousness lodged in it," has "become a harlot" and is full of "murderers." "Thy princes are rebellious and the companions of thieves; every one loveth gifts, and followeth after rewards; they judge not the fatherless,

neither doth the cause of the widow come unto them."
"Woe unto them that decree unrighteous decrees, and
that write grievousness which they have prescribed; to
turn aside the needy from judgment, and to take away
the right from the poor of my people, that widows may
be their prey, and that they may rob the fatherless"
(x, 1 and 2; *cf. Mark* xii, 40). "Woe unto them that
call evil good, and good evil; that put darkness for light,
and light for darkness: that put bitter for sweet, and
sweet for bitter. Woe unto them that are wise in their
own eyes, and prudent in their own sight" (v, 20).
Compare with this the charges which Jesus brings against
the Pharisees and scribes, and it will be seen that here
again Isaiah was the model of the evangelists. Jesus
calls the Pharisees "blind leaders of the blind" (*Matthew*
xv, 14) and "blind Pharisees," and blames them for the
perverse ways they have chosen to attain salvation
(*Matthew* xxiii, 16, 19, 24, and 26). But we read in
Isaiah (iii, 12): "O my people, they which lead thee
cause thee to err, and destroy the way of thy paths," and
the prophet returns incessantly to the blindness of the
people and their leaders. Jesus reproaches the Pharisees
with hypocrisy, and tells them that their service of God
is mere lip-service, and that by their refining and multi-
plying commandments they have made the way of salvation difficult for themselves (*Matthew* xv, 8). Isaiah
also complains to "the Lord" that his people approaches
him only with its lips, but its heart is far from him; that
its fear of God is only learned from the precept of men
(xxix, 13), and it does not honour him in the right way.
"For......your lips have spoken lies, your tongue hath
muttered perverseness. None calleth for justice, nor any
pleadeth for truth; they trust in vanity and speak lies;
they conceive mischief and bring forth iniquity" (lix,
3 and 4). Jesus calls the Pharisees "serpents and generation of vipers," as John is supposed to have done (*Matthew*
xxiii, 33). Here again he merely does what Isaiah had

done: "They hatch cockatrice' [vipers'] eggs, and weave the spider's web; he that eateth of their eggs dieth, and that which is crushed breaketh out into a viper. Their webs shall not become garments, neither shall they cover themselves with their works; their works are works of iniquity......their thoughts are thoughts of iniquity...... they have made them crooked paths" (lix, 5–8).

We have, therefore, every reason to doubt the historical truth of the relevant passages in the gospels, and this doubt increases when we find that even so important a scene as the expulsion of the merchants from the temple and the words put into the mouth of Jesus on that occasion are inspired by Isaiah, and closely follow passages in the prophet. What does "the Lord" say in the first chapter of the prophet?

> To what purpose is the multitude of your sacrifices unto me? saith the Lord: I am full of the burnt offerings of rams, and the fat of fed beasts; and I delight not in the blood of bullocks, or of lambs, or of he-goats.
>
> When ye *come to appear* before me, who hath required this at your hand, to tread *my courts?*
>
> Bring no more *vain oblations;* incense is an abomination unto me.

"Behold," says the prophet Malachi (iii, 1), continuing this,

> I will send *my messenger*, and he shall prepare the way before me; and *the Lord, whom ye seek, shall suddenly come to his temple*, even the *messenger of the covenant*, whom ye delight in; behold, he shall come, saith the Lord of hosts.
>
> But who may abide the day of his coming? and who shall stand when he appeareth? for he is like a refiner's fire and the fullers' soap.
>
> And he shall sit as a refiner and purifier of silver, and he *shall purify the sons of Levi*, and purge them as gold and silver, that they may offer unto the Lord *an offering in righteousness*.
>
> Then shall the offering of Judah and Jerusalem be pleasant unto the Lord, as in the days of old, and as in former years.
>
> And I will come near to you to judgment; and I will

R

be a swift witness against the sorcerers, and against the adulterers, and against false swearers, and against those that oppress the hireling in his wages, the widow, and the fatherless, and that turn aside the stranger from his right, saith the Lord of hosts.

Add the words of Zechariah (xiv, 21) :—

Yea, every pot in Jerusalem and in Judah shall be holiness unto the Lord of hosts; and all they that sacrifice shall come and take of them, and seethe therein; *and in that day there shall be no more the Canaanite* [merchant] *in the house of the Lord of hosts.*

And if we further conclude that the words of Jesus, " My house shall be called of all nations the house of prayer, but ye have made it a den of thieves " (*Mark* xi, 17), are a combination of *Isaiah* lvi, 7 (" Mine house shall be called an house of prayer for all people "), and *Jeremiah* vii, 11 (" Is this house, which is called by my name, become a den of robbers in your eyes ? "), the historicity of the narrative breaks down altogether. The seventh chapter of Jeremiah also describes a closely similar situation, as the first chapter of Isaiah and the narrative of the cleansing of the temple :—

Stand in the gate of the Lord's house, and proclaim there this word, and say, Hear the word of the Lord, all ye of Judah, that enter in at these gates to worship the Lord.

Thus saith the Lord of hosts, the God of Israel: Amend your ways and your doings, and I will cause you to dwell in this place......

For if ye throughly amend your ways and your doings; if ye throughly execute judgment between a man and his neighbour;

If ye oppress not the stranger, the fatherless, and the widow, and *shed not innocent blood* in this place, neither walk after other gods to your hurt;

Then will I cause you to dwell in this place, in the land that I gave to your fathers, for ever and ever.

We see from this why Jesus had to go to Jerusalem and begin his work with the cleansing of the temple, and why his threatening speech on the Pharisees and his prediction of the destruction of Jerusalem must be connected with the episode. It is all foreshadowed in the words of the prophet, and there is no guarantee of historical reality. In the thirteenth chapter of Mark and the twenty-fourth chapter of Matthew we do, indeed, detect an historical reality; but the events referred to have, as Graetz has shown, the colouring of the terrible time of the Bar-Kochba war in the second century, when Jews and Christians opposed each other in deadly enmity and made each other responsible for the judgment, when the name of the followers of Jesus was hateful to the Jews, when the "Minæans" were openly cursed, and Jews and Christians alike were executed with fearful cruelty during the religious persecution under Hadrian.[1] Yet here again the model for the prediction of Jesus, or for the Jewish Apocalyptic which is at the base of it, was the prophet Isaiah, when he says, in regard to the judgment on Jerusalem and the accompanying horrors: "And the people shall be oppressed, every one by another, and every one by his neighbour; the child shall behave himself proudly against the ancient, and the base against the honourable" (iii, 5; see *Mark* xiii, 12). When Jeremiah (vii, 30) says, in the same connection, "They have set their abominations in the house which is called by my name, to pollute it," we are reminded of the "abomination of desolation" which is, according to Mark (xiii, 14), to be a sign for Christians to fly, and in connection with which Jesus himself appeals to *Daniel* ix, 27. How far the whole story in the gospels has been influenced by the prophets is seen by the cursing of the fig-tree, which is supposed to have occurred about the time of the cleansing of the temple, since even this detail was, apparently, furnished by Isaiah (i, 29 and 30): "Ye shall be confounded for the gardens that ye have chosen, for ye shall be as an oak whose leaf fadeth." We may

[1] Lublinski, *Das werdende Dogma*, p. 75; compare K. Lippe, work quoted, p. 245.

add the words of Jeremiah (viii, 13), who in the same connection makes the "Lord" say: "There shall be [there are] no grapes on the vine, nor figs on the fig-tree, and the leaf shall fade [has faded], and the things that I have given them shall pass away from them" (see also *Hosea* xiii, 15).

It is still disputed how far the movement initiated by Jesus was a movement of the proletariate. The gospel of Luke represents the saviour chiefly as a friend of the poor and oppressed. Anyone who carefully considers the circumstances will see that this feature also has been taken from Isaiah. In the prophet "the Lord" is, above all, the saviour of the poor and the unjustly treated and suffering, reproaching the higher class for their conduct and charging them with violence and injustice: "The Lord will enter into judgment with the ancients of his people and the princes thereof; for ye have eaten up the vineyard; the spoil of the poor is in your houses. What mean ye that ye beat my people to pieces and grind the faces of the poor?" (iii, 14). It is very probable that the Jesus-sect consisted mainly from the start of the lowest sections of the people, such as had nothing to lose and nothing to hope for in life, and whose whole thoughts and feelings were bound up so much the more intimately with the promise of a happy future in the world beyond, which was connected with the coming of the Messiah. Here, again, it is to Isaiah, not to Jesus, that we must trace the sympathy with the poor, who unites pity and goodwill to the enslaved with anger against the rich and the oppressor, and has thus provided the basis of the philosophy of Christianity. When *Wisdom* describes the opponents of the Saviour and servant of God as being especially the wicked and unjust, it is merely developing the lesson of Isaiah, and declaring that they are the enemies of the poor and weak, the oppressors of the lower people, a proud, hypocritical, and self-righteous class; thus we get the picture of the Pharisees and scribes as we find it in the gospels, though it is the Pharisees of the second, rather than the first, century who have contributed to its concrete features, as these were, in point of fact, the bitterest and most irreconcilable opponents of the poor members of the Jesus-sect. And if this was the quality of the opponents of the Saviour, there was all the more reason to represent him as a *poor* man, springing from the lower class, and the antithesis of Jew and Gentile, just and unjust, of which there had originally been question in Isaiah's " servant of God," received in the historical clothing of the mythical ideas the character of a struggle of the poor against the rich and powerful, the laity against the arrogance of the priests and scribes, the honest search for salvation against hypocrisy, the plain piety of the prophets against the law and the pride of its official representatives.

(*k*) *Further Modifications of Prophetical and Historical Passages*.—In these circumstances no historical importance will be attached to the attitude of Jesus towards places which were hostile to him (*Matthew* xi, 20; *Luke* x, 13). It is in itself very improbable that Jesus would curse a place because it was not converted by his miracles to faith in him, as his own relatives and nearest disciples are represented as at times not believing in him; and here again the Evangelists seem to have had in mind the prophet Isaiah, who is never tired of calling his woes upon the heathen cities and predicting their destruction, and whose threatening words are unmistakably echoed in the words of Jesus.[1]

A classical illustration of this connection of the words of Jesus with those of Isaiah and invention of situations for them is found in *Matthew* xvi, 15, where we have the famous confession of Peter and subsequent appointment of the disciple as successor in the power of the keys. Who can fail to see that there is here a combination of *Isaiah* xxviii, 16 ("Behold I lay in Zion for a foundation

[1] Cf. *Isaiah* xiv, 12, and *Matt.* xi, 23; *Isaiah* xiii, 19, and xvii, 9; and *Matthew* xi, 22 and 24.

a *stone, a tried stone, a precious corner stone,* a sure *foundation;* he that believeth shall not make haste [become weak] "), and *Isaiah* li, 1 (" Hearken to me, ye that follow after righteousness, ye that seek the Lord; look unto the rock whence ye are hewn......look unto Abraham your father......for I *called him alone,* and *blessed* him, and increased him "), with the prophet's remarkable reproaches of Shebna, the "treasurer" and head of the king's house, because he had had his tomb hewn out of a rock. The prophet threatens that Jahveh will drive him from his occupation for this, and continues (xxii, 20):—

> And it shall come to pass in that day, that I will call my servant Eliakim the son of Hilkiah;
> And I *will clothe him with thy robe, and strengthen him with thy girdle, and I will commit thy government into his hand;* and he shall be a father to the inhabitants of Jerusalem, and to the house of Judah.
> *And the key of the house of David will I lay upon his shoulder; so he shall open, and none shall shut; and he shall shut, and none shall open.*
> And I will fasten him as a nail in a sure place; and he shall be for a glorious throne to his father's house.

Zechariah also makes the high-priest Joshua be clothed ceremoniously by the Lord with the insignia of his *office,* and appointed as *head* of his house and *overseer* of its courts. And the high-priest Joshua is in the same relation to the Messiah Zerubbabel as Peter is to Jesus, and in the end takes his place.

That Jesus was to die at Jerusalem and, in the sense of Isaiah's "servant of God," expiate the sins of men by his death, was the starting-point of the whole of this inquiry. To what extent mythical and Old Testament motives have co-operated in the description of the trial and influenced the gospel story I have already shown in the first part of the *Christ-Myth.* Here I will be content to draw attention to a further circumstance, which, in all probability, has had a very decisive influence on the gospel narrative of the sufferings and death of Jesus. In his history of the Jewish War (vi, 5, 3) Josephus says that a certain *Jesus* (!), son of Ananus, an unlettered provincial, *went to Jerusalem for the feast of tabernacles* four years before the war broke out, when the city still enjoyed perfect peace and prosperity, and suddenly began to cry out: "A voice from the east, a voice from the west, a voice from the four winds, a voice over Jerusalem and the temple, a voice over bridegrooms and brides, a voice over the entire people." He cried this day and night, passing through all the streets of the city. Arrested and beaten, he merely repeated his words *without saying a word in his defence or against his captors.* Brought before the Roman authority and scourged until the flesh was stripped from his bones, he neither craved mercy nor shed tears, but accompanied each stroke with the mournful cry: "Woe to Jerusalem." When Albinus, the official, asked him who he was, whence he came, and why he cried thus, *he made no reply*, and Albinus, convinced that the man was insane, *set him free.* "*He cursed none that beat him*," Josephus continues, "nor thanked those who gave him food; he gave no other reply to any man than his prophecy of misfortune. He was especially loud in his cry on feast-days." In the end he was killed by a stone during the siege.

8.—HISTORIANS AND THE GOSPELS.

When we consider these things, we see that the claim that the gospel narrative could not have been invented is an empty phrase. It would be well if those who use it would be more explicit, and tell us precisely what there is that could not be invented in the narrative.

No one will question that the figure of Jesus in the gospels has a certain nucleus, about which all the rest has gradually crystallised. But that this nucleus is an historical personality, and not Isaiah's "servant of God," the "just" of *Wisdom*, and the sufferer of the twenty-second psalm, is merely to beg the question; and this is the less justified since all the really important features of the gospel life of Jesus owe their origin partly to the myth, partly to the expansion and application of certain passages in the prophets.

Theologians triumphantly point to the fact that even scholars who are not influenced by theology have not doubted the historical existence of Jesus. When we look closely into the matter, however, we find that these scholars have not given any critical consideration to the question, that in this matter they have spoken as laymen, not as experts, and that they adhere to the historicity of the man Jesus, not on personal scientific grounds, but out of conventional feeling. This is true of profane historians, who, as far as I can see, have almost all avoided up to the present a serious discussion of the question. It is true of Zimmern, who, as an Assyriologist, has certainly discovered the striking parallels between the Christ-myth and the Babylonian myth, and even admitted that these are not mere casual analogies, but proofs of a direct dependence and historical connection at important points, yet who, as a former theologian, adheres to the belief in the historicity of Jesus, without finding any foundation for it.[1] In this Zimmern appeals to Wundt and to Hermann Schneider, who says in his *Kultur und Denken der Babylonier und Juden* that we must retain the historicity of Jesus for reasons drawn from the history of the evolution of religion. But what Schneider leaves intact of the personality and story of Jesus is so meagre, and so devoid of solid foundation, that it cannot claim any historical significance. One can see for oneself. "That the wise teacher," says Schneider of Jesus, "first appeared in adult age, and first taught in the synagogues and open air of his native place, is *very*

[1] *Zum Streit um die Christusmythe: Das babylonische Material in seinen Hauptpunkten dargestellt*, 1910.

probable; also that he gathered about him a circle of disciples of his own social sphere. That in this way he came into collision with the professional interpreters, the scribes, and the professionally pious, the Pharisees, is *very probable* in view of the character of his teaching. It must *remain an open question* whether he went to Jerusalem and was executed there (!); that he should seek disciples of his new teaching in the centre of Judaism *would not be surprising;* that he was confused on account of some imprudent remark with the Messianic pretenders of that excited world, and executed, is *not unthinkable,* but *it is just as possible* that he never left Galilee and died there in obscurity (!). The gospel story of the entrance into Jerusalem and death of the Messiah swarms with historical and scientific impossibilities, and is, in view of the central position of these elements in the dogma, rather a disproof than a proof of their contents" (p. 464).

This, then, is the opinion of the historical Jesus of a scholar without theological prejudice—and at the same time a typical example of the blending of the method of subtraction with the practice of deducing reality from possibility, as we generally find in this department. I should imagine that a theologian would say in face of such witnesses: "Save us from our friends."

9.—THE WORDS OF THE LORD.

(a) *The Tradition of the Words of the Lord.*—Wundt also holds, as quoted by Zimmern, that "the story of the Passion is, with the exception of a few [which?] details of sufficient (!) historical credibility, a tissue of legends." "But," he says, "what we do not find affected by these legends, or in any of the mythological prototypes, are the *sayings and discourses of Jesus,* as they are reported in the synoptic gospels."[1] Schneider also sees in his teaching

---

[1] *Völkerpsychologie,* ii, 3, 528.

the best proof of the historical existence of Jesus (p. 465). What must we make of this statement ? In other words, what evidence do the words of Jesus afford of his historical reality ?

We have already pointed out that the contents of the gospels point to two sources—a record of the actions of Jesus and a collection of his sayings, which we obtain from the parallels in Matthew and Luke as compared with Mark. But we also pointed out how uncertain our knowledge of this collection of sayings is—so uncertain that we may justly speak of this source as " a completely unknown x."

What makes this tradition of sayings so valuable to theologians is the circumstance that they believe it brings them much nearer to Jesus than the gospel of Mark. It is true that they cannot deny that, even if they succeeded in entirely and confidently reconstructing this tradition, of which there is as yet no question, we should still have only a book with a certain literary form or composition, arranged on the lines of literary composition. " By means of the sayings-source we do not at once reach Jesus, but the community. To put it precisely : in suitable cases we learn from the source what seemed to the community the characteristic, distinctive, and indispensable thing in Jesus " (Weiss, p. 159).

Now, in view of the entire constitution of the so-called primitive community, that is not a great achievement. It is even less when we reflect that, as we have previously pointed out, we are not at all sure that the traditional " words of the Lord " are the words of a single historical individual—namely, the historical Jesus. Theologians assume this; but they are again merely begging the question—a vice which infects the whole of their historical method. " Words of the Lord "—we cannot repeat it too often—are in Scripture so frequently merely words which the Lord (namely, Jahveh) gives to his followers through the " spirit " that, even granting the existence of an historical Jesus, it would be impossible to discriminate between what is due to the "spirit" in the collection and what is due to Jesus.[1] We do not know whether the collection of sayings expressly contained only the words of Jesus, or also included sayings which were on other grounds thought worthy of being admitted. We cannot say whether words which were believed to have been spoken under the influence of the "spirit" were not afterwards incorporated in the gospels and put in the mouth of Jesus simply because the best and most important sayings *must* have come, in the opinion of his followers, from the lips of him whom they venerated as "the Lord" in the specific sense of the word.

That a great deal that is tendentious, partisan, misunderstood, and of late origin has found its way among the "words of the Lord" in the gospels, that different phases of religious thought have found expression in them and armed themselves with the authority of the "Lord of Lords," is admitted by all critical students. Some idea can be formed of how much breaks down in this way if one takes the trouble to strike out of the gospels the words of Jesus which are recognised as interpolations.

But have we any guarantee of the substantial truthfulness at least of the tradition? We are referred to the form of the tradition, the deep impression of the words of the teacher in the memory of his hearers, the accurate, almost verbal, retention of detail that distinguishes the rabbinical instruction.[2] We are told that the

---

[1] Just as in the collection of sayings it is supposed to have been written, "Jesus says," etc., so in the prophets we find the words of Jahveh introduced by "A word of Jahveh," "Thus says Jahveh," etc. We have already seen that Jesus is possibly only another name for Jahveh.

[2] If this be true, how is it that such an important detail as the Lord's Prayer has been handed down to us in such various forms? No one knows exactly what words Jesus used in this prayer. According to Harnack, the earliest version is: "Father, the bread for to-morrow give us to-day, and forgive us our sins as we forgive others, and lead us not into temptation." *Sitzungenbericht der Preussichen Akademie der Wissenschaften*, 1904, Bd. V. Cf. Steudel in *Berliner Religionsgespräch*, "Hat Jesus gelebt?" 1910. 59 f.

Talmud shows the tenacity and conscientiousness of such a tradition. Granting, however, that the circumstances of the tradition were really so favourable, how came the various sayings of Jesus to be handed down to us in so many different forms as we actually have them? How can we explain that so much was lost of the words of Jesus that was certainly important, while so much that is unimportant was preserved? Yet we cannot suppose that Jesus said and preached no more than we have in the gospels as his words. "What was a precept of the school to the pupils of the rabbis," says Weiss, "became for the disciples of Jesus a question of beatitude. The words of the master were a matter of life and death; they were the foundation of the community, and the accurate determination of the words was their most important duty" (p. 162). It is remarkable, however, that the ostensibly earliest Christian writings lay so little stress on the words of Jesus that Clement, James, *The Teaching of the Apostles*, etc., quote the words of the Lord without expressly describing them as sayings of Jesus;[1] that Paul himself seems to know nothing of them, since, as we saw, there is not a single clear case of his referring to sayings

---

[1] Thus we read in *Clement* (xlvi, 8) the saying of Jesus: "Woe unto that man......it had been good for that man if he had not been born" (*Matthew* xxvi, 24), but with no reference to Jesus. Again, in xlix, 1, we find a hymn to love which is closely related to 1 *Corinthians* xiii, 1, though Paul is not mentioned. We read in 1 *Clement*, xiii, 1: "Let us before all things be mindful of the words of the Lord Jesus which he spoke, teaching meekness and patience. For he also said: Have mercy, that ye may find mercy. Forgive, that ye may find forgiveness. As ye do, so will it be done unto you. If ye are meek, ye shall find meekness. With what measure ye mete, it shall be measured to you again (*Matthew* vii, 1; *Luke* vi, 36-38; *Matthew* v, 7, and vi, 14; *Luke* vi, 31). With this command and these rules we will confirm ourselves in lowliness, so that we may walk in obedience to his holy words." But we also read on one occasion: "For the holy word says: To this man will I look, even to him that is poor and of a contrite spirit, and trembleth at my word"—a quotation from *Isaiah* (lxvi, 2). In *The Teaching of the Apostles* (i, 2) the doctrine of the two ways is developed, and it is also quoted in the Epistle of Barnabas (xviii, 1); and we find words which echo the Sermon on the Mount, though Jesus is not mentioned as their author, and no indication is given that they are not common Jewish sayings, as the quotation of the twelve Mosaic commandments suggests.

of Jesus, even where the similarity of idea ought to have reminded him of them, or the context should have actually compelled him to quote the authority of the master for his views.

How is it that, if Weiss is right, the words of Jesus played hardly any part in the early days of Christianity? Weinel's statement (p. 15) that the sayings of Jesus, not Christology, were the chief concern of the first Christians cannot be vindicated by a single historical fact. According to *Acts*, the first Christian sermon was not a repetition of the teaching of Jesus, but a discourse about Jesus, as we learn in the instances of Peter, Stephen, Philip, and Apollo.[1] If they really believed that these sayings belonged to an historical Jesus, why have they not been more carefully preserved? How was it possible for this collection of sayings to be lost? One would think that so valuable a thing as the words of their Lord and master would have been guarded by the community as a sacred treasure, copied innumerable times, and handed on from one generation to another. Instead of this, it seems that the mere memory of the existence of such a collection was entirely lost by Christians for centuries, and it was reserved for modern critical theologians to establish the former existence of such a source. As if providence had wished to reserve this material for their learned investigations.

(b) *The Controversies with the Pharisees.*—An attempt has recently been made to provide a proof that the "sayings of the Lord" in the gospels really come from the historical Jesus. These sayings and teachings, it is said, these conflicts with the Pharisees, these conversations with the disciples, parables, etc., are so "unique" and "inimitable," stand so far above all the rest of ancient literature, and have so pronounced a personal character, that they could only come from a personality, and, indeed,

[1] *Acts* ii. 14 : iii. 12 : vii. 2 : viii. 5 and 32 : xviii. 24.

from the Jesus of the gospels. The logical defect of this deduction is obvious. No one has ever questioned that the words of Jesus in the gospels have a thoroughly personal and individual colouring, that they convey an impression of definite historical situations, and that they reflect the feelings and thoughts of a personal inner life. But whether this was the life of a single individual, or a number of individuals in different circumstances contributed to the "sayings of the Lord" in the gospels—whether this single personality was the Jesus of the gospels or some prominent rabbi—is the great point in question.

The many irreconcilable contradictions that we find in the sayings of Jesus rather suggest that several persons, not one only, are behind them. And if they really belonged to one single personality, they could be traced to Jesus only *in so far as he was known to us from other sources;* in that case only should we have a right to say that none but so "unique" a person as this Jesus could have uttered such "unique" sayings. But we know this Jesus and the "uniqueness" of his inner life only from the words ascribed to him in the gospels. Thus the argument *always runs in a circle* when one attempts to prove the "uniqueness" of Jesus from the character of his words, and the "unique" character of his words from the "uniqueness" of the Jesus of the gospels.

Are these sayings really of such a character that they must be due to so extraordinary a personality as Jesus?

Take his conflicts with the Pharisees. The Evangelists are eager to show the superiority of their Jesus to the Pharisees and scribes in certain distinctive circumstances, and to put it in the clearest possible light. Over and over again the Pharisees approach the Saviour to put him to the test or ensnare him in the coils of their rabbinical dialectic, and over and over again they retire confounded and shamed by the clearness of his mind. Yet in very many cases the way in which Jesus confounds his learned opponents is such that we hardly know which is the more surprising, the utter unsoundness and meaninglessness of his replies, or the simplicity of the Pharisees in accepting them.

Thus, for instance, the disciples pluck ears of corn on the Sabbath, and when the Pharisees reproach Jesus for this he replies: "Have ye not read what David did, when he was an hungred, and they that were with him? How he entered into the house of God, and did eat the shewbread, which was not lawful for him to eat, neither for them which were with him, but only for the priests? Or have ye not read in the law, how that on the Sabbath days the priests in the temple profane the Sabbath, and are blameless?" (*Matthew* xii, 3). As if the action of the disciples could be in any way compared with the conduct of a hungry army, to which, moreover, the Jewish law even permitted the eating of unclean food! And as if the offering of sacrifice in the temple on the Sabbath were forbidden![1]

On another occasion the Sadducees put him the captious question, to which husband a woman would belong after death who had married seven brothers in succession, and Jesus reproaches them with not knowing the law, since in the next world people would neither marry nor be given in marriage, but be like the angels in heavens, and he adds: "As touching the resurrection of the dead, have ye not read that which was spoken unto you by God, saying, I am the God of Abraham, and the God of Isaac, and the God of Jacob? God is not the God of the dead, but of the living. And when the multitude heard this"—the Evangelist observes—"they were astonished at his doctrine" (*Matthew* xxii, 30–33). Why were they astonished? Can they really have supposed that the words of Jesus were a refutation of the Sadducæan view that there was

---

[1] See the *Tractate Schabboth*, fol. 17, col. 1: "The operations involved in offering sacrifice are not considered as work—that is to say, as breaking the Sabbath." See also *Rosh hashana*, fol. 21, col. 2, etc.

no resurrection of the dead? That God is the God of the living does not prove that life is not extinguished at death. And what the object is of bringing in the patriarchs it is impossible to say. When, moreover, Jesus accuses the Sadducees of ignorance of the law, he clearly forgets that precisely according to the law the woman never ceases to be the wife of her first dead husband, however many husbands she may subsequently wed.[1] How, then, could he silence the Sadducees, or "stop their mouths," as Luther puts it, with such a remark?

Another time the Pharisees ask him, as he teaches in the temple, by what authority he does this; and Jesus replies with a question about the origin of John's baptism, whether it was from heaven or from men; and when they dare not reply—for certain very improbable reasons—he answers, arrogantly: "Neither tell I you by what authority I do these things" (*Matthew* xxi, 23), and thus evades their question.

The greatest victory of Jesus over the Pharisees is supposed to have been when he asked them whose son the Messiah was, and they said, the son of David. He then said to them: "How then doth David in spirit call him Lord, saying, The Lord said unto my Lord, Sit thou on my right hand, till I make thine enemies thy footstool [*Psalm* cx, 1]? If David then call him Lord, how is he his son?" (*Matthew* xxii, 43–45). The gospel says that this reply so confounded the Pharisees that they dared not answer him, and put no more questions to him from that day. As a matter of fact, the reply of Jesus contains so obvious a fallacy that at the most we could only understand the behaviour of the Pharisees as a reluctance to have anything further to do with a man who answered in such a way.

Generally speaking, the Pharisees in the gospel description are anything but plausible. These zealots of the

---

[1] K. Lippe, work quoted, p. 228.

law who ask Jesus for a proof of his Messianic mission
(*Matthew* xii, 38; xvi, 1), while the law expressly forbids
them to attach any importance to the signs and wonders
of a false prophet (*Deut.* xiii), these heads of the community who allow themselves to be called by Jesus
hypocrites, blind, serpents, and generation of vipers,
calmly submit to these insults before the crowd, put
their hands in their pockets, plot the destruction of Jesus,
and meantime allow him to teach in the temple and the
synagogue—these are certainly not historical personalities,
especially when we observe that none of them is personally
described or named, whereas the Talmud scarcely ever
omits to name the persons in its record of the innumerable discussions of the rabbis with their opponents. We
have already seen the origin of these Pharisees who are
silenced by Jesus on every occasion and quietly allow
themselves to be "struck on the mouth" or instructed
by him; they come from the book of *Job*, where we read
in the twenty-ninth chapter: "The princes refrained
talking, and laid their hand on their mouth. The nobles
held their peace, and their tongue cleaved to the roof of
their mouth. When the ear heard me, then it blessed
me......After my words they spake not again; and my
speech dropped upon them. And they waited for me as
for the rain, and they opened their mouth wide as for the
latter rain"—that is to say, they looked forward eagerly
to the words of Job, which the Evangelist has perverted
into the sense that the Pharisees sought to destroy Jesus,
not to be inwardly strengthened by him. In any case,
we have no reason to be "surprised" at the way in which
Jesus escapes the toils of his enemies. His dialectic is
by no means of a high order, as anyone will perceive
who compares the conflicts of Jesus and the scribes and
Pharisees with the way in which Socrates confounds his
opponents in the Platonic dialogues. There is no
question whatever of "uniqueness" in this respect in the
case of Jesus.

s

(c) *Sayings of Jesus on the Weak and Lowly.*—Among the finest characteristics of Jesus we must place, it is said, his relation to the lowly, his love of children, his sympathy with the least conspicuous objects in nature. It is assuredly a touching and amiable feature in a man like Jesus to stoop so lovingly to the weakest of the weak, to look with tender eye on the flowers of the field and the birds of heaven, to contrast their indifference to the future with man's constant concern about his maintenance (*Matthew* vi, 26). But that this feature is not "unique" we learn from the Talmud, where we read: "Hast thou ever seen a bird or a beast of the forest that must secure its food by work? God feeds them, and they need no effort to obtain their nourishment. Yet the beast has a mind only to serve man. He, however, knows his higher vocation—namely, to serve God; does it become him, then, to care only for his bodily wants?" (*Kidushin* 4, *Halach* 14). "Hast thou ever seen a lion bearing a burden, or a stag gathering the summer's fruits, or a wolf buying oil? Yet all these creatures are sustained, though they know no care about their food. But I, who have been created to serve my creator, must be more concerned about my nourishment."[1]

Further, one might hold that Isaiah's description of the Saviour as especially sympathetic to the weak and needy would suffice of itself to "invent" the feeling of Jesus for children and embody it in the figure of his human personality. Children were, as the Talmud shows, greatly cherished among the Jews, and the love of them is deep-rooted in the Jewish character. "Out of the mouth of babes and sucklings," says the psalmist (viii, 2), "hast thou ordained strength [praise]"; and Jesus repeats this to the high-priests and their followers, when they are indignant at the cry with which the children greet him in the temple (*Matthew* xxi, 15). In

---

[1] See also *Ps.* cxxxvi. 25 : cxlvii. 9.

the same psalm it is said (4 and 5): "What is man that thou art mindful of him? and the son of man that thou visitest him? For thou hast made him a little lower than the angels, and hast crowned him with glory and honour." "About the Messiah," says the Talmud, "will all gather who seek in the law, especially the little ones of the world; for by the boys who still frequent school will his strength be increased."[1]

From these words we understand, even from the mythic-symbolical point of view, the saying: "Suffer little children, and forbid them not, to come unto me, for of such is the kingdom of heaven" (*Matthew* xix, 14) or the scene where Jesus calls a child, sets him in the midst of the disciples, who have asked who is the greatest in the kingdom of heaven, and says: "Verily, I say unto you, Except ye be converted, and become as little children, ye shall not enter into the kingdom of heaven. Whosoever therefore shall humble himself as this little child, the same is greatest in the kingdom of heaven" (*Matthew* xviii, 2–4). We read in the Talmud: "A young man deserves praise when he becomes [in mind] like the children" (*Tanchuma*, fol. 36, col. 4), and "Whosoever humbles himself in this life for love of the law, the same will be reckoned among the greatest in the kingdom of heaven" (*Baha Mezia*, fol. 84, col. 2). It is not clear, moreover, that the meaning of the relevant passages in the gospels is not symbolical, and the "children" for whom Jesus cares are not, as W. B. Smith says, proselytes to the belief in Jesus. For the Talmud speaks of those who have recently joined Judaism as "children."[2] "Whoso shall *receive* one such little child *in my name* receiveth me. But whoso shall offend one of these little ones *which believe in me*, it were better for him that a millstone were hanged about his neck, and that he were drowned in the depth of the sea" (*Matthew* xviii,

---

[1] Sohar to *Exodus*, fol. 4, col. 13.
[2] *Jebamoth* 22a. 48b. 97b: *Necharoth* 47a.

5 and 6). We must remember the many conflicts among the first Christians, even in the second century, as to whether a pagan on embracing the Christian faith should submit to the Jewish law and be circumcised or not, and the disdain of the Jew-Christians for the Gentile-Christians. "Take heed that ye despise not one of these little ones; for I say unto you, that in heaven their angels do always behold the face of my Father which is in heaven. For the son of man is come to save that which was lost......Even so it is not the will of your Father which is in heaven that one of these little ones should perish" (*Matthew* xviii, 10, 14). This should make an end of such sentimental stuff as Weinel puts before his readers on p. 86 of his work, as a sort of Indo-Germanic importation into the feelings and ideas of Jesus, when he says that Jesus was enabled to "hear the voice of God in bush and tree, in the harvest and the song of birds, in the blooming flowers and the play of children."

Jesus says in *Matthew* xi, 25 :—

> I thank thee, O Father, Lord of heaven and earth, because thou hast hid these things from the wise and prudent, and hast revealed them unto babes.
> Even so, Father; for so it seemed good in thy sight.
> All things are delivered unto me of my Father; and no man knoweth the Son, but the Father; neither knoweth any man the Father, save the Son, and he to whomsoever the Son will reveal him.
> Come unto me, all ye that labour and are heavy laden, and I will give you rest.
> Take my yoke upon you, and learn of me; for I am meek and lowly in heart; and ye shall find rest unto your souls.
> For my yoke is easy, and my burden is light.

These words are among the finest attributed to Jesus, but they are based on literary borrowing. The place that Jesus ascribes here to himself in regard to his father is precisely the relation of wisdom to Jahveh in the book of *Wisdom* (vii, 14; viii, 3; xvii, 28). In the book of Jesus

Sirach also it is written: " Secure wisdom, which is not bought with gold. Bend your necks under its yoke, and let your soul receive justification. Close is it to him who desires it, and whosoever gives himself to it, he findeth it. See it with your eyes; little have I laboured, and have found much refreshment in it " (li, 25). In fact, *Wisdom* itself makes Sirach speak thus: " Come unto me, ye that desire me, and sate yourselves with my fruits. For the thought of me is better than sweet honey, and the possession of me better than virgin honey. They that eat me shall ever hunger after me, and they that drink me shall ever thirst after me. He that heareth me shall not be ashamed, and they that use me shall not sin " (xxiv, 19). The idea of the supper in which the blood of the Lord is drunk and his body eaten, to purify from sin, is perceived in these words. But we fully realise that these words of Jesus were really taken from the Scriptures and put into the mouth of Jesus by the Evangelist when we find that the first conception goes back once more to the prophet Isaiah, the great source of the gospels:—

> Ho, everyone that thirsteth, come ye to the waters, and he that hath no money; come ye, buy, and eat; yea, come, buy wine and milk without money and without price.
> Wherefore do ye spend money for that which is not bread? and your labour for that which satisfieth not? hearken diligently unto me, and eat ye that which is good, and let your soul delight itself in fatness.
> Incline your ear, and come unto me; hear, and your soul shall live; and I will make an everlasting covenant with you, even the sure mercies of David (*Isaiah* lv, 1-3).

In this sense Jesus sends away the rich young man who cannot bring himself to abandon his wealth for the sake of the kingdom of heaven: " Verily, I say unto you, That a rich man shall hardly enter into the kingdom of heaven......It is easier for a camel to go through the eye of a needle than for a rich man to enter into the kingdom of God " (*Matthew* xix, 23). This, again, is a familiar saying of the rabbis, in which the man who pretended to believe some impossibility was asked: "Are you from Pombeditha [in Babylonia], where they can drive an elephant through the eye of a needle?"[1] And when Jesus says to the disciples, who ask about their reward for following him : " Everyone that hath forsaken houses, or brothers, or sisters, or father, or mother, or wife, or children, or lands, for my name's sake, shall receive an hundredfold, and shall inherit everlasting life" (*Matthew* xix, 29), he is merely repeating the blessing of Moses (*Deut.* xxxiii, 9): "Who said unto his father and to his mother, I have not seen him ; neither did he acknowledge his brethren, nor knew his own children......bless, Lord, his substance, and accept the work of his hands." "Many that are first shall be last, and the last shall be first," Jesus continues. And the Talmud supports him, saying: "Whoso lowereth himself, him doth God exalt; whoso exalteth himself, him doth God lower; whoso seeketh greatness, from him it flees; whoso fleeth greatness, it runneth after him" (*Erubim*, 13b; cf. *Baba Bathra*, fol. 10, col. 3).

(d) *Jesus's Belief in God the Father.*—But Jesus, theologians assure us, taught a new and unheard-of conception of God, and in this especially is the "uniqueness" and unsurpassable greatness of his teaching; for such an achievement is only possible to a supreme religious genius—namely, Jesus. God as a loving father, in contrast to the wrathful and stern God of Judaism!

---

[1] *Baha mezia*, fol. 38, col. 2 ; see also *Bereschit*, fol. 55, col. 2. We saw previously how the story of the rich youth is regarded by Schmiedel as one of the "pillars of a really scientific life of Jesus," because it contains the disavowal of the epithet "good" on the part of Jesus. But, as Smith has shown in his *Ecce Deus*, there is question only of a parable. The rich youth is a symbol of Judaism, which must renounce its property—its prerogatives and prejudices—and share them with the Gentiles, and "goes away sorrowful" because it has not the courage to do so. The words, "And he was sad at that saying, and went away grieved" (*Mark* x, 22), are, as Smith has shown, strikingly based upon the words of *Isaiah* lvii, 17, where the Greek translation says of Israel: "And he was grieved, and went his way sadly." May not the whole story be merely a paraphrase of the words of Isaiah?

"God and the soul, the soul and its God"—since Harnack published his *Wesen des Christentums* the refrain has echoed in every chapel and in all the publications of the evangelical and liberal theological school. They take it for granted, of course, that the "son of God," whether this is meant in the metaphysical or merely in the metaphorical sense, must have had a quite new conception of God, throwing in the shade all earlier ideas, and they talk themselves into an ecstatic admiration of Jesus's conception of God. Yet the idea of God the Father is common to all religions; and it is sheer theological prejudice to say that, when a Greek prayed to "Father Zeus" or a German to "All-father Odin," there was no corresponding sentiment in his soul, and his piety was not coloured by a childlike trust in the goodness, the surpassing wisdom, and the power of God conceived as a father.[1] Long before the time of Jesus the idea of God as the Father was quite common among the Jews. Wendt, in his *System der christlichen Lehre* (1906), counts no less than twenty-three passages in the Old Testament in which God is conceived as Father in just the same sense as we find in Jesus.[2] Isaiah exclaims, for instance (lxiii, 16; lxiv, 7): "Doubtless thou art our father......thou, O Lord, art our father, our redeemer."

It may be urged that the Jewish Jahveh is a stern God, who visits the sins of the fathers on the children down to the third and fourth generation (*Exodus* xxxiv, 7). But we also read in the Old Testament: "The fathers shall not be put to death for the children, neither shall the children be put to death for the fathers" (*Deut.* xxiv, 16); and, on the other hand, the idea of God as a stern, punishing father is not foreign to Jesus. And where shall we find in the words of Jesus a finer utterance on God than this: "The Lord God, merciful and

---

[1] See A. Dieterich, *Mithrasliturgie* (1903), p. 141.
[2] Cf. *Exodus* xxxiv, 6; *Deut.* viii, 5; xxxii, 6; *Sir.* xxiii, 1; *Ps.* ciii; *Wisdom* ii. 16, etc.

gracious, long-suffering, and abundant in goodness and truth, keeping mercy for thousands, forgiving iniquity and transgression and sin" (*Exodus* xxxiv, 6 and 7)? Or where shall we find more fervent thanksgiving for God's fatherly goodness and mercy than in the psalmist (*Psalm* ciii) ?—

> Bless the Lord, O my soul; and all that is within me, bless his holy name.
> Bless the Lord, O my soul; and forget not all his benefits;
> Who forgiveth all thine iniquities; who healeth all thy diseases;
> Who redeemeth thy life from destruction; who crowneth thee with loving-kindness and tender mercies;
> Who satisfieth thy mouth with good things......
> The Lord is merciful and gracious, slow to anger, and plenteous in mercy.
> He will not always chide; neither will he keep his anger for ever.
> He hath not dealt with us after our sins, nor rewarded us according to our iniquities.......
> *Like as a father pitieth his children*, so the Lord pitieth them that fear him.
> For he knoweth our frame; he remembereth that we are dust.
> As for man, his days are as grass; as a flower of the field, so he flourisheth.
> For the wind passeth over it, and it is gone; and the place thereof shall know it no more.
> But the mercy of the Lord is from everlasting to everlasting upon them that fear him, and his righteousness unto children's children.

As regards the relation of God the Father to the individual soul, this "religious individualism," as it is called, is not peculiar to Jesus or Christianity, but a fundamental feature of all deeper religions, and especially of the mystery-cults. In all of them the individual sought to enter into a direct personal relation to the deity, and the subjective feeling of the presence of God in them was not less strong and deep than in the case of Jesus.

In point of fact the God of Jesus is merely the God of

the Old Testament, the one God of Israel (*Mark* xii, 29), the God of Abraham, Isaac, and Jacob (*Matthew* xxii, 32). Jesus himself, as described in the gospels, is so little conscious of teaching anything new in this respect that he makes no claim to do so. Wrede destroyed the theological legend that Jesus had taught a new and deeper conception of God.[1] Even Wendt, when he does attempt to define the difference between the God of Jesus and the God of Judaism, has at length to confess the truth, and admit, in regard to the idea of God the Father: "Jesus was not the first to strike this note; it was heard before his time both in the Jewish and Greek religious worlds." It is true that he adds that the belief in God the Father had never before been "conceived with such confidence and plainness, such power and exclusiveness, as here, and never brought into such definite relation to the personal life" (p. 25); but R. Grützmacher has rightly characterised these as "statements which, apart from their really great modesty as a description of something new and epoch-making, which Christianity is supposed to have introduced into the religious history of mankind, are not capable of proof."[2]

The God and Father of Jesus is the common God of the Jews. "Not a sparrow shall fall on the ground without your Father," says Jesus in *Matthew* (x, 29); and he adds: "The very hairs of your head are all numbered." We read the same in the book of *Job*: "Doth not he see my ways and count all my steps?" (xxxi, 4). "Without the will of God no bird falls from heaven," says the Talmud; "how much the less shall danger threaten a man's life, unless the creator himself make it?"[3] And it is the same in *Pesikta* (fol. 18, col. 4): "Do I not number every hair of every creature?" "No man strikes here below with his finger but it is known above" (*Chulin*, 7).

Much stress has been laid on the fact that Jesus does

---

[1] *Paulus*, p. 91.   [2] *Gegen den religiösen Rückschritt* (1910), p. 4.
[3] *Bereschit rabba*, 79, fol. 77, col. 4.

not speak of God in general as the father of all men, but specifically as *his* father. But in *Mark* (viii, 38; xiii, 32) Jesus calls God not so much *his* father as the father of the Christ. It is only in *Matthew* and *Luke* that we find that intimacy and familiarity in the words of Jesus respecting his relation to God, and in *John* it assumes a thoroughly mystical character.[1] But that he calls God his father is, as we saw, an expression taken from the book of *Wisdom*, where the wicked hate the "just," because he speaks of God as "his father" (ii, 16).

(*e*) *Love of Neighbours and of Enemies.*—We cannot, therefore, find in their conception of God the extraordinary feature that would justify us in ascribing the words of the gospels to so extraordinary a man as Jesus. Is it in their ethical ideas?

According to *Mark* (xii, 29), Jesus answers the scribe who asks him which is the chief commandment: "Hear, O Israel; The Lord our God is one Lord: and thou shalt love the Lord thy God with all thy heart, and with all thy soul, and with all thy mind, and with all thy strength; this is the first commandment. And the second is like— namely, this: Thou shalt love thy neighbour as thyself." The words are found in *Deut.* vi, 4, and *Levit.* xix, 18. Jesus himself is well aware that in this he is not expressing any new idea. The way in which the scribe at once agrees with him shows that he is only putting a common opinion, and this is shown also by the parallel passage, *Luke* x, 25, where Jesus makes the scribe quote the words as a commonplace of the law. In *Matthew* xxii, 40, Jesus adds: "On these two commandments hang all the law and the prophets." Further, we read in *Tobias* iv, 16: "What thou dost not wish any man to do unto thee do thou not unto another"; and we find the saying in the same negative form in the Talmud: "A heathen came to Hillel and said to him: I will embrace Judaism

---

[1] Ernest Havet, *Le Christianisme et ses origines* (1884), iv, p. 37.

on condition that thou teachest me the whole doctrine
during the time that I stand on one leg. And Hillel
said: What thou dost not like do not to thy neighbour;
that is the whole doctrine. All the rest is only explanation; go thou and learn."[1] If this is supposed to be less
than Jesus demands, we must remember that the maxim is
in a negative form in the older editions of the gospels. In
this respect, therefore, the "love" which Jesus demands
is merely the Old Testament love of one's neighbour.

In *Matthew* v, 43, however, it is said: "Ye have
heard that it hath been said, Thou shalt love thy neighbour, and hate thine enemy. But I say unto you, Love
your enemies, bless them that curse you, do good to them
that hate you, and pray for them which despitefully use
you and persecute you." Here the love of one's neighbour seems to be elevated into a command to love one's
enemies. Weiss is astonished that I have "overlooked
this, and so many other things" (p. 166). I should have
thought that Christian apologists would have been better
advised not to touch the point. If Jesus really spoke
these words, he betrayed an astonishing ignorance of the
Mosaic law. Where is it written that the Jews must
hate their enemies? In *Levit.* xix, 18, where the love of
one's neighbour is prescribed, it is expressly said: "Thou
shalt not avenge, nor bear any grudge against the children
of thy people," and "Thou shalt not hate thy brother
in thine heart; thou shalt not in any wise rebuke thy
neighbour, and not suffer sin upon him [thou shalt
freely call thy neighbour to account, that thou bear no
sin on his account]." Not only towards their own people,
but even towards strangers, the Jews must not be without
love: "Thou shalt not oppress a stranger; for ye know
the heart of a stranger, seeing that ye were strangers in
the land of Egypt" (*Exodus* xxiii, 9), and "The stranger
that dwelleth with you shall be unto you as one born

---

[1] *Tract. Schabboth.* 31a.

among you, and thou shalt love him as thyself" (*Levit.* xix, 34). Even the love of enemies is commanded in the law: "If thou meet thine enemy's ox or his ass going astray, thou shalt surely bring it back to him again. If thou see the ass of him that hateth thee lying under his burden, and wouldest forbear to help him, thou shalt surely help with him" (*Exodus* xxiii, 4 and 5). "Rejoice not," says *Proverbs* (xxiv, 17), "when thine enemy falleth, and let not thine heart be glad when he stumbleth." "If thine enemy be hungry, give him bread to eat; and if he be thirsty, give him water to drink; for thou shalt heap coals of fire upon his head, and the Lord shall reward thee" (xxv, 21 and 22). In *Job* it is represented as a crime against God to rejoice over the misfortune of one's enemy (xxxi, 29), and the psalmist boasts of having saved one who had been his enemy without cause (vii, 5). "Say not thou, I will recompense evil," it is said in *Proverbs* (xx, 22); "but wait on the Lord, and he shall save thee." "Let them curse, but bless thou," says the psalmist (cix, 28). And Jesus Sirach says: "Forgive thy neighbour the injury he has done thee; then will thy sins be forgiven thee when thou prayest" (xxviii, 1).

Not only the Old Testament but the Talmud is full of demands of love of one's enemies and examples of good feeling towards opponents. "Thou shalt not hate, not even internally" (*Menachot*, 18). "Love him that punisheth thee" (*Derech Erez Sutha*, c. 9). "How is it possible for one that fears God to hate a man and regard him as an enemy?" (*Pessachim*, 113). A rabbi used, before he went to bed, to forgive all who had injured him during the day. Another, Rabbi Josua, wished to bring the divine judgment upon a heretic who tormented him, but went to sleep, and when he awoke reflected: This sleep was a warning that the just should never call the punishment of God on the guilty (*Berachot*, 76, also 10a). "When," says the Talmud (*Sanhedrim*,

39b), "the angels wished to sing a chant of joy because the Egyptians were destroyed in the sea, God said to them: My creatures are drowned, and would ye sing?" Finally *Job* says (xxxi, 13): "If I did despise the cause of my manservant or of my maidservant, when they contended with me; what then shall I do when God riseth up?......Did not he that made me in the womb make him? and did not one fashion us in the womb?"

The Talmud by no means restricts this love of one's enemies to members of one's own people. As man is bidden to pray to God for sinners (Sohar to *Genesis*, fol. 67), so God says to Moses: "Israelite or Gentile, man or woman, slave or free, all are alike for you" (*Jalkut*, c. 20b). In accordance with this, and in agreement with *Levit.* xix, 9, the Talmud commands them not to prevent the Gentile poor from gleaning in the fields (*Gittin*, c. 5), and repeatedly represents Abraham the Israelite as a model of tolerance. The best is, however, that the words of Jesus, "Bless them that curse you, do good to them that hate you," are not found at all in the older manuscripts of the gospels, but *are* found in the Talmud, where we read: "It is better to be wronged by others than to wrong" (*Sanhedrim*, fol. 48), and "Be rather among the persecuted than the persecutors" (*Baba mezia*, 93). "Where in the world," asks Weiss, "is there a Jewish writing or a Jewish community that has ever made love of one's enemy a fundamental rule of commerce? And wherever it has been put in practice—whence came the impulse, who inspired men thereto? The Talmud, or the Old Testament, or the figure of him who sealed his word on the cross?" (p. 165). The answer is found in the above.

It is sheer theological prejudice and perversion of history to say that Jesus was "the first" to preach love of enemies, that men owe to his example alone that love of one's neighbour has become the supreme principle of moral conduct, as Weinel claims. As if the Stoics had not preached universal love of mankind long before the time of Jesus; not merely as a passive endurance, but as an active interest in the lot of others and disinterested helpfulness on the basis of descent from a common divine Father and as members of a common humanity! As if Jesus had not violated his own command in his conduct towards the Canaanite woman (*Mark* vii, 27), his refusal to allow the disciples to go and preach the gospel to the Gentiles and the Samaritans (*Matthew* x, 5), his curse of the places that would not be converted, and his anger against the Pharisees and scribes on account of their opposition to him! It is an empty theological phrase to say that Jesus "raised the altruistic ideal to a pitch of supreme intimacy" and "destroyed in principle the barriers between peoples and sects";[1] it is anything but the outcome of candid religious-scientific inquiry—it is a resolute closing of one's eyes to the facts to exalt Jesus, in face of the above quotations from the Old Testament and the Talmud, for a merit which does not belong to him, but to them, and to maintain the fiction that love of enemies was made a "fundamental rule of trade" by Jesus in any higher sense than we find in the rest of Judaism. As long as theologians continue to praise the moral maxims of Jesus in this way at the expense of non-Christian ethics, we must decline to regard their efforts as impartial, in spite of that claim of "honourableness" which they repeat so pitifully, and however proudly they may wrap themselves in the

---

[1] "Jesus by no means 'discovered' altruism in ethics. Hellenistic moralists urged altruism long before the birth of Jesus. If the ethic of Jesus seems *particularly altruistic*, this is due, apart from theological suggestion, to the fact that the altruistic maxims of Jesus may seem less restricted and more impressive than in the case of the Greeks, because the scientific capacity, and therefore the scientific control of a new ethic, were slighter in the case of the Jews and Jesus than among the Greeks and their leading thinkers" (Schneider, p. 476). We may add that, when religious education and the Church do all they can to impress on the people this false view of the ethic of Jesus, they rely not only on the thoughtlessness of the masses, but on the fact that very few know anything about Greek or Hindoo philosophy and religion.

mantle of their scientific infallibility. We do not question their *subjective* honour, but we do question their ability, in their atmosphere of theological hypnotism, to see things as they really are. And if they grant that the precept of love of enemies has in it nothing peculiarly characteristic of Jesus, there is an end of the proof of "uniqueness" that was based on it, and the historical reality of the Jesus of the gospels falls to the ground.

(*f*) *The Sermon on the Mount.*—Careful inquiry shows that the remaining moral precepts and edifying sayings of Jesus have no more title to originality than the command to love one's neighbours and enemies. Take the Sermon on the Mount, for instance, which is wanting in Mark, and was certainly never delivered in the form in which we have it; this collection of the quintessence of the ethical teaching of Jesus is a "mere compilation of existing Jewish literature," and does not contain *a single idea* that we do not otherwise find in Jewish proverbial literature. Robertson, following Rodriguez (*Les origines du Sermon de la Montagne*, 1868), has given in his *Christianity and Mythology* a whole series of parallels; and from the work of the Rabbi Dr. Emanuel Schreiber, *Die Prinzipien des Judentums, verglichen mit denen des Christentums* (1877), it will be seen that the number of coincidences, not merely with the Talmud, is incalculable.[1]

"Blessed are the poor in spirit, for theirs is the kingdom of heaven," Jesus begins the Sermon; and the psalmist (cxvi, 6) says: "The Lord preserveth the simple; I was brought low, and he helped me." "Blessed are they that mourn, for they shall be comforted," is the next sentence; and Isaiah says (lxvi, 13), "As one whom his mother comforteth, so will I comfort you," to those who mourn the loss of their country, and announces to them the glorious fulfilment of the divine promises.

---

[1] See also Nork, *Rabbinische Quellen und Parallelen zu neutestamentl. Schriftstellen* (1839); T. Eschelbacher, *Das Judentum und das Wesen des Christentums*, 1908.

"Blessed are the meek, for they shall inherit the earth," is the third maxim; and Isaiah says (lvii, 15): "I dwell in the high and holy place, with him also that is of a contrite and humble spirit, to revive the spirit of the humble, and to revive the heart of the contrite ones." "A man's pride shall bring him low," says *Proverbs* (xxix, 23), "but honour shall uphold the humble in spirit." "My son," says Ecclesiasticus (iii, 17), "do thy work in humility; the greater thou art do thou the more humble thyself, and thou shalt find favour in the eyes of the Lord." Rabbi Jochanan says: "When a man has acquired meekness, then will he also acquire honour, wealth, and wisdom" (*Midrash Jalkut Mischle*, 22); and the psalmist says (xxxvii, 11): "But the meek shall inherit the earth, and shall delight themselves in the abundance of peace."

"Blessed are they which do hunger and thirst after righteousness," Jesus continues, "for they shall be filled." "He that walketh righteously and speaketh uprightly," says Isaiah (xxxiii, 15), "shall dwell on high"; and the Talmud says: "Any age in which the doctrine is not found—that is to say, in which a righteous life, conformable to the law, is not possible—lives in hunger" (*Schemot rabba*, cap. 31; see also *Psalm* cxviii, 19). In *Proverbs* we read (xxi, 21): "He that followeth after righteousness and mercy findeth life, righteousness, and honour." This also agrees in substance with the fifth beatitude: "Blessed are the merciful, for they shall obtain mercy." Pity and sympathy, even for animals, are urged and praised both in the Old Testament and the Talmud.[1] "Blessed are the pure in heart, for they shall see God," is the sixth beatitude. "Who shall ascend into the hill of the Lord?" says the psalmist (xxiv, 3), "or who shall stand in his holy place? He that hath clean hands and a pure heart." "Blessed are the peacemakers, for they shall be

---

[1] *Deut.* xxv. 4: xxii. 6 and 10.

called the children of God." But the psalmist also exclaims (xxxiv, 14): "Seek peace, and pursue it." Indeed, peace is lifted to so lofty a position by the Talmudists that they call the Messiah himself "peace," and Isaiah has described him as above all a bringer and prince of peace. Finally, the eighth beatitude, "Blessed are they which are persecuted for righteousness' sake, for theirs is the kingdom of heaven," has an echo in the Talmud: "They who are persecuted and persecute not, who sustain ridicule and injury and themselves do no injury, are the elect of God, of whom it is said: They shine like the sun" (*Schabbeth*, 88b). We have already seen, moreover, that persecution because of their righteousness is a mark of the good in the book of *Wisdom*, and secures heaven for them.

It is not necessary to go into other details of the Sermon on the Mount. It contains, as we said, nothing whatever beyond the common Jewish ethic, in spite of the trouble the Evangelists have taken to set up an artificial contrast between the ethic of Jesus and the Jewish morality of the time, and the effort of Christian theologians to obscure the real relation of the Christian to the Jewish ethic. Thus the prohibition of anger against one's brother (*Matthew* v, 22) is from *Lev.* xix, 17.[1] The maxim that merely to look upon another's wife is equal to adultery (*Matthew* v, 28) is covered by *Job* xxxi, 1, and *Ecclus.* ix, 5 and 8, and similar strict maxims in the Talmud, such as: "Whoever regards even the little finger of a woman has already violated matrimony in his heart" (*Bereschit*, 24 and 24a). When Jesus insists on purity and goodness of heart before a man approaches the altar to offer sacrifice (*Matthew* v, 23), he is merely following Isaiah and the other prophets who place piety of heart above the external piety of sacrifices and good works.[2]

---

[1] See also *Gen.* xlix, 7; *Prov.* xii, 16, and xiv, 16.
[2] *Isaiah* i, 11; *Jer.* vi, 20; vii, 22; *Hosea* vi, 6; *Amos* v, 22; *Micah* vi, 6; *Mal.* i, 10; *Eccles.* vii, 9, etc.

Indeed, it seems that the much-quoted maxim, that one must not resist evil, but present the other cheek to the smiter (*Matthew* v, 39), can be traced to *Isaiah* l, 6, and the description of the servant of God, who presents his back to those who beat him and his cheeks to those who plucked the hair. There is, moreover, a famous Jewish proverb: "If any demand thy ass, give him the saddle also" (*Baba kama*, 27).

Again, the advice as to almsgiving, doing good in secret (*Matthew* vi, 1-4), praying and fasting (5), and forgiving injuries (14) is founded on Jewish teaching, and is echoed in similar maxims of the Old Testament and the Talmud. Isaiah demands an inward, not an external, fast (lviii). The preacher bids his readers avoid many words in praying (v, 1; see also *Ecclesiasticus* vii, 14). As to the "Lord's Prayer," not only are the several phrases contained in the Old Testament[1] and in the Talmud, but it is certain that it was not uttered by Jesus in its present form.[2] The warning against the accumulation of earthly treasures and against the dangers of wealth (*Matthew* vi, 19), and the counsel to look first to the kingdom of God, are quite in accord with the prophets (*Ecclesus.* xxvii, 1, xxxi, 3; *Eccles.* v, 9, xii). The saying, "Judge not, that ye be not judged" (*Matthew* vii, 1), runs in the Talmud: "Judge everyone as favourably as possible" (*Abot*, i, 6), and "Judge not thy neighbour until thou hast stood in his place" (*Abot*, ii, 4), and "With the measure with which a man measures shall it be meted unto him" (*Sota*, 8b). The saying about the beam and the mote (*Matthew* vii, 4) is found word for word in the Talmud (*Baba bathra*, 15), and runs, in the mouth of the Rabbi Nathan: "The fault from which thou art not free blame

---

[1] See, for instance, *Ecclesiasticus* xxviii, 2.
[2] See Robertson, p. 450, and the above note concerning the Lord's Prayer. It is quite unintelligible to me how, in face of this plain fact, a Jewish rabbi like Klein can say: "Students of the evolution of religion have not as yet made any attempt to bring forward parallels to this unique(!) prayer. It is the most personal thing that we have of Jesus" (p. 84).

not in another" (*Baba mezia*, 59). The sentence, "Ask, and it shall be given to you; seek, and ye shall find; knock, and it shall be opened unto you," corresponds to the words of the prophet Jeremiah (xxix, 13): "And ye shall seek me, and find me, when ye shall search for me with all your heart," and to "The doors of prayer are never closed" of the Talmud (*Sota*, 49). Jeremiah, like Jesus, warns against false prophets, and urges to true repentance and good deeds.

In view of all this one does not see why the people should be "astonished" at the teaching of Jesus (*Matthew* vii, 28), since all the moral principles which the Evangelists put in the so-called Sermon on the Mount had long been, as Renan says, "the small change of the synagogues." Perhaps it will be suggested that the finest sayings of Jesus which are also found in the Talmud have been taken by the latter from the gospels. But at the time of the compilation of the Talmud the mutual hatred of the two parties was so great that a pious Jew would quite certainly not have admitted into his collection sayings which he knew to be represented by the Christians as the "words of Jesus." If it were done unwittingly, it would only show how slight the difference was from the first between the Jewish and the Christian morality; and it would be difficult to avoid the conclusion that the Christians had taken their "words of Jesus" from the common proverbial wisdom of the Jews.

Naturally, it was only the best in the available literature that seemed to the Christians good enough to be put in the mouth of Jesus. We are, of course, dealing with a "spiritualised and intimate Judaism," a philosophy of life and deity that had, among the dispersed Jews, been permeated by the finer thought and feeling of the Greek spirit. Anyone who doubts the possibility of this must have in mind only the description of Judaism in the pages of the gospels themselves, and take it to be an historical fact that Judaism was in the time of Jesus as fossilised and spiritless as it is described in the gospels. Such an assumption is a sheer *petitio principii*, and runs counter to the familiar experience that, when the religious leaders of a people lapse into formalism, the stream of inner religious life runs freely in other channels, and may produce new and remarkable phenomena. Remember the ancient mystics in the time of the scholastics of the Middle Ages, or the pietists during the predominance of the driest theological rationalism.

It is usually among the laity, the secret sects and conventicles, that the religious life pulses all the more vigorously and becomes all the deeper in proportion to the formalism of the official religion. Certainly, in contrast to the spirit of the Pharisees and scribes about the beginning of the second century, it is a " new spirit " that lives in the Jesus-sect, and finds expression in the words and ideas which Jesus is supposed to have uttered. But it is not a new spirit in the creative sense, since all that it contains of moral value has been derived from the great fund of Jewish proverbial wisdom, not produced by itself. They are the ideals of men who, no one knows how long before, had brooded over the writings of the prophets, especially Isaiah, lit the fire of the inner religious world from the plain and penetrating piety of the psalms and proverbs, absorbed their spirit, and never ceased to remain in continuous contact with the " everliving in the Scriptures." They could not, it is true, have transferred these finer flowers of Judaism to their own garden if they had not been personally disposed to this religious intimacy. But that one single personality gave them this spirit, as theologians say, it is just as superfluous to suppose as in similar cases of the rise of a pietistic and mystic fervour among the laity by the side of the official teaching of the sect. These first Christians had not to seek the pearls—the true and eternal—in the wilderness of official knowledge of the law, as they had never expressly looked there for them. And when it is said that only a quite exceptional religious genius like Jesus could have done this, it is forgotten that *the words of Jesus which have come down to us were not selected by him, but by the Evangelists, out of tradition;* since they certainly represent only an insignificant part of what Jesus could have taught.

Thus the fall of Jerusalem, the collapse of the political and national conditions of the Jewish religion, the increasingly bitter antagonism of the legal piety of the Pharisees to the Christian sectaries, and their inner conception of the Jewish faith, wholly suffice to explain not only the outburst of Messianic hope among them, but why the Christians precisely at this time—a time of the deepest humiliation and trouble—announced that the Messiah was coming immediately, and directed all their efforts to a preparation for his coming. All the lofty moral maxims and promises on which the community had long brooded, and which they may possibly have gathered into a collection of so-called " Sayings of the Lord," now sprang to the lips of the Christians, in contrast to the official legal righteousness, took the form of sayings of the expected Messiah himself, of warnings, consolations, and promises given during his earthly life, which they regarded as a condition of his coming again in splendour as the Messiah; and while the vague image of the Isaian servant of God and Saviour that lived in their hearts, perhaps fed by visionary experiences, assumed the shape and features of an historical Jesus, the word and image blended involuntarily, not consciously, in their inflamed imaginations into an inseparable unity, just as religious sects are accustomed to regard the most profound and important of their rules and customs as revelations of the deity or of their supposed founder.

(*g*) *Further Parallel Passages.*—Thus we see that from the words of Jesus no proof can be drawn of his historicity; indeed, even Weiss admits that it is "possible" that "not a single word of Jesus has been preserved, and that everything has been put into his mouth" (p. 168). We think that we are quite justified in assuming this when we find that it would be hard to quote a single expression of Jesus that might not be taken from the Talmud or the Old Testament. To what even apparently small details this extends is seen in *Matthew* viii, 22: "Follow me, and let the dead bury their dead." This corresponds to the command in the Talmud to postpone the burial of the body of a relative to reading in the law (*Megillah*, fol. 3). In fact, the peculiar expression of Jesus can only be understood when we learn that the godless living are said in the Talmud to be "dead" (*Jalkut Rubeni*, fol. 177, col. 3). Even such a saying as that in *Matthew* x, 40-42, and *Luke* x, 16, is found in the Talmud: "He who takes his neighbour into his house has the same reward as if the *Schechina* [divine spirit] itself entered his house" (*Shir hashirim rabba*, fol. 13, col. 3). "He who feeds one learned in divine things will be blessed by God and men" (*Sohar* to *Gen.*, fol. 129, col. 512). "If ye give ear to my angel, it is as if ye hearkened unto me" (*Schemoth rabba Abschn.*, 32, fol. 131, col. 3). "If thou honourest my commandments, thou honourest me; if thou despisest them, thou despisest me in them" (*Tanchuma*, fol. 16, col. 3).

Take such a saying as that in *Matthew* x, 35: "I am come to set a man at variance against his father, and the daughter against her mother, and the daughter-in-law against her mother-in-law," and compare it with *Micah* vii, 6: "For the son dishonoureth the father, the daughter riseth up against her mother, the daughter-in-law against her mother-in-law; a man's enemies are the men of his own house." The advice of Jesus as to the method of reconciliation with a brother who has offended (*Matthew* xviii, 15-17) corresponds to the procedure enjoined by Joma (fol. 87, col. 1), except that in the one case it is the injured, and in the other the injurer, who must act. *Matthew* xviii, 20—"Where two or three are gathered together in my name, there am I in the midst of them"—runs in the Talmud: "Where there are two persons, and they make not the law the subject of their discourse, is the seat of the scoffer [*Ps.*. i, 1]; but where the law is the subject of discourse, there also is the *Schechina*"—*i.e.*, the spirit of God (*Pirke Aboth*, col. 3). Jesus says in *Luke* x, 18: "I beheld Satan as lightning fall from heaven." In Isaiah it is similarly said of Babylon: "How art thou fallen from heaven, O Lucifer, son of the morning! how art thou cut down to the ground, which didst weaken the nations!" (xiv, 12), and the context makes it clear how easily the words might be applied to Satan.

We have previously shown how the Talmud agrees as to the story of the coin of the taxes and the answer of Jesus to the question of the Pharisees, whether it was lawful to give tribute to Cæsar or no. The story of the anointing of Jesus at Bethany has obviously grown out of *Psalm* xxiii, 5 ("Thou preparest a table before me in the presence of mine enemies; thou anointest my head with oil; my cup runneth over"), and *Deut.* xv, 11 ("For the poor shall never cease out of the land"). The scene in the garden of Gethsemane is provoked by *Genesis* xxii, 3 and 5, where Abraham takes with him his son Isaac and two servants, and bids them wait and pray while he goes with Isaac to sacrifice the boy. There is also a reference to the story of Elisha, when he falls asleep under a bush as he flies before Ahab, and is twice awakened by an angel, who gives him a loaf and a vessel of water, and bids him strengthen himself for the journey. It is significant that we find here the words which occur in the gospels: "It is enough. Take now my life, Jahveh" (*Mark* xiv, 36 and 41). Then there is the phrase: "My soul is exceeding sorrowful." "Why art thou cast down, O my soul? and why art thou disquieted in me? hope thou in God; for I shall yet praise him for the help of his countenance"; so runs *Psalm* xlii, 5, in accord with *Mark* xiv, 34. And verses 35 and 36 suggest *Ecclesiasticus* (xxiii, 1 and 4) : " O Lord, my Father and the author of my life, let me not fall through them [my sins]......abandon me not to the attack they plan against me."

10.—THE PARABLES OF JESUS.

The parables come after the phrases of the Sermon on the Mount as the most important of the sayings of Jesus. They are so greatly esteemed, and have such a repute for "uniqueness" and unsurpassable excellence that in the opinion of many they would suffice of themselves to establish the authorship of Jesus.

All these parables deal with " the kingdom of heaven," the manner of its spread, the way to become worthy of it, and the attitude which the Jews and Gentiles assume in regard to the promise of it in the Jesus-cult. The connection with Isaiah is thus obvious.

"Go and tell this people," Jahveh bids the prophet, " Hear ye indeed, but understand not ; and see ye indeed, but perceive not. Make the heart of this people fat, and make their ears heavy, and shut their eyes; lest they see with their eyes, and hear with their ears, and understand with their heart, and convert, and be healed " (vi, 9 and 10). " With stammering lips and another tongue will he speak to this people. To whom he said, This is the rest wherewith ye may cause the weary to rest; and this is the refreshing ; yet they would not hear" (xxviii, 11 and 12). These words have had a general influence on the description of the conduct of the Jews to Jesus, but they have had the special effect of causing the Evangelists to make Jesus speak in parables (*Matthew* xiii, 13). In this way we can understand the otherwise unintelligible saying in *Mark* iv, 12, that the Saviour speaks in parables to the people in order that they may *not* understand him and be converted and receive forgiveness for their sins. There is simply question of a quotation from Isaiah. More than elsewhere we here recognise the mystery-character of the original Christianity of the Jessæans, who thus reveal their dependence on Isaiah. The doctrine is communicated in parables which are unintelligible to "outsiders" and are not intended to be understood by them. Only the disciples or initiated are permitted to perceive "the mysteries of the kingdom of heaven." Hence we read in *Matthew* xiii, 34 and 35 : "All these things spake Jesus unto the multitude in parables; and without a parable spake he not unto them; that it might be fulfilled which was spoken by the prophet, saying, I will open my mouth in parables; I will utter things which have been kept secret from the foundation of the world " (*Psalm* lxxviii, 2). Mark, moreover, says that he explained all to his disciples (iv, 34).

In these circumstances we are not surprised to find one of the chief parables, that of the sower (*Matthew* xiii, 3 ; *Luke* viii, 5), first among the Naassenes, the pre-Christian Gnostic sect, the close relation of which to Christianity we have already pointed out. In this parable, however, we have, as W. B. Smith has shown at length, a modification and adaptation of a much older allegory in which the Gnostic teaching illustrated the sowing by God of the seed springing from the Logos which produces the world.[1] In the case of many other parables of Jesus, also, the source can be traced, and they are not reproduced as sayings of Jesus with any great improvement. Thus the parable of the merchant who exchanges all his goods for a single pearl is found in the Talmud (*Schabbat*, fol. 119, col 1), and goes back to *Proverbs* viii, 10 : " Receive my instruction, and not silver; and knowledge rather than choice

---

[1] *Der vorchristliche Jesus* (1906), pp. 108-135. Moreover, we read in the first Epistle of Clement : " The sower went forth and cast all his seed on the earth. They fall dry and naked on the soil, rot, and then the care of the Lord causes them to rise again out of their corruption, and from the one many are produced, and they bring forth fruit " (xxiv, 5). We see that the parable was told in many forms. Which form comes from Jesus?

gold. For wisdom is better than rubies; and all the things that may be desired are not to be compared to it." Even the parable of the net, which follows it in Matthew, seems to be inspired by the same passage in the Talmud, according to which the pearl is lost in a storm, swallowed by a fish, and recovered by the catching of the fish, and restored to its original owner, who sells it and obtains great wealth.

We read as follows in the Talmud: "God said to man: How great is thy guilt for betraying me? Thou sinnest against me, and I have patience with thee. Thy soul comes daily to me, when thou sleepest, and renders its account, and remains my debtor. Yet I give thee back thy soul, which is my property. So do thou each evening return his pledge to thy debtor." It is not difficult to see in this passage the parable of the dishonest servant (*Matthew* xviii, 23).

Again, we read in the Talmud: "To whom shall I liken the Rabbi Bon, son of Chaija? To a king that hath hired labourers, among whom was one of great power. This man did the king summon to himself, and held speech with him. And when the night fell, the hired labourers came to receive their hire. But the king gave to the favoured labourer the same hire which he had given unto the others. Then they murmured and said: We have laboured the whole day, and this man hath laboured but two hours, yet there is given unto him the same wage that we have received. And the king sent them away, saying: This man hath done more in two hours than ye have done during the whole of the day. Even so had the Rabbi Bon done more in the study of the law in the twenty-eight years of his life than another would have done who had lived an hundred years" (*Berachoth*, fol. 5, col. 3). The parable is quite consistent and unassailable. But the Biblical parallel—the parable of the workers in the vineyard—is clearly distasteful, since the king attempts to justify his conduct by a purely arbitrary feeling, and regards his lack of justice as a virtue (*Matthew* xx, 15). It has not been improved in the mouth of Jesus, where it is made to illustrate the theme that in the kingdom of heaven the last shall be first, and the first last; that many are called, but few chosen (xx, 16).

The parable of the two sons recalls the saying of the Talmud: "The just promise little, but do much" (*Baba mezia*, fol. 76, col. 2). The parable of the rebellious vine-workers is inspired by *Isaiah* v:

> My well-beloved hath a vineyard in a very fruitful hill.
> And he fenced it, and gathered out the stones thereof, and planted it with the choicest vine, and built a tower in the midst of it......and he looked that it should bring forth grapes, and it brought forth wild grapes.
> And now, O inhabitants of Jerusalem, and men of Judah, judge, I pray you, betwixt me and my vineyard.
> What could have been done more to my vineyard, that I have not done it? Wherefore, when I looked that it should bring forth grapes, brought it forth wild grapes?
> And now go to: I will tell you what I will do to my vineyard. I will take away the hedge thereof, and it shall be eaten up; and break down the wall thereof, and it shall be trodden down:
> And I will lay it waste......For the vineyard of the Lord of hosts is the house of Israel, and the men of Judah his pleasant plant; and he looked for judgment, but behold *oppression*; for righteousness, but behold *a cry*.

The parable of the royal marriage-feast runs in the Talmud: "A king held a great banquet, to which many guests were invited. They were requested to bathe, anoint themselves, and put on their festive garments, in order to appear worthily before the king. But the hour of the banquet was not definitely fixed. The more shrewd were seen walking up and down before the door of the palace about the ninth hour of the day, awaiting the moment when they should be permitted to enter. The more short-sighted thought otherwise, and each one went about his business, as on other days. Suddenly the summons was sent forth that those who were invited should come to the king's table. Then the former came in splendid garments, but the others in their soiled workday-clothes, on account of the haste of the summons. The king looked with friendly eye on those who had shown themselves prepared at his invitation; but the others, who had paid less regard to the king's command and had entered the palace in unfitting garments, had to receive as their reward the displeasure of the king. Those who were successful had a place at the royal table; the unsuccessful had to witness this, and had in addition to undergo severe punishment."[1] The parable is not very happy, on account of its many improbabilities; but in the New Testament it is altogether absurd. The invitation to a banquet already prepared; the reluctance of the guests to go to the marriage-feast, so that they even kill some of the servants; the blind fury of the king, who burns the town in revenge; his anger against one who is brought in from the road because he has not on the wedding-garment, and the terrible punishment inflicted on him—all this is so unnatural, grotesque, and ridiculous that it can only be pronounced a complete perversion of the Talmud original.

The parable of the ten virgins (*Matthew* xxv, 1), which embodies the same ideas, is no better. Ten maidens going out to meet a bridegroom at night, and some of them forgetting (!) the oil for their lamps and being rejected by the bridegroom for this slight negligence—these are not pictures taken from life, but untrue constructions of a flighty imagination. The same may be said of the master in the parable of the loan of the talents (*Matthew* xxv, 14), who is angry with the servant who brings back his talent without interest, deals hardly with him, and casts him into the darkness, where there was weeping and gnashing of teeth. We may note in passing that *Matthew* xxv, 29, is a rabbinical proverb

[1] *Koheleth rabba*, 9, 8. See also *Bereschit rabba*, sect. 62, fol. 60, col. 3; and *Sohar Levit.*, fol. 40, col. 158.

from the Talmud, where we read: "He who gathers shall have more added unto him; but he who suffers a loss, from him shall yet more be taken."[1]

Of the parables in Luke, that of the lost sheep (xv, 4) runs as follows in the Talmud: "A muleteer drove twelve span before him, all laden with wine. One of them strayed into the yard of a Gentile. Then the driver left the others, and sought the one that had broken loose. Asked how he had ventured to leave the others for the sake of one, he answered: The others remained on the public road, where there was no danger of any man seeking to steal my property, as he would know that he was observed by so many. So it was with the other children of Jacob [besides Joseph]. They remained under the eye of their father, and were moreover older than Joseph. He, however, was left to himself in his youth. Hence the Scripture says that God took special care of him."[2]

The parable of the lost piece of silver (xv, 8) repeats and weakens the same idea, and is likewise found in the Talmud: "When a man loses a piece of gold, he lights many lamps in order to seek it. If a man takes all this trouble for the sake of temporal things, how much the more should he when there is question of treasures that keep their worth in the world to come?" (*Midrash Schir hashirim*, fol. 3, col. 2). It is also the theory of the rabbis[3] that penitent sinners are dearer to God than the virtuous (*Luke* xv, 10).

The parable of the unjust steward (*Luke* xvi, 1) runs as follows in the Talmud: "A king had appointed two overseers. One he chose as master of the treasure; the other he put in charge of the straw-store. After a time the latter fell under suspicion of unfaithfulness. Never-

---

[1] *Tikkunim in Sohar Chadash*, fol. 75, col. 4.
[2] *Bereschit rabba*, sect. 86, fol. 84, col. 3.
[3] See *Sohar* to *Gen.*, fol. 29, col. 1113, where it is said that the penitent was a stage above the pious; and *Sohar* to *Lev.*, fol. 7, col. 56.

theless he complained that he was not promoted to the post of master of the treasure. Then was he asked, in astonishment at his words: Fool, thou hast incurred suspicion in charge of the stores of straw: how couldst thou be entrusted with the treasure?" (*Jalkut Simeoni*, (sect. 1, fol. 81, col. 1). The parable is not profound; but it is not quite inconceivable, as is the case with the parable in the gospel, when it says: "And the lord commended the unjust steward," and "Make to yourselves friends of the mammon of unrighteousness.......He that is faithful in that which is least is faithful also in much; and he that is unjust in the least is unjust also in much. If, therefore, ye have not been faithful in the unrighteous mammon, who will commit to your trust the true riches? And if ye have not been faithful in that which is another man's, who shall give you that which is your own?" (8–12). One asks in astonishment how such a parable could find admission into the New Testament.

The parable of the rich man and poor Lazarus (*Luke* xvi, 20) reminds us of the Talmud story of two men who died at the same time, one of whom had lived virtuously and the other viciously, and whom a rabbi saw, the one enjoying great delight, the other painfully licking with his tongue the edge of a spring, the water of which he could not reach.[1] We read much the same in *Midrasch Koheleth*, fol. 86, col. 14: "Of two sinners one had been converted before his death; the other remained in sin. When the latter went to hell, he marvelled to see the former companion of his evil deeds taken into heaven. Then he heard a voice: Fool, know that thy frightful death brought thy companion to repentance; why didst thou refuse during thy life to turn thy heart to penance? To this the sinner replied: Let me do penance now. Fool, the voice cried once more, knowest thou not that

---

[1] *Tractat. Chagiga*, fol. 77, col. 4, Jerusalem Talmud.

eternal life is like the Sabbath? He who does not prepare his food for the Sabbath on the day of preparation [Friday], whereof will he eat on the Sabbath? He who does not penance before he dies shall have no share in eternal life." In fact, the very words of *Luke* xvi, 25, are found in the Talmud, where it is said of the godless: " Because you have no share in that life you receive your reward in this world " (*Berachoth*, fol. 61, col. 2).

In order to illustrate the words, " Ask, and it shall be given you; knock, and it shall be opened unto you " (*Luke* xi, 9), Jesus tells the parable of a man who goes to a *friend* at midnight and asks for *three loaves*, which he at length receives, not from good-feeling or affection, but because of his importunity. The widow also (*Luke* xviii, 1) obtains her deliverance from her adversary after long entreaty only because she was so troublesome to the judge. These parables are harmless in themselves, but what an unworthy idea of God is embodied in them!

The comparison of the Messiah to a bridegroom (*Matthew* ix, 15; *John* iii, 29), and his coming to that of a thief in the night (*Luke* xii, 39), must have been very common among the Jews, as we find it also in *Revelation* (iii, 3, and xix, 7), and we saw that this was originally a Jewish work, subsequently modified in the Christian sense; perhaps it belonged to the circle of Gnostic sects from which Christianity issued.[1]

After all this it is impossible to say that the parables of Jesus could not be " invented " or are " unsurpassable." On the contrary, they are often defective, sometimes quite inconceivable, and are closely related to the Jewish parables both in form and contents; indeed, they are in part imitations of the latter, and are at times weakened, instead of being improved, in reproduction. It is mere theological hypnotism, which more or less affects all of us, that makes so much of the parables of Jesus. And

---

[1] Also compare *Isaiah* lxi, 10, and *Mark* ii, 19.

when Fiebig says, in his *Die Gleichnisreden Jesu* (1899), that these parables "have in themselves the guarantee that no one but Jesus could have created them" (p. 162), we know what to think of such extravagances.

The parables of the good Samaritan (*Luke* x), the prodigal son (*Luke* xv), and the Pharisee and the publican (*Luke* xviii) are really beautiful and important. The first, however, has a parallel in a Buddhistic parable which is believed to have had some influence on the gospel story;[1] the coincidence proves at all events that such a parable could be "invented." The parable of the good Samaritan corresponds in substance with *Deut.* xxii, 1. It is in harmony with Jewish morality, but not with the command which Jesus laid on his disciples not to go to the Samaritans. Possibly it is a later invention belonging to the time when the Christian mission was extended to non-Jewish places. Both of the first two parables give ground for reflection in the fact that they are found only in Luke, not in Matthew and John. This looks as if they were not in the so-called collection of sayings. As to the parable of the Pharisee and the publican, so excellent a story may have been invented late, just as well as that of the woman taken in adultery (*John* viii, 3). How can we say that it was impossible for any but Jesus to have told the story?

11.—GENERAL RESULT.

This examination of the parables contained in the gospels confirms our conclusion that it is impossible to see in the words of Jesus any proof of his historicity. Theologians are shocked that the *Christ-Myth* is unable to agree with the usual unrestrained admiration of the ethical principles of Jesus. Yet it has a companion in this in Schneider, who writes:—

> Jesus remains pre-Hellenic in ethic. He is a prophet,

---

[1] Pfleiderer, *Urchristentum* (1902), i, p. 447; Van den Bergh van Eysinga, *Indische Einflüsse auf evang. Erzählungen* (2nd ed. 1909, p. 57).

not a philosopher; an instrument of God, not a freethinker. His highest conceptions are anthropomorphic; his whole nature is semi-scientific, scholastic, clear in collecting instances to support his statement, but incapable of appreciating and properly presenting instances to the contrary. If we look only at details, we imagine that Jesus has exhausted all the possibilities of ethics; if we regard the whole, we see that he skims the surface and thinks he can hold all things, because he can penetrate none. It is only children that can unite everything. *Thus Jesus is not the highest and freest personality of history, but only the highest in ancient Judaism, restricted and not free in comparison with the greatest Greek thinkers.* If, in spite of this, he had succeeded to their heritage with his ethic, he owes this to his *reactionary character.* The romanticists of Hellenism, sated with the rational, were impressed by the irrationality, the paradox, the authoritative and primitive, the sentimental-social element in his teaching; romanticists easily become Catholics. To the masses the prophet of Nazareth becomes a Tammuz-form; the authoritative foundation of his ethic becomes a blunt command of a strong God to weak men; the utilitarian idea of redemption in this world (?) becomes a common (immoral, in the sense of the highest Greek morality) and material hope as regards the other world, of which Jesus himself knew, and could know, nothing (p. 478).

Thus we can sufficiently understand the "mighty, life-controlling impression" which the gospel figure of Jesus has made on millions of people. "Some magic or power must have gone forth from him," says Weiss, and he points to the fact that art has at all times gone to the gospels for material. "The true artist has a sure feeling for the sincere and living; he is for us an impartial witness that"—Jesus was an historical personality? No, no; but that—"the gospel tradition, however it arose, is not an insignificant thing, but something alive and true" (p. 46). As if that were in contradiction to our thesis that the "words of the Lord," because they are supposed to come from Jesus, are *immeasurably overrated* and their defects overlooked, and therefore in no circumstances can they be used to prove the historical reality of the god-man Jesus in the usual

sense! This argument—we cannot repeat it too often—
runs in a circle, like all the others. No one betrays this
more clearly than Weiss himself when he exclaims to
the reader at the close of his work: "Take and read!
......Read the words of Jesus, *as if they came from
Jesus,* and thou wilt recognise that this is not merely the
simplest, but the safest, theory" (p. 170). That is
exactly what we charge against theology, even when it
professes to be critical: it has hitherto always read the
words of the gospels *as if* they came from Jesus, without
considering the opposite theory. This may very well be
the "simplest" and most convenient way of dealing with
the gospels; but is it on that account the correct way?
In such circumstances theologians naturally find what
they *assumed* in advance, just as the believer finds in the
gospels the Jesus whom he seeks—the Jesus that heredity,
education, and custom have suggested to him. But that
this is a "scientific method," or has anything whatever
to do with sound historical research, is exactly what
we deny.

12.—THE "STRONG PERSONALITY."

When we regard all that we have seen as to the
mythic, Old Testament, and Talmudic character of the
actions and words of Jesus, it is difficult to maintain
with good conscience the existence of an historical Jesus.
Of which of his actions or words could it be said with
confidence that they really go back to an historical Jesus?
The situation is not that certain things in the gospels
are found to be fictitious, and that this by no means robs
all the rest of historical value. The fact is that there is
nothing, absolutely nothing, either in the actions or words
of Jesus, that has not a mythical character or cannot be
traced to parallel passages in the Old Testament or the
Talmud, and is therefore under suspicion of being derived
from them. Let us hear no more of the "uniqueness"
of and "impossibility of inventing" the Jesus of the

gospels! Until the passages in the gospels are positively shown to us on which such a claim is made, we are justified in ignoring it.

It is a complete *misunderstanding of the facts* to say that this admitted "mythical woof" of the gospels proves nothing against their substantial accuracy, and to attempt to convict those who reject the historical Jesus of defective method. The wrong method is altogether on the side of those who believe in an historical Jesus, although there is *not a single passage in the gospels* they can show to be historical. "When the throne falls, the duke must go." If all the details of the gospel story are resolved in mythical mist, as they are resolved in the hands of historical criticism, then, precisely from the methodological point of view, we lose all right, not merely to say what Jesus was, but to make the bare assertion that there ever was such a person. "It is uprooting the foundations of history, we are told, not to believe in the existence of Christ and the truth of the narratives of his apostles and the sacred writers. Cicero's brother also said: 'It is uprooting the foundations of history to deny the truth of the Delphic oracles.' I would ask Christians if they think they destroy the foundations of history when they reject these oracles, and whether the Roman orator would have thought that he was destroying the foundations of history if he had rejected their oracles, supposing that he had known them. Each man fights for his own chimera, not for history."[1]

But "our confidence in tradition and in historical reason will be profoundly shaken if there never was such a person as Jesus," exclaims Herr von Soden—and hundreds echo the lament. For in that case "the whole of civilisation has been deceived for 2,000 years" (p. 8). The answer to this difficulty—so profoundly penetrated with the "historical sense"—was given by Steudel.[2] It

---

[1] Dupuis, *Ursprung des Gottesverehrung*, p. 228.
[2] *Wir Gelehrten vom Fach*, p. 8.

almost looks as if the old French scholar Dupuis had foreseen von Soden when he says that "in matters of religion the belief of many generations proves nothing but their own credulity; Hercules was assuredly the sun, whatever the Greeks may have believed and said of him. A great error is propagated more easily than a great truth, because it is easier to believe than to reflect, and men prefer the wonders of romance to the plain facts of history. If we were to adopt that rule of criticism, we might urge against Christians that the faith of any people in the miracles and oracles of its religion proved its truth; I doubt if they would admit the argument, and we will do the same with theirs. I know that they will say that they alone have the truth; but the other people say the same. Who shall judge between them? Sound reason, not preformed faith or pre formed opinion, however widespread it may be" (p. 227). For the rest, have not nearly eighteen centuries believed in the "god-man" Christ, and died in the belief, though a more enlightened age has shown that the belief was a mythological illusion, and our liberal theologians have succeeded it with their human Jesus? Our confidence in historical reason will be shaken if there never was such a person as Jesus! But must not this confidence in reason be shaken if it should be true that a man has been made a god, and for centuries has been honoured as Jesus was in Christianity? One defends, so to say, the honour of human reason, when one shows it the error of what liberal theology calls history and the origin of Christianity. Liberal theologians would do well to reflect before they cut the ground from under their own feet with such arguments.

There is still one difficulty to consider, and, although it has not a very firm basis in our opponents, it has played a great part in the public discussion—the difficulty, namely, that so mighty a spiritual movement as Christianity can only be explained by a "strong personality," who must, of course, have been Jesus. This difficulty also may be described as "simple." It assumes something that needs proving—that only a great individual personality can bring about a spiritual movement, and that such a movement must in all circumstances be traced to a single outstanding personality. What instances are there of this in history? Are we referred to the personality of Luther in relation to the Reformation? But historians are agreed that Luther would never have accomplished his task if he had not been preceded by Huss, Jerome of Prague, Savonarola, the mysticism of Eckehart and Tauler, etc. And beside Luther are other "strong" personalities, such as Zwingli, Calvin, and Hutten, men who helped to clear the stifling religious atmosphere of the time by their contemporary appearance and work in the direction of the Reformation. And would all these men together have done anything if they had not found the masses prepared for their ideas, and an age that pressed for the settlement of a crisis?

Great personalities are by no means always the initiators of a new spiritual movement. It is usually prepared in numbers of individuals, and at length the inner need reaches its height and a few clear-minded and energetic personalities take the lead, though these need not at all be the "greatest" of their age. When the harvest is ripe, the seed falls, and no superhuman force is needed. It may be questioned whether Luther could have established the Reformation if he had been born fifty years earlier. The importance and power of a movement, therefore, are by no means proportionate to the importance of the personalities in whom it takes shape, and who give the first impulse to its becoming an open force. If the time has come, a slight impulse will often suffice to discharge the accumulated energy; just as a small stone detached on the precipice suffices to launch an avalanche that thunders down the mountain and sweeps away forests, houses, and men. So mighty a movement as the Renascence, which entirely changed the intellectual condition of Europe in less than two centuries and ended the Middle Ages, did not start from a single personality. The French Revolution was essentially the work of the masses, from which a few gifted, but by no means "powerful," personalities—Mirabeau, Danton, Robespierre, etc.—stood out; and they were, to some extent, rather swept along by it than leaders of it.

Who was the founder of the Babylonian, the Egyptian, or the Greek culture? Who created the ancient religions of Zeus, Dionysos, and Osiris? Who founded Judaism? Was it Moses? The more advanced representatives of science have long since given up the historicity of Moses, and even those who still adhere to it are compelled to restrict his significance to such an extent that it is quite absurd to call him the "founder" of the Jewish religion. Post-exilic Judaism was created, quite independently of this legendary Moses, by the joint work of the priests at the temple of Jerusalem who, under the influence of the prophetic reform, codified and elaborated "the law"; only a few names have come down to us, and even in their case we have no guarantee that even the smallest share of the work can be ascribed to them. In the case of the religion of Mithra even these few names are wanting. Yet Mithraism was a religious movement that spread with irresistible force from the east over Europe about the beginning of the present era, and was the most dangerous rival of Christianity in the fourth century. It has been said that Mithraism failed, in contrast with Christianity, precisely because it did not spring from a strong personality such as Jesus. There is this much truth in the statement, that the Persian Mithra was a very shadowy form beside Jesus, who came nearer to the heart, especially of women, invalids, and the weak, in his human features and on account of the touching description of his death. But that shows at the most that the more concrete idea has the better prospect of triumphing in a spiritual struggle than the more abstract; it proves nothing as regards the historical reality of the idea. Moreover, history teaches us that it was quite different causes—partly external and accidental causes of a political nature, such as the death in the Persian war of the Emperor Julian, one of the most zealous followers of Mithra — that gave Christianity the victory over Mithraism.[1]

There is, therefore, no proof whatever in such general assertions as that only a great and powerful personality like Jesus could have given birth to Christianity. That is a very convenient way of proving one's thesis. It is merely a relic of the childlike conception of history that we often find in elementary schools—the conception that history is "made" exclusively by what are called heroes, among whom must be numbered the ancestors of the ruling house. A great spiritual movement *may* be brought into being by strong personalities, but need not be; and the claim that such a movement *must* have been brought about by a *single* outstanding personality is a monstrous absurdity, and the absurdity only increases when this individual is supposed to be so "unique" as to transcend all human levels, as Jesus is represented by theological "historians."

Naturally, the early Christian movement had "great" personalities to give it a definite aim, control its organisation and direction, and defend its right to be heard. Peter, James, John, etc., may have been among these individuals, whose merits were so much appreciated by a later Christian generation that they became direct disciples of Jesus in the "history" of the Saviour. But

---

[1] Cf. J. M. Robertson, *Pagan Christs*, 2nd ed., 1911, 327 ff. As Robertson shows in this work also, the historicity of Zarathustra and Buddha is not so well founded as one commonly thinks. Only of one single great religion (Mohammedanism) do we know positively that its founder was an historical person. But Mohammedanism is in its essence not an original religious creation, but an eclectic composition of ancient Arabic and Jewish fragments, and the great influence which it exerted in history depends upon quite other things than its inner religious truth.

it does not follow that they were inspired in their work by an historical Jesus, any more than that the Virgin Mary must be an historical personality because a French peasant-girl thought that she saw her with her bodily eyes in a lonely grotto, and in consequence thousands go every year to Lourdes to be healed of their maladies. For the rest, if anyone persists in thinking that Christianity must have been founded by a single powerful personality, may it not have been Paul? If not Paul, have not our inquiries shown that in the long run the contents of the gospels may be traced to the prophet Isaiah, whose "predictions," sayings, penitential appeals, and promises reappear in the gospels, in the form of a narrative? *Hence Isaiah, not Jesus, would be the powerful personality to whom Christianity would owe its existence.*

13.—THE HISTORICAL JESUS AND THE IDEAL CHRIST.

If, then, the historical individual Jesus cannot be regarded as the founder of Christianity and the one who inspired the followers of the new religion and impelled them to sacrifice their lives for their faith, what can we substitute for him as the determining principle of the whole movement? Isaiah's suffering servant of God, offering himself for the sins of men, the just of *Wisdom* in combination with the mythic ideas of a suffering, dying, and rising god-saviour of the nearer Asiatic religions —it was about these alone, as about a solid nucleus, that the contents of the new religion crystallised. The *ideal Christ*, not the historical Jesus of modern liberal theology, was the founder of the Christian movement, and made it victorious over its opponents. It is more probable that *Jesus and Isaiah are one and the same person* than that the Jesus of liberal theology brought Christianity into existence; that the first Christians, the Jessæans, were followers of the prophet; and that in their over-heated imaginations the figure of the prophet himself was transformed into the Saviour and Redeemer.[1]

From the first we find Christianity as the religion, not of the historical man Christ, but of the *super-historical god-man Jesus Christ*, who merely passes through history. It is he who is supposed to have appeared to Paul and revealed himself as the true Saviour (*Gal.* i, 12 and 16). His figure is discerned clearly enough beneath the human clothing in the gospels, the purpose of which it is, not " to raise to a higher sphere the life of the historical Jesus by means of fanciful myths and stories of miracles, but to bring home to readers by an historical representation the superhuman divine nature of Jesus."[2] That God himself has exchanged his heavenly glory for the lowliness of earth; that Christ became "the son of God" and descended upon the earth; that God divested himself of his divinity, took on human form, led a life of poverty with the poor, suffered, was crucified and buried, and rose again, and thus secured for men the power to rise again and to obtain forgiveness of sins and a blessed life with the heavenly father—*that is the mystery of the figure of Christ;* that is what the figure conveyed to the hearts of the faithful, and stirred them to an ecstatic reverence for this deepest revelation of God. There is not in the centre of Christianity one particular historical human being, but *the idea of man*, of the suffering, struggling, humiliated, but victoriously emerging from all his humiliations, "servant of God," symbolically represented in the actions and experiences of a particular historical person. How much grander, loftier, and more spiritual is this idea than the prosy belief of liberal theologians in the "unique" personality of Jesus of Nazareth of 1,900

---

[1] As is known, there was a legend of Isaiah having been taken up into heaven, like Moses, Elijah, Enoch, etc.—a proof that about the beginning of the present era the figure of the prophet had actually assumed superhuman characters.

[2] Ferd. Jak. Schmidt, *Der Christus des Glaubens und der Jesus der Geschichte* (1910), p. 29.

years ago, which has played hardly any part in the whole Christian development, and which, on account of its temporal, national, and temperamental limitations, would never have been able to fill the religious thought of nearly two thousand years.

Those who believe in an historical Jesus tell us that personalities, not ideas, make history. Apart, however, from the fact that this is no proof of the historicity of Jesus, as, of course, the idea of the Christian Saviour had to be made the centre of the new religion by personalities, until three generations ago the personality was not prominent at all in the historical conception of Christianity, but was used merely as an "illustration" in explaining the unfolding of the divine idea, without having any independent significance as the leading and shaping factor in history.

In his work, *Idee und Persönlichkeit in der Kirchengeschichte* (1910), Walther Köhler has shown by means of historical facts how little interest Christianity has in "great" personalities, since the most distinguished members of the religion, such as Augustine, Thomas Aquinas, Eckehart, Tauler, Huss, Luther, etc., conceived the world-process as a divine phenomenon, made the individual secondary to the development of ideas, and merely introduced it occasionally to illustrate the ideal history. When Master Eckehart speaks of Christ, he is by no means thinking of the historical individual, but merely of the idea of the Christ, whose actions and sayings in the gospels he interprets symbolically, and converts into the super-historical of his speculative mysticism. When Lessing pens the famous words, "The accidental truths of history can never furnish proof of the necessary truths of reason," he shows that he attaches no importance in his religious feeling to the historical person of Jesus. According to Kant, the historical serves "only to illustrate, not to demonstrate." In his work, *Die Religion innerhalb der Grenzen der blossen Vernunft*, Christ is to him nothing but "the ideal of human perfection," and he says that it contains its reality "in itself" for practical purposes: "We need no example from experience to serve as a model to us of the idea of a man morally pleasing to God; it is found as such in our reason." Indeed, Kant regards it as "the utmost absurdity conceivable" to take an historical belief, like that in Jesus, however proportioned it be to human capacity, and however deeply it may be rooted in the hearts of men on account of its long prevalence, as a condition of a universal and exclusively saving faith (p. 280).

How far from this view are our modern liberal theologians—who, nevertheless, swear by Kant—when they make the belief in the historical man Jesus, the "personal life of Jesus," in their fine phrase, the essential element of Christianity! What they really appreciate in Kant is his hostility to metaphysics, which enables them to refrain from positive statements on transcendental things, and continue to use Biblical expressions because no more correct expressions are yet available. Liberal theology is an offspring of the time which chose science for a leader after the collapse of speculative philosophy about the middle of the last century, and, under the banner of modern empiricism and positivism, branded the belief in ideas as a superstition. It was the time when the emphasis of personality, which had begun with Erasmus, and increased in the pietism of the eighteenth century, in Schleiermacher, Humboldt, Neander, and others, at length became generally popular. The idea is nothing; the individual is everything. Man, Feuerbach had taught, creates the idea, not the idea man. From the psychology of the academic school and the general appreciation of facts of experience theologians adopted a new way of looking at things. A tendency got the upper hand among them which, apart from religious speculation, rejected the hitherto prevailing view of Christianity as obsolete, and substituted the mere man Jesus for the discarded dogma. "Personalities, not ideas, make history." The cult of the "great man" began. By introducing personality as the decisive factor in the mechanism of history, it was hoped to find the necessary foundation for the cult of "the greatest personality in history," the historical Jesus. The fact was overlooked that modern empiricism and psychology are merely the complement of scientific materialism. It was not noticed that to do away with the belief in the objective idea was to destroy the foundation of the belief in providence and a divine control of human events; and with this belief all religion disappears. People talked themselves into an ecstatic reverence for the "unique" personality of Jesus, although the advancing criticism of the new figure of Jesus left less and less positive historical facts in support of it, and it became increasingly difficult to maintain this reverence. How did it fare with the professors when they found the traditional figure of Jesus becoming fainter and fainter as their "historical criticism" advanced? The clergy continued to breathe new life into the fading figure, and found it possible still to feel themselves personally "overpowered" by their Jesus. They were proud that they now knew the real "essence of Christianity" for the first time. And when an objection was raised at times to this methodical Jesus-cult, they consoled themselves resignedly with the words of Carlyle: "Man knows nothing more sacred than heroes and reverence for heroes."

In this condition of self-sufficient ecstasy about Jesus, in which it was no longer thought necessary to trouble about the great questions of general philosophy from some excessive tenderness about the "supersensuous," and the "unknowable" was silently ignored, *The Christ-Myth* fell like a bomb, with startling effect. The inadequacy of their own theory began to dawn even upon the simplest of them. A certain nervousness and insecurity spread among theologians, and took the form of furious bitterness and hatred when the author of that work endeavoured, by

means of lectures, to interest the general public in his
denial of the historicity of Jesus. Now the whole Press
is engaged against the disturber of the peace; it is the
easier as the word "liberal" confuses the liberal in the
theological and the political sense, in spite of enormous
differences, and the "orthodox" Press is readily gained.
Opposing lectures and Protestant meetings are organised,
and J. Weiss publicly declares that the author of the
book has "no right to be taken seriously." But among
his fellows, within the four walls of the lecture-hall, and
in the printed version of his lectures, Weiss assures his
readers that he has taken the matter "very seriously,"
and speaks of "the fateful hour through which our [theo-
logical] science is passing" (p. 170). Bousset declares in
the Scientific Congress of Preachers at Hanover that the
question of the historicity of Jesus "is not worthy of
occupying public attention." But at the World-Congress
for "Free Christianity and Religious Progress" he grants
that the ideas of *The Christ-Myth*, which "have not even
been made approximately plausible," have nevertheless (?)
awakened a conviction of the need for a "certain revision"
of liberal theological views. Indeed, this protagonist of
the modern Jesus-cult, who is supposed to have proved
so "triumphantly" against Kalthoff the correctness of
his views, acknowledges that "intensive historical work
has made the situation of the present theological position
acute, and laid insupportable difficulties on the theologian," and that history, "when it is pressed resolutely
to the end, leads to a region beyond itself"; and, appealing
to Kant and Lessing, he demands a different foundation
for belief than history—namely, "reason."[1]

14.—IDEA AND PERSONALITY: SETTLEMENT OF THE RELIGIOUS CRISIS.

If liberal theologians are really in earnest in attempts
to attain a philosophical system, they can only realise

---

[1] *Die Bedeutung der Person Jesu für den Glauben*, pp. 6, 10, etc.

their aim by a renewal of belief in reason in the universe, in a metaphysical "sense" of existence, in the defining and controlling power of the "idea," and the co-ordination and subordination of human personality to the system of ends, the recognition of which is the essence and condition of all religious belief. The chief danger that has come to our time, especially to religion, under the influence of science is the denial of objective purpose in the universe. Let men be taught to believe again in ideas, and then Monism, in its idealistic form, will become the first principle of all deep religious life. From this point of view personality ceases, however great it may be, to claim an independent and unique significance in the world-process; even the great individuals of history sink to the condition of mere means and instruments; "agents," as Hegel says, of a purpose that represents a stage in the advance of the general mind. Liberalism is content with the mere cult of the great historical personality, as if it had any value as such. But when we ask how the personality stands out from its environment, what it is that raises an individual to world-significance, whence its great influence and power over men come, we find that, as Hegel says, the world-spirit is especially active in such an individual, and leads his will.

In other words, it is the *idea* that attains consciousness in such men and stirs them to action; they are what they are only by the living power of the divinity within them. In this sense it is true that in the last resort ideas, not personalities, rule the world; and this is the one really religious view, because we cannot see why Christianity, too, may not have come into being from the idea living in its adherents of a suffering, dying, and rising saviour. We see how this idea created the religions of Attis, Adonis, Osiris, Dionysos, and similar gods; how Christian mysticism has at all times drawn fresh strength from it, and German speculative philosophy has derived from it a system that, by its depth, amplitude, and religious content,

has thrown all previous systems into the shade, and which
has only been prevented by its scientific form from exer-
cising an uplifting and ennobling influence on life. It
is said that a purely ideal religion of this kind cannot
satisfy the religious needs of humanity without historical
guarantees of its truth. But it *has* satisfied immense
numbers — even setting aside India, where idealistic
Monism forms the nucleus of all religious life—in the
mysticism and piety of Eckehart and Tauler, in that
humble and self-sacrificing surrender to the all, such as we
find in the institutions of the later Middle Ages, the care
of the sick and the poor, which owed their origin, not to
the official religion of the Church, but to the mystics; it
has satisfied the best minds of Germany — Lessing,
Herder, Goethe, Schiller, Hegel, etc. How, then, can
we be asked to admit that the salvation of modern times
depends on a belief that has, in the Churches, degenerated
into a stupid superstition? All the best that the German
mind has ever conceived or felt, for which it has struggled
and suffered, all the deepest aspirations of its native
religious spirit, which were early quenched by the
missionary work of the Christian Church, owe their
emergence into light to this Monistic religion of our
great thinkers and poets. Why, then, should we be compelled to take our religious possessions from the past?
Are the ideas of a remote age and a degenerate culture
to keep us under their power for ever? Much zeal is
shown against materialism; as if it were not just as
crude a materialism to make the belief in religious truth
dependent on its visible realisation in a single human
individual of ancient times, and as if what is called the
"ideal Christ," the working of the divine spirit in us, the
one source and centre of all religious life, could be replaced
and vanquished by a belief in the historical Jesus.[1]

---

[1] See my work, *Die Religion als Selbst-Bewusstsein Gottes* (1906), and the second *Berliner Religions-gespräch* about the question, "Lebt Jesus?" 1911.

The question of the historicity of Jesus is, as things are, not merely an historical, but an eminently *philosophical*, question. In it is reflected the struggle of two hostile philosophical systems, which have stirred the human mind from the dawn of thought: on one side the belief in the idea as the ultimate determining principle of the world-process, to which the great personalities of history are related as the servants, instruments, and realisers of its content; on the other side, the view that personalities as such are the determining factors of the world-process, and something ultimate and original. On the one hand is the idealistic philosophy of history in the sense of Plato and Hegel; on the other the Leibnitzian doctrine of monads in the shape of modern psychologism and empiricism. In essence it is only the old antagonism of realism and nominalism which absorbed the Middle Ages—the question whether the personality is the product of the idea, or the idea the product of the empirical personality—that has come to a head in the question of the historical personality of Jesus. And, just as surely as the profoundly religious thinkers have adopted the realistic view and contended for the priority of the idea over the individual, so the opposite theory of the nominalist has led to the dissolution of religion and the decay of belief in the ideal connectedness of the world-process —in a " providence "—in which all religious life is rooted, and with which it stands or falls; just as surely, again, the religious settlement of the problem will be found only in a return to the belief in the idea, and a renunciation of the prevailing theological theory of the absoluteness, originality, and independence of personality. If it is a matter of experience that the value of religion increases in proportion to the decay of the belief in the absolute significance of the individual, then modern religion will only be raised to its highest pitch of intensity when we cease to elevate a single personality of history to the grade of the absolute, and to raise other human individuals above the significance of mere varying phenomena and embodiments of the idea. If modern mankind cannot be restored to a belief in the idea, if Plato, Plotinus, and Hegel are now merely figures in history, then all effort in connection with the further development of religion will be fruitless, and the doom of religion is sealed.

The desperate efforts of liberal theologians to give a central significance in faith and life to the historical Jesus, for the sake of continuity with the historical past and of the Church, seem, from the religious point of view, to be as absurd as they are superfluous. Jesus is said to be "the greatest personality in the history of the world," the "realised ideal of man," the creator of Christian symbolism (?), and even a symbol of the Christian life of faith (Bousset); he is glorified as "the ever newly issuing embodiment of higher religious power, whose heart-beat pulses throughout Christendom" (Tröltsch); his historical existence is guaranteed to us by the "immediate results" of his action. Yet it is merely self-deception and confusion of ideas to say that in this way his relation to Christianity can be honestly maintained. It is precisely the aim of religion to free man from dependence on the world, and therefore from the dependence and relativeness of temporal existence. Hence a single historical fact, like the life and death of a man Jesus, cannot in any sense be made a ground of faith. In religion the individual avoids history; "he shakes it off, to live his own life." Neither in the last resort nor in the ultimate aim of his life does he tolerate this "entanglement in the confused lines of history."[1] How, then, can the historical man Jesus be made the foundation or keystone of religion? And how can the salvation of man be made dependent on his attitude to this supposed founder of the Christian religion?

At the base of all the deeper religions lies the idea of a suffering god, sacrificing himself for humanity, and

---

[1] S. Eck, *Religion und Geschichte* (1907), p. 14.

obtaining spiritual healing for man by his death and his subsequent resurrection. In the pagan religions this idea is conceived naturalistically: the death of the sun, the annual dying of nature, the happy revival of its forces in spring, and the victorious conquering of the power of winter by the new sun—this is the realistic background of the tragic myth of Osiris, Attis, Adonis, Tammuz, Dionysos, Balder, and similar deities. The great advance of Christianity beyond these nature-religions is that it spiritualised this idea by applying it to the man Jesus Christ, blended the many saviour-gods in the idea of the one god-man, and gave it the most plausible form by connecting it with an historical reality. But this standpoint is not yet the best. The historical clothing of the Christian idea of redemption is ruined as soon as it is, as in our time, made the express object of scientific inquiry and historical criticism, on account of the rise of historical science and the stimulation of the sense of reality. *The purely historical conception of Jesus cannot satisfy the religious consciousness of our age.* It owes its prestige in reality to the effects of a way of thinking that is regarded by its adherents themselves as obsolete. A single historical personality can no longer be the redeeming principle of a humanity that has not merely broken with the geocentric and anthropocentric view of the origin of Christianity, but has seen through the superstitious nature of ecclesiastical Christology. What was once the prerogative of Christianity—that it superseded the polytheism of pagan antiquity, and conceived the idea of the divine Saviour in the singular and historically—is to-day the greatest hindrance to faith. Modern humanity has, therefore, the task of again universalising the idea of divine redemption, or enlarging the idea of a god-*man*, which is common in Christendom, to the idea of a god-*humanity*.

With this belief in a plurality of "god-men," religious development returns in a certain sense to pre-Christian religion and its numerous "god-men," but enriched with the partial truths of Christianity, through which it has passed, filled with the idea of the one reality and its spiritual nature, to which the various individuals are related only as *modi*, phenomena, or revelations, confiding in the divine control of the world, and therefore in its rationality and goodness, in spite of all the apparently accidental obstacles which the world-process encounters here and there. Thus man secures a faith in himself, in the divine nature of his being, in the rationality of existence; thus he is placed in a position to save himself, *without a mediator, simply on account of his own divine nature*. Self-redemption is not a redemption of the ego by itself, as our opponents misrepresent, but of the ego by the *self*, of the *phenomenon* by the *divine fund of being* in man. Christianity recognises only one redemption through Christ; it makes the possibility of redemption dependent on belief in the reality and truth of the historical god-man. The religion of the future will either be a *belief in the divine nature of the self*, or will be nothing. And if there is no other redemption of man than redemption by himself, *by the spiritual and divine nature of the self*, no Christ is needed for it, and there is no ground for concern that religion may perish with the denial of the historicity of Jesus.

In a Monistic religion, which alone is compatible with modern thought, the idea of a religious significance of Christ is not only superfluous, but mischievous. It loads the religious consciousness with doubtful historical ballast; it grants the past an authority over the religious life of the present, and it prevents men from deducing the real consequences of their Monistic religious principles. Hence I insist that the belief in the historical reality of Jesus is the *chief obstacle to religious progress;* and therefore the question of his historicity is not a purely historical, but also a philosophic-religious, question.

The more progressive theologians would be ready to-day to accept this Monistic broadening and deepening of religion if they were not compelled by their clerical condition, and the connection of the Church with the State, to adhere to Jesus in some sense or other, no matter how slender it be. They support this position with the claim that a religion without Jesus would not do justice to the importance of the great personality and of history for religious life. In reply to this objection we hardly need to appeal to Hegel, the philosopher of historical development, to whom this high appreciation of the present above history may be traced, as well as this vindication of "personalities of world-history." The great personality has clearly a value even in our own view: in it the unity of God and man, the God-humanity, attains a clearer expression. It serves as proof to the religious consciousness that God raises up the right man at the right time. It reveals the living connection of the common individual life with the universal spiritual life. In the chain of historical events the pious mind finds a guarantee of a pervading rational control and a purposive development of earthly life, however obscure the paths of this development may be, and however difficult it may be at times to recognise the sense in existence. The divinity lives in history, and reveals itself therein. History is, in union with nature, the *sole* place of divine activity. The divinity, however, does not chain itself to history in order to unite past and future to a single historical event; but one continuous stream of divine activity flows through time. Hence it cannot wish that men shall be bound up with some such single event; in virtue of its divine character the detail may at any point of history be raised above the conditions of time and nature.

To bind up religion with history, as modern theologians do, and to represent an *historical religion* as the need of modern man, is no proof of insight, but of a determination to persuade oneself to recognise the Christian religion alone.[1]

---

[1] See my *Die Religion als Selbst-Bewusstsein Gottes*.

APPENDIX

In the course of the work we have many times drawn attention to the remarkable details which Psalm xxii supplies in connection with the crucifixion of Jesus. The psalm is one of those that have presented very great difficulties to interpreters. It is obvious that it deals with the lament of one who is in dire straits. Hitzig connects the psalm with Jeremiah xxxvii, 11-21, and the story narrated there of the captivity of the prophet.[1] According to Olshausen the situation it describes fits best with the Maccabæan period, and it pictures the prayers and plaints of the sufferers according to the experience of the poet and the other faithful.[2] More recent scholars despair of determining the age, and would see in the words of the psalm only the general sufferings and laments of the great mass of the despised and maltreated "pious or quiet of the land."

Whatever one may think, the enumeration of the animals that surround the sufferer is in any case striking and curious. The composition and peculiar choice of surroundings for the ill-treated, and the minute description of his sufferings and the threats made to him, suggest that we have here a very unusual case. The original Hebrew text seems to say nothing of fetters on the sufferer. In verse 14, however, it is said: "All my bones are out of joint"; and verse 16 is translated in the Septuagint: "They pierced my hands and my feet"; and the early Christians, who applied the psalm to their saviour, had in mind a crucifixion, and, like Justin and Tertullian, saw in the "horns of the unicorns [wild oxen]" (verse 21) the arms of the martyr's stake.

If we now glance at the globe of the heavens, at the spot where Orion is found, we see at once that all the details of the psalm agree and are intelligible, if an astral interpretation is put on it.

[1] *Die Psalmen* (1836), p. 60.   [2] *Die Psalmen* (1853), p. 121.

On the "world-tree," the Milky Way, which plays the part of a tree elsewhere in the astral myth, hangs Orion with arms and legs outstretched in the form of a cross.[1] Above his head he is threatened by the Bull with gaping jaws, the Hyades, which are in the corner on his left; we may also recall the lion's jaws in the constellation Leo, which is distant ninety degrees from the Hyades, and is therefore astrally related to them. Behind Orion are the "wild oxen," the herd of *re'ēms*, which on the celestial globe take the form of the Unicorn, which seems about to pierce the hanging figure with its horn. In harmony with this are the words of the psalm: "Many bulls have compassed me: strong bulls of Bashan have beset me round" (verse 12).

"I am poured out like water," says the sufferer. Does not the river Eridanus flow beneath the feet of Orion? It seems to flow from his raised left foot; and the Milky Way also may be taken as water. See also Psalm lxix, 2 and 15.

"Dogs have compassed me" (Sirius and Procyon).

"The assembly of the wicked have inclosed me"—the Bulls, the Dogs, the Hare, the Heavenly Twins, who are described as "wicked" (criminals, robbers) in the astral myth. (Cf. *Gen.* xlix, where they are related to the twins Simeon and Levi and are called "bull-slayers," because they drive the Zodiacal bull before them and push him out of the heavens.)

"Like the lion are my hands and feet," the original Hebrew text of verse 16 continues. The phrase has hitherto eluded explanation. It may mean that the "wicked" surround the hands and feet of the sufferer in the fashion of the lion (*sicut leo*), as is usually understood by interpreters. But the words may possibly contain a cryptic reference to the constellation Leo: whether because the chief stars of that constellation are distributed as in Orion, and represent a lying Orion, or because of the astral relation of Orion to the Lion which we have previously mentioned, or with reference to the lion's-skin which Orion carries on his left arm and which recalls the lion's-skin of Hercules. The Septuagint substituted the words: "They pierced my hands and my feet." Now the hand of Orion

---

[1] Also *Job* xxxviii, 31. Orion is represented as a giant fastened to the heavens with chains. (Cf. Jeremias, *Das Alte Testament im Lichte des alten Orients*, 560.)

which carries the lion's skin goes with the arrow of one of the Twins (Castor), piercing the hand; and in the period of Taurus the constellation of the Arrow is in opposition to the arrow of Castor, the arrow rising in the east when the former sets in the west.

The sword in verse 20 is the sword of Orion, which is drawn up against his body. The dogs are Sirius and Procyon once more. The lion's mouth (verse 21) refers again to the Hyades or to the constellation Leo, which seems to be coming on from a distance, while the "wild oxen" indicate the herd of *re'ēms*.[1]

We may even go further, and explain other details of the psalm with reference to its fundamentally astral character. Thus, when we read in verse 17, "I may tell all my bones," we recall that no other constellation shows as plainly as Orion, on account of the number and distribution of its stars, the shape of a human being with extended limbs. At the same time the shape may be regarded as a cup, with the three stars of the belt as dice in it. In this sense we may read verse 18: "They part my garments among them, and cast lots upon my vesture." The vesture of Orion is the heavens, which are often conceived as a "starry mantle," and seem to be divided among the various constellations. Or we may take the Milky Way as his garment, the "seamless robe," because it runs continuously across the sky, which is divided at the Twins into two halves by the passage of the sun.

We are now in a position to understand the real meaning of the psalm. The constellation Orion is in astral mythology an astral representative both of the sun and the moon.[2] In it

---

[1] The Septuagint translates *re'ēms* as *monokeros*, and this is translated "unicorn" in the German [and English] versions; in point of fact, our celestial globes have, instead of the "wild oxen," the constellation of the "Unicorn," the remarkable beast of which Ktesias (about 400 B.C.) writes. This must, as Eberhard Schrader has shown, be due to a misunderstanding, the Greek writer having mistaken the figure of a buffalo with one horn on the forehead in the ruins of Persepolis for a peculiar animal, whereas the one horn is really due to the inability of the artists of that people to draw with perspective. See details in F. Delitsch's second lecture on *Babel and Bible* (1904). In view of the astral significance of the psalm, Luther was right in inserting "unicorn," and the real meaning of the passage is lost when people learned in philology insist that the "unicorn" was really a buffalo.

[2] Compare the identity of Orion with the sun and moon-god Osiris among the Egyptians. Boll, *Sphaera*, 1903, p. 164.

their fate is symbolised or vicariously represented. Orion, says Fuhrmann, has many names in astral mythology. Like the moon, he is the "many-shaped" (Proteus), giving to all the gods their particular harmonic form, and astrology sees the most diverse forms of the myth in the constellation Orion. Thus we have already recognised in it John the Baptist at the Jordan, about whom the "people" gather (p. 192), and the water-wheel (p. 211). It is Noah coming with his animals out of the ark (Argo), and stretching his hands gratefully to heaven, while the Milky Way (rainbow) arches over the earth as a sign of the new covenant (year). It is Phæton sinking with uplifted arms in the waters of Eridanus, the Hyades and Pleiades hastening in flight at his fall, and lamenting his death, while his "chariot" runs, wheelless and uncontrolled, round the pole of the heavens. It is Jason landing in Colchis with the Argo, fighting the bronze oxen of Ætes and hurrying after the Ram ("golden fleece"=the sun at the vernal point). It is Prometheus fastened cross-wise to the rocks. It is also Mithra fighting the Bull, which the Scorpion makes harmless by biting its organs of generation, as the Bull disappears when the sun enters the sign of the Scorpion.

In these cases there is question of the sun and the moon when they are distressed and need help; that is to say, of the lowest altitude of the sun during the year, or of the moon before its temporary disappearance.

The sun is far away; it is in the winter half of the ecliptic. Orion seems to cry for help with raised arms: "My God, my God, why hast thou forsaken me? Why art thou so far from helping me, and from the words of my roaring? O my God, I cry in the daytime, but thou hearest not; and in the night season, and am not silent. But thou art holy, O thou that inhabitest the praises of Israel. Our fathers trusted in thee: they trusted, and thou didst deliver them. They cried unto thee, and were delivered: they trusted in thee, and were not confounded. But I am a worm, and no man." Orion, the most human-looking of all the constellations, is the sun, which in the winter-time, pale and despised, creeps over the earth like a worm.[1] "A reproach of men and despised of the people.

---

[1] It has also been pointed out that the Milky Way, in which Orion is,

All they that see me laugh me to scorn; they shoot out the
lip, they shake the head, saying, He trusted on the Lord that
he would deliver him; let him deliver him, seeing he delighted
in him." Thus also it is said of the scoffing "wicked": "They
gaze on me, and show their pleasure in me." In point of fact,
they look down on Orion from the higher point of the ecliptic.[1]
Why should not the Twins at the highest point of the
ecliptic "mock" the sun, as it moves heavy and dull on the
lowest stretch of its annual path? Compare also *Psalm
lxix, 7-16*.[2] Now it crosses the equator, and rises higher and
higher. The situation changes. God has heard the cry of
the abandoned. The better season begins: "The meek shall
eat and be satisfied." In fervent strains of praise the delivered
sings, amid the chorus of stars ("in the great congregation"),
the grace of the Lord. Jahveh resumes the lordship of the
world, and all peoples gladly praise his name.[3]

Thus the interaction of earth and heaven, man and God,
which was so familiar to the whole of antiquity, is reflected
in the heavens, both the enchained and enfeebled sun (moon)
and Orion corresponding to "the son of man," who cries for
help against the dangers of the winter that threaten him.
From this point of view the twenty-second psalm may, as I

stretches like a worm across the sky when Orion sets in the beginning of
winter. In the Babylonian myth the Milky Way was a worm (Tiâmat),
which the sun (Marduk) split into two halves.

[1] The Twins are the little boys who in 2 *Kings* ii, 23, scoffed at Elisha,
when he had divided the "Jordan" with the "mantle" of Elijah, crossed it
dry-shod, reached the "city of the moon," Jericho, at the "source of the
waters" (watery region of winter, the vessel of Aquarius), and is now
rising again. They cry to him: "Go up, thou bald head," because the
sun has lost its hair at the lowest part of its path (Samson and Hercules,
see p. 165). In this connection also we must take the "fifty men" who
sought the vanished Elijah (Helios) in vain for three days (months), and
the "miscarriage" that is supposed to cause the water of the city. The
men refer to the weeks of the year (compare the fifty sons of Danaus, the
waterman), and the latter to the sterile season which is ended by the sun.

[2] It is admitted that verse 21 ("They gave me gall for my meat, and in
my thirst they gave me vinegar to drink") has been taken literally from
the psalm and applied to the crucifixion of Jesus, like the second verse of
the twenty-second psalm. In view of the affinity of the psalms this is a
fresh proof that the sentence, "My God, why hast thou forsaken me?"
is not historical. (See also lxix, 9.)

[3] I would ask the reader not to pass judgment on all this until he has
studied the constellations. There are too many who shrug their shoulders
at astral mythology and never glance at the heavens or have the least
idea about the corresponding speculations of the ancients.

pointed out in *The Christ-Myth*, be a song of the cult to the suffering and rising son-god—Gressman sees a similar song in the fifty-third chapter of *Isaiah*—whether the movements described are taken to be purely celestial or whether they had an earthly counterpart in a corresponding cult-action after the manner of the festivals of Attis, Tammuz, Adonis, Osiris, etc. If we substitute for the "crucified" Orion of the twenty-second psalm the two other important celestial crosses—the vernal cross with the Ram (Lamb) and the autumnal cross with the Cup (skull) below it, the Virgin, Berenice's Hair (*megaddela*=Mary Magdalene), etc.—we have all the astral elements of what Niemojewski calls the "astral *via dolorosa*" (p. 413). May we suppose, in fine, that Orion itself plays the part of the crucified Saviour? In that case the (weeping) women at the cross are represented by the Pleiades (the "rain-sisters"), one of which bears the name of Maja (Maria). The Pleiades also are hair-dressers (*megaddela*), as they are represented in medieval manuscripts on the basis of an old tradition,[1] and they culminate when Berenice's Hair rises above the eastern horizon. Electra is supposed to be the centre of the Pleiades. She is the mother of Jasios (Jesus), and is represented as a mourner with a cloth over her head, just in the same way as the Christian Mary. But as Jasios was also regarded, according to another genealogy, as the son of Maja, the mourning Pleiad may also stand for her. As is known, the mother of Jesus also is a dove (*peleids*, Pleiad) in the early Christian conception.

According to Niemojewski, the cup (*gulguleth*=skull) represents the heavenly Golgotha. But we may refer it to the skull of the Bull and the head of Medusa, and regard "the place of skulls" as the region of the heavens where Orion is found. On this supposition the two evil-doers are recognised in the Twins, which we have already ascertained to be the astral criminals. Castor is regarded as evil on account of his relation to winter, and Pollux good on account of his relation to summer. Niemojewski sees the two evil-doers in the Dogs (Sirius and Procyon). The difference is not great, as the Dogs

---

[1] Boll, *Spæra*, p. 380. Compare the drawing in Thiele's *Antike Himmelsbilder* (1898), p. 112.

culminate at the same time as the Twins, and may therefore be substituted for them.

Here we have firm ground on which to establish the originally astral and mythical character of the remainder of the story of Jesus, and we seem to have a very strong proof that there was a cult of "the crucified" before the time of Jesus, and that the nucleus of the figure of Jesus is in reality purely astral.

All the oriental religions, including Judaism, are essentially astral religions. We have previously (p. 223) shown that *Revelation* is a Jewish-Gnostic work, the Jesus of which is more primitive than the Jesus of the gospels. But *Revelation* is entirely and certainly of an astral character. It is a further proof that Christianity is no exception to the rule.

INDEX

ABGAR, letter of Christ to, 1
Acts of Peter, 30, 35
Acts of Pilate, the, 1
Adonis, 67, 163, 209, 214
Akiba, R., 15, 16
Ambrosian Choral, 190
Annas, 158, 212
Apollonius of Tyana, 177
Apostolic Fathers, 132
Aquarius, 190, 211
Asclepios, 78, 196, 199
Attis, 67, 163
Augustus, 164, 213

BASILIDES, 112
Bethany, 144
Bracciolini, Poggio, 46, 47
Brahma, 22
Brothers of Jesus, 10, 84–91, 146
Bull, the, 310

CAIAPHAS, 158, 212
Capernaum, 212
Celsus, 57
Children, love of, 259
Chrestiani, 49, 50, 52
Chrestus, 19, 49, 53
Christianity, beginning of, 233–5
Christus, the name, 43
Clement of Rome, 27, 29, 31, 72
Cluvius Rufus, 23, 24
Crucifixion, date of the, 215

DANAIDS, 29, 30
Dio Cassius, 31, 42
Dionysios of Corinth, 32
Dionysos, 67
Divorce, 236

EASTER-STORY, the, 163, 164, 166
Ebionite gospel, 129
Elias, 78
Emmanuel, the name, 195
Enemies, love of, 266–70
Epiphanius, 196, 217, 218
Eridanus, 191, 192, 211, 212, 310

Essenes, the, 2, 218, 220
Ethic of Christ, 94–7, 258–62
Eusebius, 9, 32, 33, 87, 125

FISHES, 190, 211
Flavius Subrius, 42
Frederick the Great, 130, 133

GADARENE swine, the, 140, 178
Galilee, 209
Gamaliel, R., 14
Genesareth, Sea of, 212
Gethsemane, 208–9
Gibbon, 25
Gnostics, the, 55, 67, 68, 107, 111-17, 216, 227
Golgotha, 209
Gospels, chronology of the, 212
—— style of the, 156–7, 160

HADRIAN, 52
Hannas, 109
Heavenly Twins, 159, 310, 311, 314
Hegel, 302
Hegesippus, 27, 32, 87
Heracles, 67, 136, 292
Hermes Necropompos, 192, 196
—— Psychopompos, 191
Herod, 158
Herod Antipas, 193
Herodotus, 191
Hosea, 198
Hyades, the, 208, 211, 310

IDEAS and realities, 304–6
Isaiah, 69, 72, 169, 174, 175, 184, 189, 241, 246, 258, 296
Isis, 50, 51

JAIRUS, daughter of, 140
James, the Apostle, 89, 90
James, Epistle of, 183
Jasios (*see* Jason)
Jason, 67, 164, 191, 196, 197, 312
Jerusalem, 205–9
—— destruction of, 243, 247

Jessæans (*see* Jessenes)
Jessenes, the, 2, 42, 44, 217
Jesus, birth of, 161
—— death of, 159, 164, 213
—— the name, 195
—— son of Ananus, 215, 247
Jews at Rome, the, 44, 51
—— and Christians, 6, 12, 40, 108, 231
Job, 179
Job's Testament, 181
John the Baptist, 183–194
Jonah, 165
Jordan, the, 191, 312
Joseph, 214
Josephus, Flavius, 3–10
Joshua, 164, 165, 191, 195, 197, 199, 218, 222, 226
Judas the Betrayer, 83
—— the Gaulonite, 5
Julius, 197
Justin, 198
Justus of Tiberias, 2

KANT, 298, 299
Krishna, 214

LAST SUPPER, the, 80–4
Leo X., 130
Lessing, 298
Longinus, 55
Lysanias, 158

MAIA, 164, 197
Marcion, 112
Marcus Aurelius, 19, 32
Marduk, 67
Mark, 123, 124, 125
Martha, 144
Martyrs, number of the, 40
Mary, 86, 90, 91, 164, 314
Matthew, 127
Matthew, original gospel of, 13, 14
Melito of Sardis, 32
Messiah, the name, 195
Milky Way, the, 191, 192, 211, 300
Miracles of Jesus, 137–40, 175–8, 218
Mithraism, 294
Monism, 303, 307
Moses, 78, 198

NAASSENES, 220, 281
Nasiræans, 204
Nave, 197, 198
Nazarenes, the, 2, 42, 44, 201–4, 217
Nazareth, 200–5, 211
Nazoræans (*see* Nazarenes)

Neighbour, love of, 266–70
Neronian persecution, the, 21–48

OANNES, 190, 191
Ophites, 220, 221
Origen, 9, 35
Orion, 192, 211, 309–13
Orosius, P., 37
Osiris, 67, 163

PALESTINE, 159
Papias, 123, 124, 126, 127
Parables, the, of Jesus, 280–8
Paul, conversion of, 114–16
Paul, death of, 28–9
Paul, historicity of, 61–5
Paul not a Jew, 117–19
Paul, style of, 102, 103
Paul, theology of, 65
Paul, vision of, 78
Pauline Epistles, the, 62–4, 101 102–21
Pentecost, 166
Perseus, 165
Personality in history, 293
Peter, 124, 125
Peter, death of, 28–9
Pharisees, the, 230, 235–45, 253–4
Philo, 2, 67, 225
Phœnix, the, 213, 214
Photius, 3
Pilate, 4, 22, 55, 158
Plato, 170
Pliny, 18–19, 26
Porphyry, 18, 57
Pre-Christian Jesus, 200, 216–28
Presbyter Johannes, 124
Primitive Mark, 128
Primitive Matthew, 13, 14
Procyon, 311

RABBIS, the, 11
Resurrection, the, 77–80, 163–6
Revelation, 223–5

SABBATH, the, 236, 254
Sadducees, the, 230, 255
Samaritans, the, 270, 288
Saviour, expectation of, 67, 68, 162
Schmiedel's Main Pillars, 144–55
Scribes, the, 235–45
Serapis, 50, 52, 78
Sermon on the Mount, the, 271–5
Shakespeare, 159
Sibylline Oracles, 34, 222
Simon the Magician, 30, 54
Sirius, 311
Socrates, historicity of, 133

Solomon, 219
Stoics, the, 269
Suetonius, 19-20, 49
Sulpicius Severus, 43, 45

TACITUS, 20-56
—— manuscripts of, 47, 49
Talmud, the, 10-17
Talmud (quoted), 92, 95, 96, 97, 236, 237, 258, 259, 262, 265, 268, 269, 272-4, 278, 281-7
Tammuz, 232
Teaching of the Twelve Apostles, 223, 252
Tertullian, 33
Therapeuts, 218, 220, 225
Theudas, 5
Tiberius, letter to, 1

Tongues, gift of, 107-8
Trajan, 18
Trypho, 16

UNIQUENESS of Jesus, 142-4

VALENTINE, 112
Vopiscus, Fl., 51

WATER-WHEEL, the, 211
Wisdom, 69, 170, 173
Words of the Lord, the, 91, 127, 249-53

XIPHILINUS, 42

ZECHARIAH, 238